CATHOLIC PRACTICAL THEOLOGY

A Genealogy of the Methodological Turn to Praxis,

Historical Reality, & the Preferential Option for the Poor

Bob Pennington

PACEM IN TERRIS PRESS

Devoted to the global vision of Saint John XXIII,
prophetic founder of Postmodern Catholic Social Teaching,
and in support of the search for a Postmodern Ecological Civilization,
which will seek to learn from the rich spiritual wisdom-traditions
of Christianity and of our entire global human family.

www.paceminterrispress.com

ISBN-13: 978-0999608845
ISBN-10: 0999608843

*Pacem in Terris Press publishes scholarly books directly or indirectly related to
Catholic Social Teaching and its commitment to justice, peace, ecology,
and spirituality, and on behalf of the search for a Postmodern Ecological Civilization.*

*In addition, to support ecumenical and interfaith dialogue, as well as dialogue with
other spiritual seekers, Pacem in Terris Press publishes scholarly books from other
Christian perspectives, from other religious perspectives, and from perspectives
of other spiritual seekers, which promote justice, peace, ecology,
and spirituality for our global human family.*

*Opinions or claims expressed in publications from Pacem in Terris Press
represent the opinions and claims of the authors and do not necessarily represent
the official position of Pacem in Terris Press, the Pacem in Terris Ecological Initiative,
Pax Romana / Catholic Movement for Intellectual & Cultural Affairs - USA
or its officers, directors, members, or staff.*

PACEM IN TERRIS PRESS
is the publishing service of

PAX ROMANA
Catholic Movement for Intellectual & Cultural Affairs
USA
*1025 Connecticut Avenue NW, Suite 1000,
Washington DC 20036
www.paceminterris.n*

*I dedicate this work to all those people who changed my life in
ways I will never be able to fully express...
yet my gratitude to each of them abounds...*

*To my wife, for her countless, everyday sacrifices
so my writing would flourish...*

*To my children, because their joy and innocence
remind me that the Kingdom of God is at hand...*

*To my mother and father, without their patience
with my personal growth and constant support
I would be incarcerated or dead.*

*To my aunt Mary and deceased grandmother Pauline, for
their fidelity to the gospel and
the Catholic Church...*

*To my mentors Bryan Froehle, Joe Holland, Joe Bracken,
Gillian Ahlgren, and Bob Lassalle-Klein,
for their unwavering assistance in my
professional development ...*

*A todos personas in La Cucarita, gracias
por abriendo mis ojos a Dios...*

*And, to all my friends who've come and gone,
for their passion, energy, and creativity, I am who I am because of each of you...*

TABLE OF CONTENTS

PREFACE

One Sunday, in 2007, at Mass at Our Lady of Lourdes Catholic Church, in Ormond Beach, Florida, I heard an appeal for mission volunteers from Bishop Thomas Wenski.[1] I responded to his call by contacting Sister Bernadette Mackay O.S.U., the Director of the Mission office at the Diocese of Orlando. A few months later, I was in the bed of a pick-up truck as it ascended a steep mountain path made of nothing but dirt and rock. My destination was La Cucarita, a remote town in the Cordillera Central Mountains of the Dominican Republic, near the border of Haiti.

La Cucarita proved to be a liminal place for me, a place where I crossed a threshold into a new and unfamiliar reality. The new, daily realities provoked confusion and consternation in me. I did not understand how everyday experiences caused me to sometimes feel like I had "encountered God" through interactions with joyful, hospitable people, or, through the contemplation of the natural

---

1 Thomas Wenski is now Archbishop of Miami.

landscape.[2] I also struggled to understand how I could feel the presence of God in a cultural context marked by a lack of material resources like water and electricity. Such a lack of resources necessary for daily life provoked in me a sense that: "This should not be!" Something was "not right."

Seven years later, in my Ph.D. program, I learned that I had what Edward Schillebeeckx describes as a "negative contrast experience." LaReine-Marie Mosely writes that, for Schillebeeckx, a negative contrast experience is something that has the power to evoke not only "outrage at excessive human suffering," but also "protest and eventual praxis to ameliorate and end the suffering."[3]

Before I arrived in La Cucarita, I could have never imagined that people could express so much joy and happiness while living in a cultural context marked by extreme poverty. La Cucaritan reality ultimately changed my life because I was forced to confront a paradox I did not understand.

As my mission work came to an end, the paradox of Cucarita remained a puzzle I could not solve. After I returned to Florida, I reflected on my mission experience and realized that my "social imaginary" had been annihilated.[4] Charles Taylor explains that a

---

2 What I mean when I say "I encountered God" is analogous to the way in which Karl Rahner, S.J. spoke as if he were Ignatius of Loyola speaking to a modern Jesuit: "I encountered God; I have experienced him." For more see, Karl Rahner, *Ignatius of Loyola Speaks*, trans. Annemarie S. Kidder, (St. Augustine's Press: South Bend, Indiana, 2013), 6-9.

3 For more on this topic see LaReine-Marie Mosely, "Negative Contrast Experience: An Ignatian Appraisal," *Horizons* 41, no. 1 (2014): 74-95. What is central to Schillebeeckx's claim is when individuals and communities face evil and suffering — their own and that of others — the universal pre-religious response is "This cannot be allowed to continue!" What is most crucial about Schillebeeckx's argument for my present and future work is that the feeling of pre-religious indignation becomes the "specific starting point for ethics."

4 Charles Taylor, *A Secular Age*, (Cambridge, MA: Belknap Press of Harvard University Press, 2007), 171-2. In *Desiring the Kingdom: Worship, Worldview, and*

social imaginary is the way people "imagine their social existence, how they fit together with others," and how things ought to go.[5] The paradoxical reality of Cucarita forced me to question my ideals and my goals. My mission experience ultimately annihilated my desire to pursue the social imaginary I associated with the "American Dream."[6] I realized I no longer wanted to be a postmodern American whose "idiosyncratic preferences are their own justifications" for happiness.[7]

The change I underwent could be described as a *metanoia*, a conversion where my "eyes were opened" and my "former world faded and fell away."[8] La Cucarita had not only opened my eyes to

---

Cultural Formation (Grand Rapids: Baker Academic, 2009), James K.A. Smith writes that, in regard to the phrase "social imaginary," Taylor acknowledges his debt to Benedict Anderson's *Imagined Communities* (London: Verso, 1991), 65 n46.

5 Taylor, *A Secular Age*, 171. Commenting on Taylor's concept, James K.A. Smith suggests that the imagination (an imaginary) is a "quasi-faculty whereby we construe the world on a precognitive level, on a register that is fundamentally aesthetic precisely because it is so closely tied to the body. As embodied creatures, our orientation to the world begins from, and lives off of, the fuel of our bodies, including the 'images' of the world that are absorbed by our bodies." Heuristically, then, the "imagination" (an imaginary) names a kind of faculty that is kinesthetic because it is closely tied to the body and how we make sense of our world. For more see, *Imagining the Kingdom: How Worship Works* (Grand Rapids: Baker Academic, 2013), 17-19n37, n38.

6 James K.A. Smith argues that the modern American social imaginary is conditioned by a narrative of autonomy that indicates that one gives oneself (*autos*) the law (*nomos*). Such a picture rejects "heteronomy," the idea that the law comes from another (*heteros*). For more, see James K.A. Smith, *Desiring the Kingdom*, 175n50.

7 Joseph A. Tetlow, "The Most Postmodern Prayer: American Jesuit Identity and the Examen of Conscience, 1920-1990," *Studies in the Spirituality of Jesuits* 26, no.1 (1994): 33.

8 Bernard Lonergan, *Method in Theology*, (Toronto: University of Toronto Press, 1990), 130. A richer description of Lonergan's insight is that conversion is "a transformation of the subject and his world. Normally it is a prolonged process though its explicit acknowledgement may be concentrated in a few momentous judgments or decisions." And, "conversion, as lived, affects all of a man's conscious

real social injustice but also to a new vision of happiness. I felt compelled to act, I felt inspired to do something. But, what? I chose to pursue graduate studies in theology.

After I earned a master's degree in Theology at Xavier University in Cincinnati, I enrolled in a Practical Theology Ph.D. program at St. Thomas University in Miami, Florida. In Miami, I learned that my vocation is to be a Catholic theologian, ethicist, and educator. As a Catholic theological ethicist, I believe one of my primary professional goals is to teach young adults that the Catholic Church turned from an "ahistorical"[9] methodological "habitus"[10] and toward a praxis-based methodology that interprets "historical reality"[11] as a *locus theologicus*, especially the reality of the poor, whom

---

and intentional operations. It directs his gaze, pervades his imagination…it enriches his understanding, guides his judgments, reinforces his decisions." 130-131.

9 "Ahistorical" means lacking historical perspective (consciousness). To contrast "ahistorical" and "historical" styles of theologizing, the phrases *"a priori"* and *"a posteriori"* may help illuminate the difference. While the situation is more complicated than simple contrast, *a priori* methods generate knowledge independent of experience, in the case of deduction from pure reason (e.g., ontological proofs). A *posteriori* knowledge is dependent on experience or empirical evidence, as with most aspects of science and personal knowledge. Ahistorical methods of theologizing would be analogous to *a priori* methods, while "historical" forms of theologizing would follow an *a posteriori* approach.

10 *Habitus* is defined by Pierre Bourdieu as "systems of durable, transposable dispositions…structured structures predisposed to function as structuring structures, that is, principles of the generation and structuring of practices." 72n1. In the explanatory footnote, Bourdieu adds that *habitus* "designates a way of being." 214n1. For more see *Outline of a Theory of Practice* (Cambridge: Cambridge University Press, 1977).

11 Ignacio Ellacuria claims that "historical reality" is the proper object of philosophy and theology. Ellacuria explains that "historical reality is the 'last stage of reality' in which the material, biological, sentient, personal, and social dimensions of reality are all made present in human history, and 'where all of reality is assumed into the social realm of freedom.'" For more on this see Robert Lassalle-Klein's *Blood and Ink: Ignacio Ellacuria, Jon Sobrino, and The Jesuit Martyrs of the University of Central America,* (Maryknoll: Orbis Books, 2014), 196-7. It is also important to note that "historical

Ignacio Ellacuria names the "crucified people."[12] And, derivative of this aim, I strive to teach students how to master the craft of using a theological method to make a critical moral choice of siding with the poor in a civic and political context.

To meet these learning goals, I designed a methodology that draws mostly from Cardinal Joseph Cardijn's See-Judge-Act method and Joe Holland and Peter Henriot's Pastoral Circle Method.[13] My method, what I refer to as eschatopraxis,[14] also aims to build on the work of David Tracy, who is recognized as one of the first Catholic theologians in the United States to develop a "practical theology."

While Tracy claims that there are three types of theology "fundamental, systematic," and "practical," my project only aims to build on Tracy's practical theological approach.[15] It is not that I do

---

reality" needs further qualification in regard to how reality is produced by systems as well as the achievements of individuals.

12 Ellacuria writes that "what is meant by 'crucified people' here is that collective body, which as the majority of humankind owes its situation of crucifixion to the way society is organized and maintained by a minority that exercises its dominion through a series of factors, which taken together and given their concrete impact within history, must be regarded as sin." For more see, Kevin Burke, *The Ground Beneath the Cross: The Theology of Ignacio Ellacuria*, (Washington D.C.: Georgetown University Press, 2000), 181n16.

13 My pedagogical project also builds on the teaching theories and practices of other scholars. The work of Thomas Groome is foundational to my project. Also, my focus on the crucified people is similar to the way Miguel de la Torre focuses on *Doing Christian Ethics from the Margins*, (Maryknoll: Orbis, 2014). And, like Christina Astorga, I argue for an ethical methodology that is rooted in Christian scripture and takes its point of departure in context-dependent sociocultural experience. For more see her *Catholic Moral Theology and Social Ethics: A New Method.* (Maryknoll: Orbis, 2014).

14 Carl E. Braaten, *Eschatology and Ethics: Essays on the Theology and Ethics of the Kingdom of God*, (Minneapolis: Augsburg Publishing, 1975), 121; 141.

15 For more on Tracy's descriptions of the "three disciplines of theology; fundamental, systematic, and practical" see, David Tracy, *The Analogical Imagination: Christian Theology and the Culture of Pluralism*, (New York: Crossroad, 1986), 54-59.

5

not recognize the importance of "fundamental theology" with its focus on "dialectic and metaphysics," or the importance of "systematic theology" with its focus on "hermeneutics, rhetoric, and poetics." It was simply necessary to limit the scope of my work to a sole focus on "practical theology" since my primary pedagogical aim is to bring "ethics and politics" into dialogue with classic Christian texts ranging from the bible to Catholic Social Teaching.[16]

My practical theological methodology, for example, first asks students to question the bias and prejudice that each uses to mediate their understanding of reality. After this first movement I teach students how to: gather empirical and ethnographic data about a present sociopolitical practice or economic reality with the goal of developing new cultural and historical knowledge in an interdisciplinary way; then question and judge these realities with a critical eschatological hermeneutic, specifically through reflection on the Bible and classic texts from the Christian tradition; and, transform the critically integrated knowledge into ethical Christian action.

In other words, my goal is to open students' eyes to sociocultural practices and historical realities they are unaware of; then juxtapose this reality to what Charles Taylor may say is Jesus' social imaginary: "the Kingdom of God." By focusing on the eschatological wisdom related to Jesus phrase "Kingdom of God," students are able to learn how to question what actions ought to be embodied to show solidarity with the poor and outcast, actions that embody what Jon Sobrino calls the *bonum morale* (moral good) of Christian morality.[17]

---

16 David Tracy, "The Foundations of Practical Theology," in *Practical Theology*, ed. Don Browning, (New York: Harper and Row, 1983), 81.

17 Jon Sobrino, *Jesus in Latin America*, (Maryknoll: Orbis, 1987), 140-145.

INTRODUCTION

W hy study theological method and methodology?[1] Moreover, how can a scholarly text on method and methodology help students and instructors in Catholic high schools, colleges, and universities? Allow me to explain.

My experience as a high school theology teacher and university religious studies professor has taught me that, if you ask most young adult Catholic Americans "Where is God found?," typical answers may include "up there," "in here," "everywhere," or, "in the Eucharist." Rarely is "the poor," "the land," or "a mountain" the first response given by a student when asked "where is God found."

Teaching students who have been formed with such theological habits helped me learn why it is important to teach students how to use a praxis-based theological method to develop the ability to think in a critical and theological fashion when analyzing

---

1 The English word "method" is derived from the Greek "*met hodos*," which means "the way," or "path." The English word "methodology" is derived from the Greek "*meta hodos*," which refers to the intellectual logic underlying how a method proceeds.

socioeconomic, political, and environmental practices that produce historical realities.

However, because most students cannot define praxis, one of the initial movements of my pedagogy is to provide a brief history of praxis in classic and modern contexts, both philosophical and theological. And, because it is germane to my thesis, it is also necessary that I provide a history of praxis in this "Introduction."

Philosophical Interpretations of Praxis

Academic discussions of praxis generally include Aristotle and Karl Marx, so let us now review how they understood it. Richard J. Bernstein explains "The Greek term *'praxis'* has an ordinary meaning that roughly corresponds to the ways in which we now commonly speak of 'action' or 'doing,' and it is frequently translated into English as 'practice.'"[2] According to Bernstein, Aristotle used *praxis* "to signify the sciences and arts that deal with the activities characteristic of man's ethical and political life."[3]

Aristotle also differentiates *praxis* from "*theoria*," which "signifies those sciences and activities that are concerned with knowing for its own sake."[4] Moreover, Aristotle also makes a "distinction between *'poesis'* and *'praxis,'*" where the former is distinguished as activities and disciplines which are primarily a form of making or the production of an artifact (building a house, writing a play).[5]

Aristotle's argument is that there are three distinct ways of relating intelligently to life, each having a different *telos*, that is, a

---

2 Richard Bernstein, *Praxis & Action: Contemporary Philosophies of Human Activity,* (Philadelphia: University of Pennsylvania Press, 1971), xiii.

3 Bernstein, *Praxis & Action*, xiii.

4 Bernstein, *Praxis & Action*, xiii.

5 Bernstein, *Praxis & Action*, xiii-xiv.

different goal:[6] 1) *theoria* (a speculative life of contemplation and reflection); 2) *praxis* (a practical life lived in a political context); and 3) *poiesis* (a productive life devoted to making artifacts or artistic endeavors).[7] But, why is Aristotle's differentiation of *praxis* from *theoria* and *poeisis* important?

Joe Holland explains that for Plato, Aristotle's teacher, "truth was not discovered through investigation of the sensate material world," but, rather through "the rationalist intuition of abstract intellectual ideas, usually translated in English as 'forms.'"[8] And, "The truth of these forms" could be "ethically 'applied' from higher rational heights to the lower and limited material world."[9]

According to Holland, this meant that "for the Platonic tradition, ethics implicitly involves two methodological moments: (1) the articulation of moral 'axioms' (abstract 'values' or 'ideals') based on intelligible forms; and (2) the application of these ideals to the less real world.[10]

Holland explains that "in contrast, for Aristotle the material world, known through the senses, was the original source of our knowledge, and so the search for abstract truth grew only out of concrete knowledge of the real world."[11] For Holland, this means that Aristotle made a "distinction, not found in Plato, between theoretical reason and practical reason."[12]

---

6 Thomas Groome, *Christian Religious Education: Sharing Our Story and Vision*, (San Francisco: Jossey-Bass, 1980), 153.

7 Groome, *Christian Religious Education*,153.

8 Joe Holland, "Introduction," *The Pastoral Circle Revisited: A Critical Quest for Truth and Transformation*. eds. Frans Wijsen, Peter Henriot, Rodrigo Mejia, (Maryknoll: Orbis, 2005), 10.

9 Holland, "Introduction," 10-11.

10 Holland, "Introduction," 11.

11 Holland, "Introduction," 11

12 Holland, "Introduction," 11.

Unlike Plato, Aristotle approached ethics as practical reason via three methodological moments: (1) rational-empirical study of reality; (2) reflection on reality by way of general moral principles stemming from historical traditions and careful observations; and (3) prudential recommendations on how to act according to right reason.[13] But, why is the difference between Platonic and Aristotelian philosophical ethics crucial in regard to contemporary philosophical and theological methodology?

In the twentieth-century there was a philosophical resurgence of Aristotelian praxis, strongly influenced by German philosopher Karl Marx. Richard Bernstein explains that "praxis is the central concept in Marx's outlook," and "it is the basis for comprehending what Marx meant by 'revolutionary practice.'"[14] Bernstein adds that Marx's focus on praxis is first and foremost a response to the work of German philosopher Georg Wilhelm Friedrich Hegel.

Hegel's notion of *Geist* (Spirit) "fascinated and deeply influenced Marx."[15] However, Marx was critical of Hegel's philosophical project because he claimed that it failed to comprehend existing political institutions.[16] To go beyond Hegel's limited claim that "the task of philosophy is to interpret the world,"[17] Marx added "the point is to change the world."[18] Marx's critique of Hegel was

---

13 Holland, "Introduction," 11. Holland claims that the "Platonic approach to social ethics" has been dominant in Kantian variants of liberal Protestantism while the Aristotelian approach to social ethics has been dominant in Catholicism to some degree since the time of Aquinas.

14 Bernstein, *Praxis*, 13. I have taken the liberty in the following quotations of rephrasing non-inclusive language.

15 Bernstein, *Praxis*, 21.

16 Bernstein, *Praxis*, 38.

17 Bernstein, *Praxis*, 33.

18 Bernstein, *Praxis*, 34.

therefore focused on Hegel's limiting of philosophy to *theoria*. For Marx, *theoria* "is the articulation of the rationality ingredient in praxis."[19]

Bernstein explains that Marx's understanding of praxis does, however, build on Hegel's idea that human "self-development" is "a process" that is "the result of humanity's own work."[20] In other words, what humans produce are not accidental by-products; they are the objectification and the concrete expression of what the human is.[21] Thus, echoing the Hegelian claim that the self is what it does, Marx maintained that "the very nature or character of a human is determined by what one does or one's praxis, and one's products are concrete embodiments of this activity."[22]

A second crucial aspect of Marx's understanding of praxis is his acceptance of Hegel's principle that a correct theoretical analysis of politics and political economy must involve a practical-critical understanding of existing institutions.[23] Marx's view of praxis therefore crystallizes as a "practical-critical" activity that becomes "revolutionary practice"[24] with the goal of transforming the world. The key takeaway is that "Marx does not begin," as does the Platonic method, "with a vision or norm of what ought to be, and then proceed to criticize what is, in light of this norm. His position (and Hegel's) is critical of this Kantian bias."[25]

Robert Lassalle-Klein notes that Kantian idealism and epistemology later becomes problematic in the theology of Latin

---

19 Bernstein, *Praxis*, 34.

20 Bernstein, *Praxis*, 39.

21 Bernstein, *Praxis*, 40.

22 Bernstein, *Praxis*, 44.

23 Bernstein, *Praxis*, 54.

24 Bernstein, *Praxis*, 55.

25 Bernstein, *Praxis*, 71.

American liberation theologian Clodovis Boff, specifically in his description of the relationship of theology and praxis. Lassalle-Klein notes that, following Kant, Clodivis Boff speaks of "the (practical) 'leap' to span the gulf dividing theory and praxis corresponding to the (epistemological) 'leap' in the opposite direction, from praxis to theory."[26]

Like Kant, "Boff argues that theological reason constructs its object, beginning with 'the concept (*Begriff*) [which] seizes its object only theoretically that is in its ideal form.' Like Kant, Boff problematically both asserts and denies access to "the 'real,' the concrete," or the 'thing in itself.'"[27] Consequently, theological reason is given the job of the Kantian "epistemological vigilance in order to avoid an oblique relationship of terms ... pertaining to two distinct orders...(theological) theory and (social) praxis."[28]

Contra Platonic and Kantian approaches, Marx's method, following Aristotle, begins with a critical understanding of present institutions, which carries "important metaphysical and epistemological implications"[29] in regard to overcoming "the dichotomy of the "is" and the "ought."[30] Marx's position on praxis, and the critical understanding of political institutions, is integral to later developments in various theological contexts, particularly Latin American liberation theology. But, first, let us look at a forerunner to modern forms of praxis in a theological context.

---

26 Boff, *Theology and Praxis*, 213. Cited in Robert Lassalle-Klein, "The Jesuit Martyrs of the University of Central America: An American Christian University and the Historical Reality of the Reign of God" (PhD diss., Graduate Theological Union, July 26, 1995), 257.

27 Boff, *Theology and Praxis*, 71. Cited in Lassalle-Klein, "The Jesuit Martyrs," 257.

28 Boff, *Theology and Praxis*, 208. Cited in Lassalle-Klein, "The Jesuit Martyrs," 257.

29 Bernstein, *Praxis*, 71.

30 Bernstein, *Praxis*, 72.

Theological Interpretations of Praxis

The *Spiritual Exercises* of Ignatius of Loyola (1491-1556) are an early modern example of a praxis-based methodology that takes as its point of departure a person's life and integrates the lived wisdom of Christian tradition, in order to facilitate discernment about how to live a life that embodies the ethos of Jesus Christ. In fact, Ignatius' explains that the *Spiritual Exercises* are indeed a method: "By the term *Spiritual Exercises* we mean every method of examination of conscience, meditation, contemplation, vocal or mental prayer" that is used as "means of preparing and disposing our soul to rid itself of all its disordered affections and the, after their removal, seeking and finding God's will in the ordering of our life for the salvation of our soul."[31] Ignatius adds that the "Spiritual Exercises" therefore rely on "the acts of the intellect in reasoning and of the will in eliciting acts of the affections."[32]

In contemporary language, Matthew Ashley describes the *Exercises* as a "systematic method for the practice of spirituality" because they are structured with a distinct perspective, like the "one given by critical social theory, from which persons can critically contextualize their understanding of God's saving love and work in and for their own historical situation."[33]

To facilitate the methodical reflection he aimed for, Ignatius parcels the *Exercises* into "Four Weeks." Ganss writes that "The First Week consists of exercises characteristic of the purgative way....It views the whole history of sin and its consequences," as a "wrecking of God's plan for human beings endowed with the freedom to

---

31 George Ganss, S.J., ed. *Ignatius of Loyola: The Spiritual Exercises and Selected Works*, (New York: Paulist Press, 1991). 121.

32 Ganss, *Ignatius of Loyola*, 122.

33 J. Matthew Ashley, "Ignacio Ellacuria and the Spiritual Exercises of Ignatius of Loyola," *Theological Studies*, (61/1: March 2000), 19 and 25.

give or refuse cooperation."[34] And "it includes the exercitant's own role in this history," which requires the person's "intellect, will, imagination, and emotions" to come into play.[35]

Ganss explains, "The Second Week presents exercises proper to the illuminative way, the acquiring of virtues in imitation of Christ." And, "The spirit of the week is set by means of an opening contemplation on Christ's call to participate with him in spreading his Kingdom."[36]

Week Two also is where Ignatius locates the "Two Standards" meditation, respectively of Jesus Christ and of Satan, that helps the person consider whether they have been trying to serve "two masters" (Matt. 6:24).[37] The Third and Fourth Weeks bring contemplations characteristic of the unitive or perfective way: activities to establish habitual and intimate union with God, through Christ.[38] During the Third Week, the exercitant associates himself or herself closely with Christ in his sufferings, and, during the Fourth Week, in his joys.[39]

In the 1970's, Ignacio Ellacuria SJ used Saint Ignatius' *Exercises* to help Jesuits and other interested parties to "historicize" the insights of Medellin in El Salvador.[40] For Ellacuria, historicization has two primary meanings.[41] First, historicization refers to the transformative power that human praxis exerts over the historical and

---

34 Ganss, *Ignatius of* Loyola, 51-52.

35 Ganss, *Ignatius of Loyola*, 52.

36 Ganss, *Ignatius of Loyola*, 52.

37 To teach my students about the wisdom behind Ignatius' two standards meditation, as well as the gospel of Matthew 6:24, I use a modern cultural artifact, Bob Dylan's song "Gotta Serve Somebody."

38 Ganss, *Ignatius of Loyola*, 53.

39 Ganss, *Ignatius of Loyola*, 53.

40 Lassalle-Klein, *Blood and Ink*, 198n49.

41 Lassalle-Klein, *Blood and Ink*, 197.

natural dimensions of reality.[42] Second, historicization includes "demonstrating the impact of certain concepts within a particular context."[43]

Robert Lasalle-Klein explains that Ellacuria historicizes the *Exercises* to help Jesuit novices "make what is historical the essential dimension of the structure of the Christian encounter with God."[44] In other words, Ellacuria thought that because the *Exercises* "turned their attention to historical, personal, and circumstantial signs" they "can [help retreatants to] discover" how the word of God is, or is not, acting "concretely" in a particular historical reality.[45] Lassalle-Klein explains "this distinction reflects Ellacuria's high regard for the *Exercises* as a critical tool for discerning whether a given sign of the times is a reflection of grace or the anti-kingdom."[46]

Lassalle-Klein claims that "Ellacuria's treatment of the meditations of the Second Week of the *Exercises* and the Ignatian theme of contemplation in action" exemplifies the notion of historicization.[47] Citing Rahner, Ellacuria asserts that this is precisely why the *Exercises* constitute "a method to find a will of God that cannot be deduced from universal principles."[48] Lasalle-Klein adds that Ellacuria believes the historical aspect of the *Exercises* is the perfect vehicle for those seeking to answer "the challenge that the Latin American Church had set itself at Medellin: to read the signs of the times in the light of the gospel in its own specific reality, and to respond adequately to them."[49]

---

42 Lassalle-Klein, *Blood and Ink*, 197n43.

43 Lassalle-Klein, *Blood and Ink*, 197n45.

44 Lassalle-Klein, *Blood and Ink*, 198n50.

45 Lassalle-Klein, *Blood and Ink*, 198.

46 Lassalle-Klein, *Blood and Ink*, 198.

47 Lassalle-Klein, *Blood and Ink*, 198.

48 Lassalle-Klein, *Blood and Ink*, 198n56.

49 Lassalle-Klein, *Blood and Ink*, 199n57.

Perhaps Ellacuria's most important insight is that the *Exercises* help one's life become a living sign of the action of the word of God in history.[50] In other words, Ellacuria believed the *Exercises* can be used to embody a "historical continuation" or a "progressive historicization" of the mission of Jesus "governed by 'the spirit of Christ'" rather than reflecting a naive ahistorical attempt to simply recapitulate the historical details of the life of Jesus.[51] What drives Ellacuria to take such a historical approach?

From his early intellectual formation till his martyrdom Ellacuria sustains a critique of Western spirituality as ahistorical because he thought it mistakenly assigned priority to Platonic *theoria* over *praxis* which made it almost "impossible to fully unleash the power of ... contemplation in action, both generally speaking, and in its specifically Ignatian form."[52] Thus, by "historicizing" the *Exercises*, Ellacuria moves beyond a contemplation of God in things toward an approach that finds "God in all things by laboring in the midst of all things."[53]

In addition to Ellacuria's historicization of Ignatius' *Spiritual Exercises*, another exemplary praxis-based theological methodology emerged from modern Western Europe. In Belgium, at the turn of the twentieth century, priest and activist Joseph Cardijn (later Cardinal) pioneers the See-Judge-Act method to help young Christian workers question labor practices that emerge out of the historical reality produced by the Industrial Revolution, and judge said reality with sources stemming from the Christian intellectual tradition, to help workers create strategies for action that would transform society.

---

50 Lassalle-Klein, *Blood and Ink*, 199.

51 Lassalle-Klein, *Blood and Ink*, 199n58 and n59.

52 Lassalle-Klein, *Blood and Ink*, 199n64.

53 Lassalle-Klein, *Blood and Ink*, 199n58, 59, 60, 61.

Some argue that Cardijn's See-Judge-Act method develops Thomas Aquinas' description of the virtue of prudence. For example, in *Laymen, Vatican II's Decree on the Apostolate of the Laity: Text and commentary*, Dominican writer Francis Wendell OP states, "The See, Judge, Act method, conceived by Thomas Aquinas, activated by Cardinal Cardijn, and canonized by Pope John XXIII, is indeed a continuing process and a discovery that is invaluable to the layman. It keeps the person with his feet in the order of reality and his head and heart in the realm of faith."[54]

Stefan Gigacz notes that Aquinas does divide prudence into three parts: (1) Foresight (See); (2) Comparison/Counsel (Judgement); and, (3) Choice or act of the will (Act).[55] Whether or not Cardijn explicitly draws from the well of Aquinas is unknown, but the similarity does indeed make the argument plausible.

Regardless of its origins, Cardijn's See-Judge-Act method is foundational to Catholic theology in the twentieth century – as this study will later document. First, it is approved by Pope Pius XI and is canonized by Pope John XXIII in *Mater et Magistra*. Vatican Council II adds canonical weight to Cardijn's method when it is used to construct *Gaudium et Spes*. Later, Pope Paul VI confirms the canonization of Cardijn's method as he uses it to craft his theological analysis of poverty in various encyclicals and letters.

---

54 *Laymen, Vatican II's Decree on the Apostolate of the Laity: Text and commentary*, (Catholic Action Federations, Chicago, 1966) 61; cited from Mary Irene Zotti's *A Time of Awakening: The Young Christian Worker Story in the United States, 1938 to 1970.* (Chicago: Loyola University Press, 1991), 263. In addition to Wendell, Kristien Justaert notes the root of Cardijn's method is Thomistic. For more see, Kristien Justaert, "Cartographies of Experience: Rethinking the Method of Liberation Theology," in *Horizons*, Vol. 42, No. 2, December 2015, 249.

55 For more on the connection between Cardijn's method and St. Thomas Aquinas' description of prudence see *http://cardijnresearch.blogspot.com/2012/10/seek-judge-act-sertillanges-side-of.html*.

After Vatican II, Latin American bishops and theologians appropriate Cardijn's See-Judge-Act method at successive meetings of the *Consejo Episcopal Latinoamericano* (CELAM), known in English as the Episcopal Conference of Latin American. What emerges from the Latin American turn to Cardijn's method, and praxis-based methodologies, is a prophetic call for a preferential option for the poor.

In addition to the Latin American development of Cardijn's method, U.S. theologians like Joe Holland reinterpret the See-Judge-Act method as the praxis-based pastoral circle method.[56] And, more recently, Pope Francis makes use of Cardijn's method to highlight the need for a praxis-based approach to issues concerning our common home in the encyclical *Laudato Si.*

In the next section, I explain how the remaining chapters unfold an analysis of various philosophical, theological, and magisterial figures who contribute to the epoch-defining Catholic turn toward theological methods rooted in a praxis-based methodology that interprets historical reality, especially poverty, as a *locus theologicus*.

Chapter Development

In this study, I argue that in the twentieth century the Catholic Church makes an epoch-defining magisterial, philosophical, and theological turn from an "ahistorical" methodological "habitus" and toward a praxis-based methodology that interprets "historical reality," especially the reality of the poverty, as a *locus theologicus*.

I claim that the development of this turn begins in pre-conciliar Western Europe, flourishes during the pontificates of John XXIII and Paul VI and at Vatican Council II, becomes vital to liberation

---

56 Another excellent resource for a contemporary understanding of praxis is Stephen B. Bevans, *Models of Contextual Theology: Revised and Expanded Edition*. (Maryknoll, NY: Orbis Books, 2013), 70-87.

theology in post-conciliar Latin America, and eventually grows into the paradigm of "practical theology."

To support of this claim I will review the contributions of a range of twentieth-century Catholic philosophers, theologians, and members of the Magisterium, all of whom lived and worked in Western Europe, Latin America, and North America. (This study does not include additional and important contributions from philosophers, theologians, and magisterial voices in Africa and Asia, due to my limited knowledge of those global regions.)

The study presents the documentation in six chapters which I parcel into three parts. Part I, which includes Chapters 1 and 2, addresses "Western European Foundations." Part II, which includes Chapters 3 and 4, addresses "Latin American Praxis." Part III, which includes Chapters 5 and 6, describes the development "From Praxis to Practical Theology."

In Chapter 1, I show that a member of the Magisterium, a lay Catholic philosopher, and an activist priest all prepare the foundation for what becomes the conciliar and post-conciliar canonical turn to praxis-based methodologies that interpret historical reality, especially the reality of poverty, as a *locus theologicus*.

First among these figures is Pope Leo XIII (1810-1903), who, through his encyclical letter *Rerum Novarum*, turns the church toward social questions such as economics, labor, and the rights of poor workers.

Second, I turn to lay French philosopher Maurice Blondel to retrieve insights from his *L'Action* (1893), *Letter on Apologetics* (1896), and *History and Dogma* (1903). These texts show that at the beginning of the twentieth century Blondel sparks a change in Catholic philosophical methodology through his critique of Neo-Scholastic Thomism and his focus on action and history.

Third, I present the work of activist priest, and later Cardinal, Joseph Cardijn, whose See-Judge-Act method, with its praxis-based methodology, becomes the canonical foundation of the Catholic Church's epoch-defining turn to historical reality as a *locus theologicus*.

In Chapter 2, I draw from the work of Saint Pope John XXIII and Pope Paul VI to show how the Magisterium canonizes Cardijn's method and the turn to praxis. To support my claim, I appeal to *Mater et Magistra* (1961) and *Pacem in Terris* (1963). I also include a discussion of how Cardijn's method is used, at Vatican Councill II, by those who draft "Schema XIII" -- the document that becomes *Gaudium et Spes*.

I conclude by presenting the work of Pope Paul VI to show how he appropriates Cardijn's See-Judge-Act method to turn to poverty as a *locus theologicus* in *Populorum Progressio* (1967) and *Octogesima Adveniens* (1971).

In Chapter 3, I discuss how members of the Episcopal Conference of Latin America [*Consejo Episcopal Latinoamericano*] appropriate Cardijn's See-Judge-Act method to interpret historical reality in Latin America as a *locus theologicus*. I show that the Latin American turn to Cardijn's method first appears in documents produced at Medellin, Colombia (1968), then in the document produced at Puebla, Mexico (1979), and, again at Aparecida, Brazil (2007).

In addition, I compare and contrast the work of Gustavo Gutierrez and Clodovis Boff to show that Latin American theologians also use praxis-based theological methodologies to interpret historical reality as a *locus theologicus*. What I argue is unique about the Latin American bishops and theologians' use of Cardijn's method and the turn to praxis is that it links the mission of the Catholic Church with the preferential option for the poor.[57]

In Chapter 4, I argue that Basque Jesuit theologian and long-time resident in El Salvador, Ignacio Ellacuria (1930-1989), embodies the epoch-defining Catholic philosophical and theological turn to praxis in El Salvador. First, I describe how Ellacuria builds on the work of his teachers Karl Rahner (1904-1984) and Xavier Zubiri (1898-1983), as well as the work of his friend Archbishop Oscar Romero (1917-1980).

I then argue that his praxis-based methodology inspires Ellacuria to see the people of El Salvador as the "crucified people whose crucifixion is the product of actions in history."[58] I conclude the

---

57 The origins of a Christian preference for the poor can be found in the words and actions of Jesus as described in the Bible. The origins of an option for the poor within contemporary papal teaching began with Pope Leo XIII. In his 1891 encyclical *Rerum Novarum* (On the Condition of Labor) Leo XIII claimed that the state "should safeguard the rights of all citizens, especially the weaker, particularly workers, women, and children." (no. 15) An option for the poor was elevated in papal teaching by Pope Paul VI, particularly in *Populorum Progressio*. The phrase "preferential option for the poor" gained theological traction with the Latin American Magisterium at post-conciliar meetings of the *Consejo Episcopal Latinoamericano* (CELAM) at Medellin, Colombia (1968), Puebla, Mexico (1979), Santo Domingo, Dominican Republic (1992), and Aparecida, Brazil (2014). Thus, the "preferential option for the poor" has since become a leitmotif in Catholic social thought on the level of the Magisterium, in social theology and ethics, and in much of the Church's pastoral discourse." For more see David Hollenbach, "Commentary on *Gaudium et Spes*," in *Modern Catholic Social Teaching: Commentaries and Interpretations*, Kenneth R. Himes, O.f.M, ed. (Georgetown University Press: Washington D.C., 2005), 287.

58 Ignacio Ellacuría, "The Crucified People: An Essay in Historical Soteriology," in Michael Lee, ed., *Ignacio Ellacuría: Essays on History, Liberation, and Salvation* (Maryknoll, NY: Orbis Books, 2013), 208. For more see, Lassalle-Klein, *Blood and Ink*, 221n104, n105, n106. For example, Lassalle-Klein notes that according to Ellacuria, the reality of the crucified people is the principal sign of the times that Christians must "become aware of," "grasp what is at stake," and "take charge of" in order to change what is counter to Jesus' notion of the Kingdom of God.

chapter with an analysis of the work of Jon Sobrino, since he is the most important commentator on the work of his confrere Ellacuria.

In Chapter 5, I claim that the turn to Cardijn's method and a praxis-based theological methodology that interprets historical reality as a *locus theologicus* initiates the discourse and paradigm of what is called "Catholic practical theology."

To support this claim, I first describe how Catholic discussions of practical theology originated in the work of Karl Rahner. Second, I show how Johannes Baptist Metz builds on the work of Rahner, his teacher, by suggesting practical theology turn to praxis instead of relying on Transcendental Thomism. Third, to show the development of practical theology in the United States, I appeal to various sources including David Tracy, Joe Holland and Peter Henriot, and Thomas Groome.

I conclude by showing that Pope Francis, specifically through his writings in *Evangelii Gaudium* (2013) and *Laudato Si'* (2015), explicitly draws from Cardijn's praxis-based theological methodology to interpret the reality of poverty and the natural environment as *loci theologici*.[59]

In Chapter 6, I describe my ethics pedagogy. I ground my pedagogical approach upon three claims. First, that teaching ethics requires a discussion of "method—how theology should approach social questions."[60] Second, that "U.S. student culture," in the context of contemporary higher education, can be described as

---

59 The study does not address ecology but this theme is on par with the theme of a preferential option for the poor in future Catholic ethics and moral theology. I look forward to being able to write something in the future about the meaning of *Laudato Si* in regard to the American business practice of mountain top removal, specifically in my home state of West Virginia.

60 Charles Curran, "Social Ethics: Agenda for the Future," in Toward Vatican III: The Work that Needs to Be Done, David Tracy with Hans Kung and Johann Baptist Metz, eds., (New York: The Seabury Press, 1978), 147.

entrance into a "liminal communal space."[61] Third, that "Eschatology is a discourse on liminality, marginality, on that which is different in an ontological, ethical and also epistemological sense."[62]

To move from these insights toward a fuller explanation of my pedagogy I explain how I teach ethics courses with a practical theological methodology that integrates a focus on praxis and eschatology in order to invite students to think about what it means to have a liminal experience, to cross a threshold, to have a *metanoia*, a conversion to seeing and judging reality with an "eschatological imaginary."

In the conclusion, I present a summary of my argument and reassert that it is plausible to argue that what links all the figures is that they all make a turn to a form of practical theology, a turn toward a praxis-based methodology that interprets historical reality, especially the reality of the poor, as a *locus theologicus*.

---

61 Philip Bergman, *Catholic Social Learning: Educating the Faith that Does Justice* (New York: Fordham University Press, 2011), 100n20.

62 Vitor Westhelle, *Eschatology and Space: The Lost Dimension in Theology Past and Present* (New York: Palgrave MacMillan, 2012), 73.

PART I

WESTERN EUROPEAN FOUNDATIONS

1

THE TURN TO PRAXIS,

HISTORICAL REALITY, & THE POOR:

LEO XIII, MAURICE BLONDEL, & JOSEPH CARDIJN

P ope Leo XIII, lay philosopher Maurice Blondel, and Rev. Joseph Cardijn (later Cardinal) are among the many late nineteenth and early twentieth-century Western-European Catholic figures who turn the Church away from a methodological habitus that
could be characterized as "anti-modern" and "ahistorical," and toward a praxis-based methodology that interprets historical reality
as a *locus theologicus*.[1]

To provide support for this claim, I present a historical over-
view of 19th century Catholicism in order to contextualize the work
of the three aforementioned figures.

---

1 "Ahistorical" means lacking historical perspective (consciousness). To contrast
"ahistorical" and "historical" styles of theologizing, the phrases "*a priori*" and "*a
posteriori*" may help illuminate the difference. While the situation is more
complicated than simple contrast, *A priori* knowledge is independent of experience,
in the case of deduction from pure reason (e.g., ontological proofs). *A posteriori*
knowledge is dependent on experience or empirical evidence, as with most aspects
of science and personal knowledge. "Ahistorical" methods of theologizing would be
analogous to *a priori* methods while "historical" forms of theologizing would follow
an *a posteriori* approach.

- First, after explaining the historical and ecclesial context I analyze the primary contribution of Pope Leo XIII. I show how Leo, via his encyclical *Rerum Novarum* (1891), initiates a turn from an "anti-modern" and "ahistorical" ecclesial outlook toward one that focuses on how the historical reality of the Industrial Revolution affects poor workers in Western Europe.

- Second, I analyze three key contributions by French philosopher Maurice Blondel: *L'Action* (1893), the *Letter on Apologetics* (1896), and *History and Dogma* (1904).[2] I claim that Blondel's critique of the classic Thomistic philosophical habitus of the Catholic Church facilitates the turn toward a more historical philosophical method.

- Third, I examine the work of Joseph Cardijn, Catholic priest and activist (later Cardinal), who develops the praxis-based See-Judge-Act method to help young Catholic workers understand the historical reality being produced by the Industrial Revolution in Belgium and France.

In sum, the goal of the chapter is to highlight the contributions of key Western European Catholic figures who play a foundational role in the Church's turn away from "anti-modern" and "ahistorical" methods and toward a praxis-based methodology and the interpretation of historical reality as a *locus theologicus*.

We begin now by asking what developments in Western European Catholicism prepare the turn to historical reality in magisterial, philosophical, and pastoral-theological work?

---

2 Maurice Blondel, *Action* (1893): *Essay on a Critique of Life and a Science of Practice.* (Notre Dame: University of Notre Dame Press, 1984). And, Maurice Blondel, *The Letter on Apologetics & History of Dogma.* trans. Alexander Dru and Illtyd Trethowan. (Grand Rapids: Eerdmans Publishing Company, 1964).

Historical & Ecclesial Context

Joe Holland explains that between 1740 and 1880, beginning with Pope Benedict XIV and ending with Pope Pius IX, the Catholic Magisterium reacts with suspicion and sometimes outright rejection of modern liberal philosophies associated with the European Enlightenment, the Industrial Revolution, the French Revolution, liberal democracy, and *Laissez-faire* capitalism. Holland adds that the Catholic Church rejects these movements because they cause an industrial, economic, and political transformation of Europe, and, because they represent intellectual positions counter to those of the aristocratic kingship model of the papacy. [3]

Moreover, as Europe underwent this modern cultural transformation, the Catholic Church experiences "cultural and political" losses due to "an anticlerical liberal movement," which aims to dismantle the "aristocratic political power of the pre-modern Catholic elites."[4] In other words, the modern "liberal challenge to Latin Catholicism in Europe took the form of an intense political conflict between the church and state."[5] The liberal forces not only want to take from Catholic hierarchy "massive amounts of property," but also want "the state to secularize society," primarily by "ending the Catholic Church's control over marriage and the education of youth." The liberal movement "became a life-threatening political issue for a papacy," because it still functions "as an aristocratic kingship" that ruled over vast feudal estates in central Italy.[6]

---

3 Joe Holland, *Modern Catholic Social Teaching: The Popes Confront the Industrial Age,* (New York: Paulist Press, 2003), 32. Most of the material I cite from Holland's book can likewise be found in Thomas Bokenkotter, *A Concise History of the Catholic Church,* (New York: Doubleday, 2005).

4 Holland, *Modern Catholic Social Teaching,* 31.

5 Holland, *Modern Catholic Social Teaching,* 32.

6 Holland, *Modern Catholic Social Teaching,* 32.

The apogee of the liberal political crisis came in 1789 with the French Revolution, which expanded across Europe with Napoleon's conquests.[7] Holland explains "with the French Revolution, the classical aristocratic Catholic paradigm was threatened with strategic devastation," with "the end result" being "the death of the European aristocratic society, the social world on which the classical Catholic strategy for evangelization had been based for more than a thousand years."[8]

Napoleon, however, is eventually defeated, first, when Paris was occupied in 1814, and, then again, in 1815 at Waterloo. Soon thereafter France's Revolutionary phase ends, and the Catholic Restoration phase begins when, at the "Congress of Vienna," Austria's Prince Metternich begins "restoration of the ancient regime by establishing the Bourbon monarchy in France."[9] By 1830, however, another "wave of liberal revolutions challenged the restoration of the ancient regime."[10] As Eric Hobsbawm notes, "The revolutionary wave of 1830… marks the definitive defeat of aristocratic by bourgeois power in Western Europe. The ruling class of the next fifty years was to be the 'grand bourgeoisie' of bankers, big industrialists, and sometimes top civil servants."[11]

Holland states "amid all this upheaval, the papal bureaucracy was divided over the best tactics for restoration."[12] The split is between two groups who prefers different approaches to modern movements. Those on the center-left prefer to seek restoration through diplomatic compromise, while the center-right oppose all

---

7 Holland, *Modern Catholic Social Teaching*, 32.

8 Holland, *Modern Catholic Social Teaching*, 35-6n13.

9 Holland, *Modern Catholic Social Teaching*, 39-40.

10 Holland, *Modern Catholic Social Teaching*, 40.

11 Eric Hobsbawm, *The Age of Revolution 1789-1848* (New York: New American Library, 1962), 86-87; cited in Holland, *Modern Catholic Social Teaching*, 40n26.

12 Holland, *Modern Catholic Social Teaching*, 42.

compromise with modernity.[13] The split develops into a debate between those who want to maintain limits on papal power versus the ultramontanists, who fought against national state power encroaching on the church.[14] What is key to understand about ultramontanism is that it is not a "monolithic movement."[15] Rather, as Holland explains, it evolves into "three divergent tendencies."[16]

Holland describes the first strain of ultramontanism as "traditionalist" and associated with the writings of the French Count Joseph de Maistre.[17] The second ultramontanist position, the progressive liberal strain, represent the first European expression of liberal Catholicism, and came to be epitomized in the voice of French diocesan priest Hugo Félicité Robert Lamennais.[18] A militant ultramontanist, Lamennais first espouse the traditionalist, conservative strain of Restorationism. However, as the French government intensify its attempt to take over the church, Lamennais shifts his perspective and becomes the leading exponent for a new liberal or democratic form of ultramontanism.[19] Lamennais' ideas are later condemned by Pope Gregory XVI in his encyclical *Mirari Vos* (1832). The third strain of ultramontanism is the "bureaucratic institutional strain," which becomes the official stance of the papal restoration strategy.[20]

While ultramontanist movements gains traction, so does strains of Liberal Catholicism. At this turbulent time Giovanni Maria Mastai-Ferretti is elected pope in 1846. It becomes evident that Mastai-

---

13 Holland, *Modern Catholic Social Teaching*, 42.

14 Holland, *Modern Catholic Social Teaching*, 43.

15 Holland, *Modern Catholic Social Teaching*, 43.

16 Holland, *Modern Catholic Social Teaching*, 43.

17 Holland, *Modern Catholic Social Teaching*, 43.

18 Holland, *Modern Catholic Social Teaching*, 43n35.

19 Holland, *Modern Catholic Social Teaching*, 44.

20 Holland, *Modern Catholic Social Teaching*, 45.

Ferretti, who takes the name Pius IX, "was not a liberal" but a "conservative."[21] The conservative nature of Pius IX is fueled by the fact that he is forced out of Rome with the revolutions of 1848.[22] When Pius IX fled to Gaeta, in the Kingdom of Naples, anticlerical republicans from all over Italy set up another Roman Republic.[23] From Gaeta, Pius IX repudiates "the revolution and all ideas of liberalizing his regime."[24]

In 1850, after Austrian troops reestablishes papal authority in the north, and French troops occupy the city of Rome, Pius IX reclaims his temporal power as king of the Papal States. By the end of 1860, however, due to conflicting military ambitions of France, Austria, and Piedmont, the pope loses control over northern lands in Umbria, the Marches, and the Legations and becomes isolated in Rome. Holland explains that the "papacy became an island fortress of clerical aristocracy threatened by a rising modern, secular, liberalism."[25]

Holland claims "with nowhere to turn, Pius IX led a reactive Catholic conservative strategy" that urges "withdrawal from the modern liberal European world."[26] From Pius' perspective, modern liberal movements are to be perceived only in negative terms.[27] As one author writes: "The Pope and the ultramontanists...came to believe that there was an absolute dichotomy between Catholicism and the contemporary world, and they actually encouraged a Catholic withdrawal from modern society as well as modern thought."[28]

---

21 Holland, *Modern Catholic Social Teaching*, 48.

22 Holland, *Modern Catholic Social Teaching*, 48.

23 Holland, *Modern Catholic Social Teaching*, 49n54.

24 Holland, *Modern Catholic Social Teaching*, 49.

25 Holland, *Modern Catholic Social Teaching*, 52.

26 Holland, *Modern Catholic Social Teaching*, 52.

27 Holland, *Modern Catholic Social Teaching*, 52.

28 Holland, *Modern Catholic Social Teaching*, 53n64.

What is significant about the Catholic ecclesial strategy based on an "anti-worldly ultramontanism" is that it coincides with Pius IX's appointment of more bishops than all the popes of the previous two centuries.[29] The appointments allow Pius to tailor the international episcopacy according to conservative, ultramontanist criteria.[30] These sociopolitical and ecclesial developments preface the most dramatic event of the papacy of Pius IX.

In 1864, Pius' *Syllabus of Errors*, appended to his encyclical *Quanta Cura*, condemns all the "errors of the modern age" and canonizes the Catholic Church's stance against liberalism, progress, and modern civilization.[31] Holland argues that the *Syllabus* presents a defensive, hostile, and anti-modern ecclesiology that rejects liberalism, industrial capitalism, and its social effects.[32] For example, Pius IX specifically condemns "the proposition that the Roman Pontiff can and should reconcile and harmonize himself with progress," particularly with ideas associated with liberalism and industrial capitalism.[33]

In 1869, after the publication of the *Syllabus*, Pius formally convenes the First Ecumenical Council of the Vatican where the bishops "approved the doctrine of papal infallibility," which fulfill the efforts of the ultramontanists to create a viable defensive papal strategy to counter the modern liberal movement.[34] In the end, Pius'

---

29 Holland, *Modern Catholic Social Teaching*, 53-4.

30 Holland, *Modern Catholic Social Teaching*, 54.

31 For more details on this see Hollenbach, "Commentary on *Gaudium et Spes*," 268-9. Also see Drew Christiansen, "Commentary on Pacem in Terris," in *Modern Catholic Social Teaching: Commentaries and Interpretations*, Kenneth R. Himes, O.F.M, ed. (Georgetown University Press: Washington D.C., 2005), 235.

32 Joe Holland and Peter Henriot, S.J., *Social Analysis: Linking Faith and Justice*. (Washington D.C.: Dove Communications and Orbis Books, 1988), 70.

33 Holland and Henriot, *Social Analysis*, 72. The authors specifically draw from No. 80 of the *Syllabus of Errors*.

34 Holland, *Modern Catholic Social Teaching*, 55.

anti-modern ecclesial strategy can only be understood as the response of a beleaguered Church to historical, socio-cultural and philosophical movements incompatible with the Church's ahistorical point of view.

The question now becomes: what type of Pontiff emerges out of this historical and ecclesial context? At the end of the nineteenth century Gioacchino Vincenzo Pecci, Cardinal Archbishop of Perugia, who becomes Pope Leo XIII, begins to lay the foundations for a magisterial position that turns away from the reactionary position of Pius IX and toward an ecclesiology that aims to reconcile with some modern developments, as well as initiate a focus on poor and exploited industrial workers.

Pope Leo XIII

Following the death of Pius IX the cardinal electors choose as the next pope one of the few remaining aristocrats, Gioacchino Vincenzo Pecci, Cardinal Archbishop of Perugia.[35] However, as Archbishop of Perugia, "Pecci published...a series of pastoral letters that...had called for reconciliation between the Catholic Church and modern civilization."[36] And, after his election to the chair of Peter "Pecci immediately sought to implement the vision of his pastoral letters."[37]

Soon after his election Leo implements his "grand design" for reconciliation of the church and modern society. Leo's design contains three main strategic lines: cultural, political, and economic. In response to the cultural shift to local and national forms of capitalism, and the new threat of socialism, Leo grounds "the intellectual base of the new papal strategy...on a revival of the philosophical-

---

35 Holland, *Modern Catholic Social Teaching*, 111-2.

36 Holland, *Modern Catholic Social Teaching*, 113.

37 Holland, *Modern Catholic Social Teaching*, 113.

theological system of the medieval scholastics, Thomas Aquinas in particular."[38] And, in the first year after his election, Leo XIII canonizes the Thomistic system in *Aeterni patris*.[39]

Pope Leo XIII's Thomistic Methodology

Holland claims "The Catholic intellectual hegemony that Leo established for Thomism had roots in the papacy of Pius IX."[40] Leo retains the Thomistic system of Pius IX because he believes that the Enlightenment had caused pernicious errors, particularly the "modern liberal epistemological split between subject and object."[41] Holland explains that Leo and the Thomists believe that "modern subjectivist epistemological models" would eventually undermine "all objective authority and were a main root of the modern cultural crisis."[42] In other words, Leo and the Thomists are convinced "the modern claim of autonomous subjectivity" would lead "to a priority of the subjective individual over objective institutions and thus to the erosion of both social community and social authority."[43]

Contra the subjectivist models that emerged out of the Enlightenment, Leo champions Neoscholastic Thomistic models of objectivity for epistemology and hierarchical institutional authority for social philosophy.[44] What is crucial to note is that "the revival of

---

38 Holland, *Modern Catholic Social Teaching*, 118.

39 Holland, *Modern Catholic Social Teaching*, 119.

40 Holland, *Modern Catholic Social Teaching*, 119.

41 Holland, *Modern Catholic Social Teaching*, 121. Prime among those thinkers who the Church condemned was Rene Descartes, Immanuel Kant and "the British tradition." 121.

42 Holland, *Modern Catholic Social Teaching*, 121.

43 Holland, *Modern Catholic Social Teaching*, 121.

44 Holland, *Modern Catholic Social Teaching*, 121.

Thomism by Pope Leo XIII" also becomes "the center of" Leo's "political strategy."[45]

Pope Leo XIII Turns to
Political & Economic Realities

According to Holland, in addition to the democratic political challenge of Chancellor Otto von Bismarck's *Kulturkampf* or "culture-war" against German Catholics, Pope Leo XIII faces a number of emerging Catholic democratic movements in France and Italy. Although an aristocratic monarchist, Leo sometimes attempts to adapt Catholicism to democratic political realities. For example, he accepts the pioneering liberal-Catholic alliance in Belgium and praises the experience of Catholics within America's liberal democracy.[46] Ironically, however, he condemns the Irish Fenian movement for independence from England and opposes Catholic participation in the democratic politics of Italy, since it threatens the restoration of his own monarchical power.[47] Overall, Holland suggests that Pope Leo XIII turns the church toward a new acceptance of political forms of democracy even if he carried it out inconsistently.

In addition to his revival of Thomistic philosophy and acceptance of political democracy (outside Italy), Leo's economic program draws inspiration from "Social Catholicism," a movement that responds to the harsh impact of capitalist industrialization upon the working class.[48] Holland claims that Leo's economic program is tied to "Social Catholicism" because it "supported a doctrine of hierarchical class harmony between capital and labor, even

---

45 Holland, *Modern Catholic Social Teaching*, 123n48.

46 Holland, *Modern Catholic Social Teaching*, 129.

47 Holland, *Modern Catholic Social Teaching*, 129n64.

48 Holland, *Modern Catholic Social Teaching*, 130n69. "Social Catholicism began after 1815, when local capitalism penetrated Belgium, France, and Germany."

while taking up the defense of workers."[49] Holland further states that Leo's economic program drastically differs from the view of his predecessors, Pope Gregory XVI and Pius IX. Holland claims that Pope Gregory "explicitly condemned the first wave of Social Catholicism in France" while Pius IX "had addressed workers in only one document," and then only urges them to be content with their lot, since 'the Catholic Church teaches...slaves to remain true to their masters.'"[50]

Holland concludes that Pope Leo XIII therefore "became the first pope ever to address the plight of modern industrial workers, albeit more than one hundred and thirty years after the start of the Industrial Revolution."[51] Where did Leo best display his concern for industrial workers? *Rerum Novarum*.

Pope Leo XIII Turns to the Poor

Pope Leo XIII issues *Rerum Novarum* in 1891. The Latin title, meaning "new things," refers to the Industrial Revolution. Rooted in the "classical Catholic-Aristotelian understanding of politics in service of the common good" the document teaches that there are "correlative rights and duties of both capital and labor" and that "workers' unions" are legitimate.[52]

Holland claims that Leo's focus on the poor in *Rerum Novarum* is seen in multiple parts.[53] First, Leo critiqued the economic context in Western Europe. For example, Leo states:

The elements of conflict now raging are unmistakable, in the vast expansion of industrial pursuits and the marvelous discoveries of

---

49 Holland, *Modern Catholic Social Teaching*, 132.

50 Holland, *Modern Catholic Social Teaching*, 132.

51 Holland, *Modern Catholic Social Teaching*, 132.

52 Holland, *Modern Catholic Social Teaching*, 144n114.

53 Holland, *Modern Catholic Social Teaching*, 177.

science, in the changed relations between masters and workmen;
in the enormous fortunes of some few individuals, and the utter
poverty of the masses; in the increased self-reliance and closer
mutual combination of the working classes.[54]

Leo also describes the harsh realities that workers and laborers face
due to:

the hard-heartedness of employers and the greed of unchecked
competition...To this must be added that the hiring of labor and
the conduct of trade are concentrated in the hands of
comparatively few; so that a small number of very rich men have
been able to lay upon the teeming masses of the laboring poor a
yoke little better than slavery itself.[55]

Second, Leo critiques socialism as providing a false philosophical remedy to the economic and social question. This false remedy
tries to convince people "to do away with private property" so all
would become "common property" to be "administered by the
state." Leo points out this philosophical position violates the fact
that "Man precedes the State" and that humans "possesses, prior to
the State, the right of providing for substance."[56]

Third, Leo claims the Church possesses the philosophical remedy to the socioeconomic ills that faced Western Europe. Leo asserts
that Thomistic philosophy provides an ethical principle that describes the relationship between rich and poor as one of mutual
rights and duties. In fact, Leo claims that the Church should be considered the best intermediary "in drawing the rich and the working
class together, by reminding each of its duties to the other, and especially of the obligation of justice."[57] In addition, Leo states that

---

54 Holland, *Modern Catholic Social Teaching*, 178n113.

55 Holland, *Modern Catholic Social Teaching*, 179n116.

56 Holland, *Modern Catholic Social Teaching*, 179n8.

57 Holland, *Modern Catholic Social Teaching*, 182n128.

Church teaching explains "capital cannot do without labor, nor labor without capital."[58] And, that the Church is concerned with advocating the position that employers have an obligation to pay a just wage:

> His great and principal duty is to give everyone what is just...wealthy owners and all masters of labor should be mindful of this - that to exercise pressure upon the indigent and the destitute for the sake of gain, and to gather one's profit out of the need of another, is condemned by all laws, human and divine. To defraud anyone of wages that are his due is a great crime.[59]

Furthermore,

> the rich must religiously refrain from cutting down the workingman's earnings, whether by force, by fraud, or by usurious dealing; and with all the greater reason because the laboring man is, as a rule, weak and unprotected, and because his slender means should in proportion to their scantiness be accounted sacred.[60]

Fourth, Leo claims that the role of the church to administer this remedy is "to teach and educate men."[61] Leo adds that this educative aspect of the Church must intervene "directly in behalf of the poor" through its many "associations which she knows to be efficient for the relief of poverty."[62]

Fifth, Leo discussed the role of the state in administering a social remedy. Leo articulated a positive role for the state, in contrast

---

58 Holland, *Modern Catholic Social Teaching*, 181-2n127.

59 Holland, *Modern Catholic Social Teaching*, 183n131.

60 Holland, *Modern Catholic Social Teaching*, 183n132.

61 Holland, *Modern Catholic Social Teaching*, 184n137.

62 Holland, *Modern Catholic Social Teaching*, 184.

to the negative understanding of *laissez-faire* liberalism.[63] Positive role meaning "the fundamental task of the state" is "to serve the common good."[64] For example, Leo argues that to serve the common good the duty of rulers is to "to act with strict justice - justice which is called distributive - toward each and every class alike." And, Leo adds that the state therefore has the "obligation to protect rights, especially the rights of the poor."[65] Leo specifies:

> *The poor and badly off have a claim to especial consideration. The richer class have many ways of shielding themselves, and stand less in need of help from the State; whereas the mass of the poor have no resources of their own to fall back upon, and must chiefly depend upon the assistance of the State. And, for this reason that wage-earners, since they mostly belong in the mass of the needy, should be especially cared for and protected by the government.[66]*

Sixth, Leo discusses the role of employers and workers in administering the social remedy, which involves an argument for the "legitimization of unions."[67] Holland explains that "While Leo argued that unions were needed because of the weakness of individual workers in defending themselves," he also argued that unions were a natural form of human community like various "confraternities, societies, and religious orders."[68]

Rerum Novarum is ultimately acknowledged as the foundation of modern Catholic Social Teaching as well as the cornerstone of a papal policy that is adopted by Leo's successors who issue encyclicals on its fortieth, seventieth, eightieth, and one-hundredth

---

63 Holland, *Modern Catholic Social Teaching*, 185.

64 Holland, *Modern Catholic Social Teaching*, 185.

65 Holland, *Modern Catholic Social Teaching*, 186.

66 Holland, *Modern Catholic Social Teaching*, 186-7n146.

67 Holland, *Modern Catholic Social Teaching*, 189.

68 Holland, *Modern Catholic Social Teaching*, 189-90n157.

anniversaries.[69] But, before seeing how the Leonine program develops in later papacies we must consider the question: what type of philosophical and pastoral-theological developments emerge along with Leo's magisterial turn toward historical reality, especially the reality faced by poor industrial workers? At the end of the nineteenth century prominent lay Catholic thinkers like Maurice Blondel begin to construct the philosophical foundations of a turn to historical reality, but not by adopting a Thomistic methodological focus, rather, by critiquing it as ahistorical.

Maurice Blondel

Maurice Blondel (1861-1949) is born November 2, 1861, in Dijon, during a revolutionary time in France. In 1881 Blondel moves to Paris to study at the *Ecole Normale* with Leon Olle-Laprune.[70] When the time comes to propose a subject for his doctoral thesis Blondel chooses *L'Action*.[71] But, why the topic of *L'Action*?

To answer this question, I first explain why Blondel wants to initiate a turn to action in philosophical discourse. Second, I show that in his dissertation Blondel's theory of action as "sign" initiates a powerful discourse that becomes canon in the work of Pope John XXIII and at Vatican Council II.[72] Third, I show that Blondel's *Letter on Apologetics* provides a critique of classic Thomistic approaches via his method of immanence. Fourth, I draw from *History and Dogma* to show how Blondel uses the hermeneutical circle to create

---

69 Holland, *Modern Catholic Social Teaching,* 144n117.

70 Alexander Dru, "Introduction: Historical and Biographical," in Maurice Blondel, *The Letter on Apologetics & History of Dogma.* Translated by Alexander Dru and Illtyd Trethowan. (Grand Rapids: Eerdmans Publishing Company, 1964), 35.

71 Action, Blondel's chosen subject, is rejected outright because the status quo at the time was that thought, not action, is the proper sphere of philosophy.

72 Maurice Blondel, *Action* (1893): *Essay on a Critique of Life and a Science of Practice.* (Notre Dame: University of Notre Dame Press, 1984).

a philosophical methodology that interprets historical reality against the Church's dogmatic teachings.

Why Action?

Blondel's turn to action seizes upon an idea that captivates him from an early age. As early as December 15, 1883, Blondel writes: "To devote oneself to the other is the rule common to man...but how? Is it to be in intellectual conflicts, in the *melee* of ideas? Or, in hand to hand fights, in the political and social fray? Is it not action alone which defines ideas?"[73]

Blondel's interest in action also stems from his Catholic roots. He wants "to study action," because he believes "the Gospel attributes to action alone the power to manifest love and to attain God."[74]

According to Oliva Blanchette, Blondel ultimately recognizes that, "In past epochs action was a prominent theme in philosophical reflection but by the late nineteenth century it all but disappeared from the philosophical vocabulary."[75] Thus, Blondel ultimate desire is "to reopen the realm of action" in philosophical discourse.[76]

Action as Sign

Blondel describes "action" as "the cement of organic life"[77] and "the geometric locus where the natural, the human, and the divine

---

73 Dru, "Introduction," 37.

74 Dru, "Introduction," 33.

75 Oliva Blanchette, "Introduction," in Maurice Blondel, *Action (1893): Essay on a Critique of Life and a Science of Practice*. Notre Dame: University of Notre Dame Press, 1984), xi.

76 Blanchette, "Introduction," xii.

77 Blondel, *Action*, 175.

all meet."[78] But why is such a description of action groundbreaking for Catholic philosophy in 1893?

Blondel's argument is novel because it overcomes the philosophical problem of subject-object dualism but not in a Thomistic way. By explaining that "the action of something else," an object, "is understood as that which modifies the subjective action profoundly,"[79] Blondel is able to make the case that: "there is no act ... that does not call for a sort of...collaboration outside the individual."[80] Moreover, all "phenomenon" are "neither from ourselves alone nor from the surrounding world alone; it is from both...indivisibly so."[81]

In other words, Blondel argues that because the "phenomenon of action supposes the convergence of two series of phenomena, one starting from the agent, the other provoked from elsewhere...every production requires the concurrence of two actors...proceeding through the mediation of the sign of the agent...and the extorted act, which comes in some way to join the sign of the phenomena that constitutes a synthesis of phenomena."[82]

Blondel's claim that action is mediated through the sign of the agent opens an argument about the need for the interpretation of "acts" as "signs" in a rigorous scientific sense. What makes Blondel's claim novel is that he suggests the science of philosophy ought to investigate action as the experimental trial of theory. For example, he writes that action "constitutes a conclusive method; it is an experimentation, in the most scientific sense of the word: a

---

78 Blanchette, "Introduction," xvi, n22,n24. Also see Blondel, *Action*, 234-245.

79 Blondel, *Action*, 208-9.

80 Blondel, *Action*, 207.

81 Blondel, *Action*, 207.

82 Blondel, *Action*, 216-217.

rigorous and demonstrative experimentation which substitutes for speculative study and for which nothing substitutes."[83]

In the end, more than sixty years later, Blondel's understanding of action as a sign becomes paramount for Catholic philosophy and theology, particularly due to John XXIII's retrieval of Jesus' call to "read the signs of the times" in the papal bull that convokes Vatican Council II. After the Second Vatican Council Gustavo Gutierrez will draw on Blondel's work to make an important distinction, that theology is a second act, but he will avoid the epistemological trap of describing theology as a later moment in a sequence. His point, like Blondel, will be that thinking is about action, the historical action of the Church in carrying on the mission of Jesus.

Blondel Critiques
Thomistic Philosophical Methodology

Blondel's text commonly known as "The Letter on Apologetics" (1896), is originally titled, "A Letter on the Requirements of Contemporary Thought and on Philosophical Method in the Study of the Religious Problem." In the article, Blondel suggests that, instead of the predominant ahistorical approach, Catholic philosophy must attend to facts and existing problems in order to better respond to real needs.[84]

In other words, Blondel argues that Catholic philosophical methodology ought to move beyond ahistorical speculation about metaphysical truths and toward the interpretation of historical reality. For example, Blondel argues that when seeking to understand faith one must first start from the fact of Christian life.[85]

---

83 Blondel, *Action*, 433.

84 Blondel, *Apologetics*, 135n1.

85 Blondel, *Apologetics*, 140.

In his article Blondel situates his claim about methodology as a critique of the ahistorical habitus of modern Catholic Thomistic philosophy that he describes as a "static."[86] Blondel claims that Thomistic methodology fails because it adheres to what "was formerly sufficient to begin with, undisputed starting-points defined as the inner coherence of truth, which presupposes a host of assertions."[87]

Blondel argues that such an approach is problematic because reason and faith "mingle their waters" yet remain separate in an uncritical dualism.[88] For Blondel, such a methodology is insufficient because it tends to uncritically presupposes speculative conclusions are realities equivalent to life actually lived, as if the speculative knowledge (theory) about reality is itself the only true reality.[89]

Contra to what he deems to be the primary defect of neo-scholastic Thomistic methodology, Blondel argues that what he calls the "notion of immanence" ought to be considered as "the very condition of philosophizing."[90] Blondel's focus on immanence contributes an important development to the methodological turn to historical reality because it adopts a philosophical standpoint that does not exclude immanent historical transcendence.[91] Rather, Blondel's method of immanence postulates that the study of religion or God must always be immanent or historical.

Accordingly, Blondel's methodology aims "to study God, and not just as God, but our thoughts, beliefs, and practices related to our understanding of God."[92] In the end, Blondel turns to a method

---

86 Blondel, *Apologetics*, 146.

87 Blondel, *Apologetics*, 146.

88 Blondel, *Apologetics*, 148.

89 Blondel, *Apologetics*, 180n1.

90 Blondel, *Apologetics*, 151.

91 Blondel, *Apologetics*, 156.

92 Blondel, *Apologetics*, 159.

of immanence and to history because he believes "only practical action, the effective action of our lives," can settle for each one of us the necessity of integrating Christian theory and practice.[93]

What is novel about Blondel's methodological approach is that it takes the lived experience of historical reality as the necessary precondition for the discovery of the "indispensable" theological supernatural.[94] The advantages of such a methodological approach are many since it does not confine itself to a dialectic of thought but, instead, makes both action and reflection on reality capital sources for philosophy and theology.[95]

History & Dogma

On November 20th, 1903 Blondel pens "History and Dogma" to add depth to his argument that Christian philosophical and theological methodology ought to proceed via a dialectical movement where the "the facts exist for the sake of ideas; and the ideas exist for the sake of the facts, for the acts."[96] Blondel's claim about the dialectical relationship between facts and ideas suggests methodology ought to integrate history (facts) and dogma (ideas)[97] in order to aim for proper ecclesial orthopraxy.[98]

In the end, Blondel argues that methodology must not "isolate the study of facts of Christian theology from the science of Christian

---

93 Blondel, *Apologetics*, 163-4.

94 Anthony J. Godzieba, Lieven Boeve, Michele Saracino. "Resurrection-Interruption-Transformation: Incarnation as Hermeneutical Strategy: A Symposium," in *Theological Studies* Vol. 67, No. 4 (December 2006). 785-6. Also see Blondel, *Apologetics*, 160.

95 Blondel, *Apologetics*, 142.

96 Blondel, *Dogma*, 252.

97 Blondel, *Dogma*, 264.

98 Blondel, *Dogma*, 282-283.

life."[99] Nor should it "set the facts on one side and the theological data on the other without going back to the sources of life and of action."[100] Blondel's point is that Christianity is not only "expressible in an ideal" but primarily as "a reality."[101]

In other words, Blondel wants philosophers and theologians to acknowledge that "in addition to dogmatic theology and exegesis there is a knowledge, a real science of action, capable of extracting, for the benefit of an experimental and progressive theology, the lessons which life draws from history."[102] And, thus, the Church ought to attend to these "profound realities"[103] as the criterion "which enables us to discern the authentic presence of God in Christian history."[104]

Now, the question becomes, who brought together into a formal theological method Pope Leo's pastoral concern for the poor worker enslaved by the Industrial Revolution and Blondel's ideas about action, history, and methodology? Enter Rev. Joseph Cardijn.

Joseph Cardijn

Léon Joseph Cardijn is born to a Catholic working-class family on November 13, 1882, in Schaerbeek, a suburb of Brussels, Belgium. His youth is defined by a historical context that reflects the effects of the democratic revolution in France, *laissez-faire* capitalism, and the industrial revolution.[105] Cardijn's youth is also "the

---

99 Blondel, *Dogma*, 283.

100 Blondel, *Dogma*, 286.

101 Blondel, *Dogma*, 283.

102 Blondel, *Dogma*, 287.

103 Blondel, *Dogma*, 272.

104 Blondel, *Dogma*, 257.

105 Stefan Gigacz, "The Role and Impact of Joseph Cardijn at Vatican II." Unpublished PhD dissertation, University of Divinity, Melbourne, Australia. Obtained in private email exchange with the author, 2006.

time of *Rerum Novarum*."[106] And, not only is young Cardijn inspired by these social, political, economic, and religious events, he is also inspired by the example of his father, who shows concern for industrial factory workers' quality of life. After attending some meetings of young factory workers Cardijn realizes his vocation is to become a priest.

After ordination Cardijn enjoys much ministerial success in Belgium, and beyond. It is arguable that Cardijn's See, Judge, Act method is the reason for his success as well as his later influence on the methodological perspective of twentieth century Catholic Social Teaching.

To support this claim, I take account of the historical roots of Cardijn's intellectual formation, with special attention to the work of Félicité Lamennais, Leon Olle-Laprune, Victor Brant's mediation of Frederic Le Play, as well as Marc Sagnier's praxis-based methodology. Second, I explore the claim that Cardijn's method resembles the Thomistic description of the virtue of prudence. Third, I present Cardijn's reflections on theological methodology. The next chapter provides a discussion of the use of Cardijn's method in authoritative teaching documents of the Catholic Church.The next chapter will also discuss Cardijn's focus on the poor at Vatican Council II.

---

106 Gigacz, "The Role and Impact of Joseph Cardijn at Vatican II."

Cardijn enters the minor seminary at Malines in 1896 and begins to "read the works of the Lamennais School."[107] At the end of 1901 Cardijn enters into major seminary philosophy studies and becomes "absorbed" in the works of many 19th century French "Social Catholics" including: Frédéric Ozanam (founder of the St. Vincent de Paul Society), Albert de Mun (founder of the French Catholic Youth Association), Alphonse Gratry, and Léon Ollé-Laprune (director of Maurice Blondel's dissertation).[108] To contextualize Cardijn's formation, due to his reading of these French figures, I present a brief excursus on Lammenais, Olle-Laprune, and Frederick Le Play (via Brants).

Felicite Lamennais is born near *Sillon* beach near the Brittany port city of Saint Malo.[109] Feli, as he was known, enters into the priesthood in 1817. As Lamennais matures intellectually he "concluded that there was no place in the emerging age of democracy for the traditional alliance of throne and altar that had stood since Charlemagne's coronation as Holy Roman Emperor."[110] What is interesting about this insight is that it reveals a change in Lamennais' perspective.

According to Gigacz, while "the young Lamennais had offered a blistering critique of liberalism," later he argues that "instead of trembling" before it, it was necessary "to catholicise it."[111] Ultimately, those who favor the Catholic Restoration movement, including Pope Gregory XVI, condemn Lamennais position. In fact, in 1832 Gregory XVI issues *Mirari Vos*, which outlines a formal

---

107 Gigacz, "The Role and Impact of Joseph Cardijn at Vatican II."

108 Gigacz, "The Role and Impact of Joseph Cardijn at Vatican II."

109 Gigacz, "The Role and Impact of Joseph Cardijn at Vatican II."

110 Gigacz, "The Role and Impact of Joseph Cardijn at Vatican II."

111 Gigacz, "The Role and Impact of Joseph Cardijn at Vatican II."

condemnation of Lamennais' position.[112] In addition to Lammenais, other figures add layers of intellectual depth to Cardijn's formation.

Leon Olle-Laprune is born in the south of France in 1839 and makes a career out of interpreting forward Alphonese Gratry's *Les sources* as well as the work of Frederick Ozanam.[113] Olle-Laprune, however, develops his own method in his major study of Aristotle's ethics, *Essai sur la morale d'Aristote* (*Essay on the Morality of Aristotle*).[114] Olle-Laprune reinterprets Aristotle's idea that "the happy life is that which is according to virtue"[115] and emphasizes that a happy Christian life is one that is rooted in the virtue of prudence as the foundation of how Christians ought to make moral decisions:

> *Practical reason discerns that which is to be done in any circumstance; it takes account of times and places and persons; it appreciates the circumstances; it determines the conduct to take: these are practical definitions, not in view of science but action. This prudence or practical wisdom is in no way moral virtue but it is the condition of it because it is the light of it. It is necessary to think well in order to act well. Such is the nature, such is the role of the applied intelligence to the discernment of moral matters, and enlightening and directing practical life. It is thought itself supporting action, phronesis.[116]*

Olle-Laprune dies in 1898 and avoids the suspicions of the Magisterium that falls upon many others, including his student Maurice Blondel. Yet, another figure is crucial to Cardijn's formation.

---

112 Gigacz, "The Role and Impact of Joseph Cardijn at Vatican II."
113 Gigacz, "The Role and Impact of Joseph Cardijn at Vatican II."
114 Gigacz, "The Role and Impact of Joseph Cardijn at Vatican II."
115 Gigacz, "The Role and Impact of Joseph Cardijn at Vatican II.."
116 Gigacz, "The Role and Impact of Joseph Cardijn at Vatican II."

While at the major seminary of Malines Cardijn learns of *Le Sillon*, the lay democratic movement and magazine organized and led by Marc Sagnier.[117] *Sillon* begins at Stanislas College as a study circle of young men who are concerned with doing social analysis.[118] To facilitate this social analysis Sagnier composes a three step methodology: "every citizen must: (1) know the state of the country; when the situation is bad, he must (2) seek solutions; and lastly, having found the solutions, he must (3) act."[119] Gigacz claims that it is clear that Sagnier's methodology has roots in the work of Olle-Laprune.[120] Thus, while it is not quite the See-Judge-Act formula, Sagnier's methodology likely provided a foundation for Cardijn's method. What is also noteworthy is that there is evidence that reveals Marc Sagnier, founder of *Sillon*, is connected to French philosopher of action, Maurice Blondel.

In 1890 Blondel is called to fill a vacancy at Stanislas College, where, for the first time, he enters into close touch with a group of Catholics interested in social questions. Blondel writes, "It was my pupils at Stanislas…who are consulting me about their plans, their program and their title, *foun'd le Sillon*. Quite a correspondence passed between us before the first number of that elegant review appeared. The first collaborators belonged to my philosophy class of 1890-91."[121]

The collaboration makes it plausible to suggest that Blondel's methodological perspective, which is undoubtedly influenced by his teacher, and chair of his dissertation, Olle-Laprune, likely affects

---

117 Gigacz, "The Role and Impact of Joseph Cardijn at Vatican II.".

118 Gigacz, "The Role and Impact of Joseph Cardijn at Vatican II." It is noteworthy that Olle-Laprune taught at Stanislas College in the mid-nineteenth century.

119 Gigacz, "The Role and Impact of Joseph Cardijn at Vatican II."

120 Gigacz, "The Role and Impact of Joseph Cardijn at Vatican II."

121 Dru, "Introduction," 39n1. For more see, Blanchette, *Maurice Blondel*, 58

Sagnier's own methodological perspective, and, therefore, Cardijn's as well.

Some suggest that Cardijn's methodology, beyond the influence of Sagnier, Lamennais, and Olle-LaPrune, also draws upon Thomas Aquinas' description of the virtue of prudence. In "Laymen, Vatican II's Decree on the Apostolate of the Laity: Text and commentary," Dominican writer Francis Wendell OP states, "The See, Judge, Act method, conceived by Thomas Aquinas, activated by Cardinal Cardijn, and canonized by Pope John XXIII is indeed a continuing process and a discovery that is invaluable to the layman. It keeps the person with his feet in the order of reality and his head and heart in the realm of faith."[122]

Stefan Gigacz claims that it is plausible to suggest Cardijn's method reflects Aquinas' description of the virtue of prudence. Aquinas divides prudence into three parts: (1) Foresight (See); (2) Comparison/Counsel (Judgement); (3) Choice or act of the will (Act).[123] Gigacz suggests that a Thomistic understanding of prudence may have been introduced to Cardijn when he came into contact with Ollé-Laprune's *La philosophie morale de St Thomas Aquin*[124] (1916), which describes a method that integrates an Aristotelian account of *phronesis* with a prudence-based Thomistic approach.[125]

---

122 Peter Foote, *Laymen: Vatican II's Decree on the Apostolate of the Laity: Text and commentary*, (Catholic Action Federations, Chicago, 1966), 61, Quoted from Mary Irene Zotti's *A Time of Awakening: The Young Christian Worker Story in the United States, 1938 to 1970*, 263. In addition to Wendell, Kristien Justaert notes the root of Cardijn's method is Thomistic. For more see, Kristien Justaert, "Cartographies of Experience: Rethinking the Method of Liberation Theology," in *Horizons* 42, no. 2 (December 2015): 249.

123 For more see: http://cardijnresearch.blogspot.com/2012/10/seek-judge-act-sertillanges-side-of.html. Prudence is defined by Thomas in Question 47, 1-3. http://www.nd.edu/~afreddos/courses/453/prudence.htm#two.

124 For more see:
http://archive.org/stream/laphilosophiemor00sert#page/220/mode/2up

125 For more see:

Aside from these roots in Lamennais, Olle-Laprune, Sagnier, and perhaps St. Thomas Aquinas, another interlocutor strongly influenced Cardijn. Enter Frederick Le Play via Victor Brants.

After Cardijn's seminary experience ends, and he is ordained in 1906, Archbishop of Malines, Desire Mercier, decided to send Cardijn to "the University of Louvain to study social sciences at the *Institut Spuerieur de Philosophie*."[126] One professor who makes a particular impact on Cardijn is Victor Brants, a disciple of French sociologist Frederic Le Play.

In 1855, Le Play publishes his path-breaking work *Les ouvriers europeens*. It begins with an expose of his "method of social observation," which "was simply the application of the scientific method of observation of the physical world to the field of social phenomena. It meant recording in detail the minutiae of life."[127] According to Gabriel Melin, Leplaysian social science consisted "purely and simply of observing facts, comparing them, classifying them, seeking the causes, understanding the effect."[128]

Cardijn's first academic paper, published in *Revue sociale catholique*, shows the Leplaysian influence as it is "packed with statistics and empirical information detailing the situation of home workers (women) in Germany."[129] A later article, *L'ouvriere Isolee* also shows the influence of Leplaysian methodology as Cardijn documented the situation of women workers with case studies and statistics as does a 1914 article on *La population feminine*.[130] But, the

---

http://cardijnresearch.blogspot.com/2012/08/see-judge-and-conclude-with-leon-olle.html.

126 Gigacz, "The Role and Impact of Joseph Cardijn at Vatican II."

127 Gigacz, "The Role and Impact of Joseph Cardijn at Vatican II."

128 Gigacz, "The Role and Impact of Joseph Cardijn at Vatican II."

129 Gigacz, "The Role and Impact of Joseph Cardijn at Vatican II."

130 Gigacz, "The Role and Impact of Joseph Cardijn at Vatican II."

important question now becomes: where does Cardijn's formation lead him?

Cardijn Methodology
Turns toward Historical Reality

Kevin Ahern explains that in 1925 Cardijn "made his first trip to Rome to make an appeal to Pope Pius XI directly."[131] After an unscheduled private meeting between Cardijn and the Pope, a papal blessing is given to "the aim, method, and organization of the J.O.C."[132] Soon thereafter "the first national congress of the *Jeunesse Ouvriere Chretienn, J.O.C.* (Young Christian Workers, Y.C.W.) was organized."[133] Cardijn later states that Pius approves the movement because his papacy is dominated by the idea that "the church must be rooted in the realities of life."[134] But, an important questions arises. How is Cardijn's method and movement of young Christian workers received?

Gigacz's research shows that the first public papal reference to the See-Judge-Act method is by Pope Pius XII in his address to the International YCW Pilgrimage to Rome on August 25, 1957. Gigacz translates the key statement from Pius XII:

> You want to live a profound, authentic, Christian life, not just in the secret of your consciences, but also openly, in your families, in your neighborhood, in the factory, in the workshop, in the office, and also

---

131 Kevin Ahern, *Structures of Grace: Catholic Organizations Service the Global Common Good.* (Maryknoll: NY, Orbis Books, 2015), 68.

132 Joseph Cardijn, *Laymen into Action*, translated by Anne Heggie (London: Geoffrey Chapman LTD, 1964), 35. In this passage, Cardin reveals that it was during his months in prison in the 1914-18 war that he drafted the main outlines of what appeared in 1925 under the title *'Manuel de la J.O.C.'*

133 Ahern, *Structures of Grace*, 68. Also see: Eugene Langdale, "Introduction," in *Challenge to Action: Addresses of Monsignor Joseph Cardijn*, (Chicago: Fides, 1955), 7-12.

134 Cardijn, *Laymen*, 35.

to show your sincere and total belonging to Christ and the Church. Your solid organization, your method summed up in the well-known formula: "See, judge, act," your interventions on the local, regional, national and international levels, enables you to contribute to the extension of the Reign of God in modern society and to enable the teachings of Christianity to penetrate with all their vigor and originality.[135]

After receiving a papal blessing and public support of his method and movement, Cardijn feels confident in his claim that the "review of life," is a "precious element in spiritual direction and formation" because it is a "means...of the total transformation of everyday life."[136] Furthermore, Cardijn adds that: "life must be one of the essential bases of a sound theology, it is...a methodological base without which we would only be making artificial gestures, aiding and abetting the divorce...between religion and the world."[137]

But, Cardijn also recognizes that beyond being "formed first of all by the discovery of facts" a sound methodology ought to help laity make "a Christian judgment, resulting in the actions they plan, the plans they carry into effect, the responsibilities they shoulder."[138]

In a key insight, Kevin Ahern suggests that Cardijn's See-Judge-Act methodology "foreshadowed, and in many ways set the stage, for what developed at the Second Vatican Council and the subsequent emergence of liberation theology."[139]

---

135 For more see: http://cardijnresearch.blogspot.com/2014/10/see-judge-act-from-john-xxiii-to-pope.html

136 Cardijn, *Laymen*, 150.

137 Cardijn, *Laymen*, 148-149.

138 Cardijn, *Laymen*, 150.

139 Ahern, *Structures of Grace*, 65.

Taking this claim as a point of departure, the next chapter explores Cardijn's effect on Pope John XXIII, the final session of the Council, the Pastoral Constitution of Vatican II, and Pope Paul VI. The next chapter also shows how important contributors at the Second Vatican Council such as "Yves Congar, OP, and Marie-Dominique Chenu, OP," who "worked closely with the JOC in France" also turn the Church toward the interpretation of historical reality via the resourcing of Maurice Blondel and the methodological insight of "reading the signs of the times."[140]

And, in chapter three, we will see the influence of Cardijn's method on Gustavo Gutierrez, a Peruvian Priest who served as "the national chaplain of the *Union Nacional de Estudiantes Catolicos* (UNEC), the IMCS federation," where he "drew inspiration from his work with students and the *jocist* method in outlining a theology of liberation in a lecture first published by the IMCS regional secretariat in Montevideo in 1969."[141]

Conclusion

In this chapter, I argued that certain early twentieth-century Western European Catholic figures made powerful arguments for a magisterial, philosophical, and pastoral-theological turn to methods that interpret historical reality as a *locus theologicus*.

---

140 Ahern, *Structures of Grace*, 70.

141 Ahern, *Structures of Grace*, 71. The author cites Gustavo Gutierrez, *A Theology of Liberation: History, Politics, and Salvation* (Maryknoll, NY: Orbis Books, 1988), 175n1. Ahern notes that both Ana Maria Bidegain and Enrique D. Dussel state that the jocist youth movements prepared the ground for the emergence of liberation theolgoy. For more see, Anna Maria Bidegain, *From Catholic Action to Liberation Theology: The Historical Process of the Laity in Latin America in the Twentieth Century*, working paper 48 (Notre Dame, IN: Kellog Institute, 1985), 22. Also see: Enrique D. Dussel, *A History of the Church in Latin America: Colonialism to Liberation* (1492-1979), trans. Alan Nely (Grand Rapids, MI: Eerdmans, 1981), 324.

To support this claim, I described how the late nineteenth century Catholic Church (as embodied by Pius IX and the "Syllabus of Errors") is suspicious of, and sometimes explicitly reject, modern liberal philosophies associated with the European Enlightenment, the Industrial revolution, liberal democracy, and *laissez-faire* capitalism.

In light of this context I then examined aspects of the work of Pope Leo XIII, lay French philosopher Maurice Blondel, and a Flemish pastoral-theologian, Joseph Cardijn. In the next chapter I will discuss members of the Magisterium, among others, whose work canonizes Cardijn's See-Judge-Act method with its praxis-based methodology that interprets historical reality as a *locus theologicus*.

2

CARDIJN'S METHOD OF PRAXIS BECOMES CANON: POPE JOHN XXIII, VATICAN COUNCIL II, & POPE PAUL VI

Overview

In the middle of the twentieth century the Catholic Magisterium canonize Cardijn's See-Judge-Act method of praxis that interprets historical reality as a *locus theologicus*.

To support this claim, I appeal to figures and sources such as Pope John XXIII, *Gaudium et Spes* (the pastoral constitution of Vatican Council II), and Pope Paul VI.

- First, I contextualize the historical and ecclesial changes that happen following the death of Pope Leo XIII and leading up to the election of Angelo Roncalli, the man who becomes Pope John XXIII.

- Second, I discuss the life of Roncalli to provide insight into the formation of a pastor who becomes a seminary professor and papal diplomat before he is elected pontiff.

- Third, I not only show that Pope John XXIII canonizes Cardijn's method in *Mater et Magistra* (1961), but also that he turns the Catholic Church further toward the interpretation of historical reality, or "signs of the times,"[1] as a *locus theologicus* in *Pacem in Terris* (1963).

- Fourth, I show that not only is Cardijn's See-Judge-Act method used to construct *Gaudium et Spes* (the pastoral constitution of Vatican Council II), but that in several speeches Cardijn himself argues that the Church ought to specifically focus on the interpretation of the historical reality of poverty as a *locus theologicus*.

- Fifth, I appeal to *Populorum Progressio* and *Octogesima Adveniens* to show that Pope Paul VI adds canonical weight to the turn to historical reality, particularly poverty, as a *locus theologicus* via Cardijn's method of theological praxis.

Historical and Ecclesial Context:
From Leo XIII to Pius XII

Holland explains that four popes carried-on the modern Leonine strategy: Pius X (1903-14), Benedict XV (1914-22), Pius XI (1922-

---

[1] Pope John XXIII convokes the Second Vatican Council with the Papal bull *Humanae Salutis* (Dec. 21, 1961). The Bull is the first time John used the phrase "reading signs of the times." John's turn to reading signs of the times marks an approach that differs greatly from the classic *ahistorical* methodological strategy that characterizes Catholic theology following the Council of Trent. The biblical roots of this hermeneutic strategy appear in the Gospel of Matthew 16:1-3. "The Pharisees and Sadducees came and, to test him, asked him to show them a sign from heaven. He said to them in reply, "In the evening you say, 'Tomorrow will be fair, for the sky is red;' and, in the morning, 'Today will be stormy, for the sky is red and threatening.' You know how to judge the appearance of the sky, but you cannot judge the signs of the times." In this passage, Jesus challenges the religious leaders to open their eyes to what is going on around them. Luke 12:57 also describes a similar scene. "You hypocrites! You know how to interpret the appearance of the earth and the sky; why do you not know how to interpret the present time?"

39), and Pius XIII (1939-1958). Holland claims that "the first three would make significant modifications to the strategy" but did not abandon it, while Pius XII "conducted himself as the most aristocratically triumphant" of all of Leo's successors.

In 1903 Giuseppe Sarto is elected as Leo XIII's successor. He takes the name Pius X in memory of the quintessentially anti-liberal Pius IX.[2] Pius X quickly changes some policies in Leo's ecclesial strategy. First, "he shifted from an optimistic view of the modern world to one that was profoundly pessimistic" and against "modernism."[3]

Pius X not only calls modernism "the synthesis of all heresies," but also condemns the writings of leading Catholic theologians and biblical scholars whose worked he believed represented aspects of modernist thinking.[4] Marc Sagnier of *Le Sillon* and the Christian Democratic movement are examples of what Pius' deems heretical. *Lamentabili* (1907) and *Pascendi* (1907) are two of his major documents that condemn modernism as a heresy. Beyond these texts, Pius institutes a policy that requires "all clergy, prior to ordination" to "take a special oath against modernism."[5]

Aside from "modernism" Pius X, like Leo XIII, continues to label socialism as the main threat to the church, but Pius' policies lean center-right as opposed to Leo's center-left policy.[6] But, according to Holland, "despite these differences, three of the four elements of the Leonine strategy still held under Pius X: (1) socialism was seen as the primary enemy of the church; (2) Thomism was used as the philosophical base to challenge liberalism; and (3) the laity were

---

2 Holland, *Modern Catholic Social Teaching*, 198.

3 Holland, *Modern Catholic Social Teaching*, 198n1, 199n5.

4 Holland, *Modern Catholic Social Teaching*, 200.

5 Holland, *Modern Catholic Social Teaching*, 201.

6 Holland, *Modern Catholic Social Teaching*, 201.

mobilized as a resistance group within democratic society."[7] Holland explains that what does not hold is Social Christianity, as Pius X associated it modernism.

In September 1914, after Pius X dies, Giacomo della Chiesa became Pope Benedict XV.[8] As Benedict XV assumes the papacy when World War I begins, he quickly "recognized the horrendous terror of modern warfare" and the "sufferings it brought on families, especially on children."[9] As the war escalates, Benedict "continued to appeal morally for peace; focused his energies on the victims of the war, especially children; and organized massive campaigns for relief. So generous was this pope's financial support for victims of the war that he nearly bankrupted the Vatican."[10]

Beyond his benevolence to those affected by war, Benedict's strategic innovations are threefold.[11] First, he establishes the modern papacy as a supranational voice against militarism and on behalf of peace and victims of war. Second, he initiated the move to decolonize Catholic missions. Third, he strongly supported the precursors of modern Christian Democratic political parties.[12] Aside from these innovations,

Benedict XV holds fast to the Leonine strategy. He continues to see socialism as the primary enemy of the Church, supports Scholasticism and especially Thomism, and deepens the overall commitment to Christian democracy.[13] Worthy of note, however, is that fact that none of Benedict's encyclicals ever mention *Rerum Novarum*.

---

7 Holland, *Modern Catholic Social Teaching*, 201.

8 Holland, *Modern Catholic Social Teaching*, 202.

9 Holland, *Modern Catholic Social Teaching*, 202.

10 Holland, *Modern Catholic Social Teaching*, 202n13.

11 Holland, *Modern Catholic Social Teaching*, 204.

12 Holland, *Modern Catholic Social Teaching*, 204.

13 Holland, *Modern Catholic Social Teaching*, 204.

In 1922, following the death of Benedict XV, the cardinals choose as pope Ambrosia Damian Achille Ratti.[14] He takes the name Pius XI and "held to the basic strategic lines of Leo XIII."[15] He maintains the strategic battle against socialism, and issues an encyclical, *Studiorum Ducem* (1923), reaffirming Leo XIII's *Aeterni Patris*.

Holland states that Pius XI also shows "support for the working class" and vehemently denounces "the capitalist class," thereby following Leo's position on the social question.[16] What shows the ultimate continuity between Pius XI and Leo XIII is that Pius issues *Quadragesimo Anno* to honor the fortieth anniversary of Leo's *Rerum Novarum*.[17]

When Pius XI dies in 1939, the cardinals quickly elected as pope the Vatican's Secretary of State, Eugenio Maria Giuseppe Giovani Pacelli.[18] Pacelli, who chooses the name Pius XII, gains wide spread respect following his negotiations for the concordant with Hitler.[19]

Holland explains that "overall, like his immediate predecessors, Pius XII still held to the Leonine strategy; he modified it only to ensure its continued viability. First, the primary focus remained the critique of socialism. Second, the philosophical base of strategic response to liberalism remained Thomism. Third, Pius continued Leo's perspective of Christian Democracy."[20] The final element in the Leonine strategy, namely "Social Catholicism," also holds under Pius XII.[21] It is not until the death of Pius XII in 1958 and the

14 Holland, *Modern Catholic Social Teaching*, 204.

15 Holland, *Modern Catholic Social Teaching*, 211.

16 Holland, *Modern Catholic Social Teaching*, 211-2.

17 Holland, *Modern Catholic Social Teaching*, 212.

18 Holland, *Modern Catholic Social Teaching*, 212.

19 Holland, *Modern Catholic Social Teaching*, 212.

20 Holland, *Modern Catholic Social Teaching*, 223.

21 Holland, *Modern Catholic Social Teaching*, 223.

election of Angelo Giuseppe Roncalli that the Catholic Church would make a definitive and canonical turn away from Neo-Scholastic Thomism and toward a more praxis based theological methodology that focuses on the interpretation of historical reality.

Angelo Giuseppe Roncalli:
Saint Pope John XXIII

Angelo Giuseppe Roncalli, the fourth of thirteen children, is born to a poor peasant family on November 25, 1881 in Bergamo, Italy.[22] As a youth, Roncalli is shaped by the rural cultural context of Bergamo, his local diocese, and by the witness of his great "uncle" Zaverio, who was active in the Catholic Action movement.[23]

In 1901 Roncalli departs home and enrolls in the *Collegio Romano* where he remains, apart from a year's military service, until 1905 when he returns to Bergamo as the secretary to the new bishop, Radini Tedeschi.[24] In 1906 Roncalli becomes professor of church history, and, shortly thereafter, is called to serve as a chaplain during WWI, an experience that convinces him "war is the greatest evil."[25]

---

22 Roncalli's father made a living as a farmer in Sotto il Monte, outside Bergamo, in central Lombardy, in northern Italy. For more see, Sean MacReamoinn, "John XXIII, Pope," in *The Modern Catholic Encyclopedia*, Michael Glazier and Monika K. Hellwig, editors. (Collegeville: Liturgical Press, 1994), 455.

23 Uncle' Zaverio inspired John to see that if he wants to be a priest in the diocese of Bergamo his theology would have to have a social dimension. For more see MacReamoinn, "John XXIII," 455.

24 MacReamoinn, "John XXIII," 455. Tedeschi is somewhat of a hero to Roncalli who admired his work in the *Opera dei Congressi*, the Rome-based coordinating body of social action and a focus for Catholic "progressive" thinking. Tedeschi's teaching that Christ's preference goes to the disinherited, the weak, and the oppressed matched his actions, which deepened Roncalli's formation.

25 MacReamoinn, "John XXIII," 455. See also, Mich, "Commentary," 192n4.

In January 1921, Roncalli becomes National Director of the Propagation of the Faith, which makes him a member of the Curia.[26] Later, Roncalli serves as apostolic delegate to Bulgaria from 1925 to 1934, and, to Turkey and Greece from 1934 to 1944.[27] In 1944, Roncalli's global experience expands when he becomes papal nuncio in Paris, where he is in contact with the democratic worker-priest movement amid the aftermath of occupation and the liberation of France. Roncalli departs Paris in 1953 due to his being named Cardinal-Patriarch of Venice.[28]

The death of Pius XII, in October of 1958, leads to Roncalli being elected Pope, a month before his seventy-seventh birthday.[29] Roncalli serves the Church as Pope John XXIII for only four years and seven months, but he successfully inaugurates a new ecclesial perspective.[30]

While most agree that Vatican Council II is *the event* that defines the Catholic Church in the twentieth century, it is crucial to ask whether or not Pope John's two encyclicals *Mater et Magistra* and *Pacem in Terris*, in addition to his stirring speech to open the council, makes plausible the argument that Pope John XXIII is *the figure* who defines the Catholic Church's canonical turn to methods of praxis, historical reality, and the poor.

---

26 MacReamoinn, "John XXIII," 456.

27 MacReamoinn, "John XXIII," 456.

28 MacReamoinn, "John XXIII," 458.

29 MacReamoinn, "John XXIII," 457. The only serious opposition to Roncalli's election seems to have been the Armenian Cardinal Agaginian.

30 Roncalli died from stomach cancer on June 3, 1963.

Mater et Magistra:
Canonization of Cardijn's Method of Praxis

In *Mater et magistra* Pope John XXIII canonizes Cardijn's method of pastoral-theological praxis that interprets historical reality as a *locus theologicus*. To support this claim, I develop an argument in three steps. First, I show that John canonizes Cardijn's See-Judge-Act method in *Mater et Magistra*. Second, I show that John adopts Cardijn's methodological approach through his analysis and description of historical realities. Third, I highlight how John's methodological approach integrates a focus on the historical reality of the poor.

In *Mater et Magistra* John wrote:

> *Teachings in regard to social matters for the most part are put into effect in the following three stages: first, the actual situation is examined; then, the situation is evaluated carefully in relation to these teachings; then, only is it decided what can and should be done in order that the traditional norms may be adapted to circumstances of time and place. These three steps are at times expressed by the three words: observe, judge, act.*[31]

John explains that "It is important for our young people to grasp this method and to practice it. Knowledge acquired in this way does not remain merely abstract but is seen as something that must be translated into action."[32]

As the authority figure of the Magisterium, these statements by Pope John XIII not only blesses Cardijn's "See-Judge-Act" method, like Pope Pius XI, they canonize it in an official Church teaching. What resulted from John's canonization of Cardijn's method is nothing short of epochal in regard to the Church's turn to a praxis-

---

31 John XXIII, *Mater et Magistra*, accessed January 15, 2015, Vatican.va, 236.

32 John XXXI, *Mater et Magistra*, 237.

based methodology that interprets historical reality as a *locus theologicus*.

Pope John XXIII Methodological Turn to Historical Reality

In *Mater et Magistra* John writes that the Holy Catholic Church ought to show concern for "the exigencies of man's daily life, with his livelihood and education, and his general, temporal welfare and prosperity."[33] Moreover, the document states that the Church ought to be concerned about practices that affect "daily life" including: the distribution of property; the distribution of goods in society; just wages; state economics and the common good; neocolonialism; and, the political dominance of the poor by the rich.[34]

John also discusses other "intimate realities" that touch the "daily lives of Christians" including: remuneration for work,[35] balancing economic development and social progress,[36] private property,[37] public property,[38] workers,[39] agriculture,[40] public services,[41] development of the economic system,[42] taxation,[43] capital,[44] social

---

33 John XXIII, *Mater et Magistra*, 3.

34 David J. O'Brien and Thomas Shannon, editors. *Catholic Social Thought: The Documentary Heritage*, (Orbis: Maryknoll, 2010), 85.

35 John XXIII, *Mater et Magistra*, 68.

36 John XXIII, *Mater et Magistra*, 73.

37 John XXIII, *Mater et Magistra*, 104.

38 John XXIII, *Mater et Magistra*, 116.

39 John XXIII, *Mater et Magistra*, 122.

40 John XXIII, *Mater et Magistra*, 123.

41 John XXIII, *Mater et Magistra*, 127.

42 John XXIII, *Mater et Magistra*, 128.

43 John XXIII, *Mater et Magistra*, 132.

44 John XXIII, *Mater et Magistra*, 134.

STUOB028

CATHOLIC PRACTICAL THEOLOGY: A
GENEOLOGY...

9780999608845

Qty: 1

BoxID: 1395765

St. Thomas University

TO REORDER YOUR UPS DIRECT THERMAL LABELS:

1. Access our supply ordering website at **UPS.COM**®
   or contact UPS at 800-877-8652

2. Please refer to Label # 01774006 when ordering.

01774006   RRD

insurance and social security,[45] price protection,[46] strengthening farm income,[47] solidarity and cooperation with rural workers,[48] the common good,[49] and the Christian vocation and mission in relation to these realities.[50]

Like *Mater et Magistra*, *Pacem in Terris* shows that John turns the Church toward "reading the signs of the times," that is, toward the interpretation of historical reality as a *locus theologicus*. Drew Christiansen explains that in *Pacem in Terris* the empirical logic of reading the signs of the times led John "to an affirmation of the values discerned in the world, as in the growing sense of equality, the claiming of rights by women, workers, and racial minorities, or the opposition to war."[51] At the same time, by reading the signs of the times John establishes "a negative dialectic between the existing political conditions"[52] and what Jesus names the kingdom of God.

John's methodology of reading the signs of the times integrates a "different moral logic, not one of moral principles alone."[53] Rather John's argument includes a call for political and economic rights: "every man has the right to life, to bodily integrity, and to the means which are suitable for the proper development of life; these are primarily food, clothing, shelter, rest, medical care, and finally the necessary social services."[54]

---

45 John XXIII, *Mater et Magistra*, 135

46 John XXIII, *Mater et Magistra*, 137.

47 John XXIII, *Mater et Magistra*, 141.

48 John XXIII, *Mater et Magistra*, 146.

49 John XXIII, *Mater et Magistra*, 147.

50 John XXIII, *Mater et Magistra*, 149.

51 Christiansen, "Commentary," 224.

52 Christiansen, "Commentary," 224.

53 Christiansen, "Commentary," 224.

54 John XXIII, *Pacem in Terris*, accessed January 15, 2015, Vatican.va, 11.

In addition, John states: "a human being also has the right to security in cases of sickness, inability to work, widowhood, old age, unemployment, or any other case in which he is deprived of the means of subsistence through no fault of his own."[55] John also argues for universal access to the human right to education and professional training.[56] And, John links economic rights with the human right to immigrate.[57]

John concludes his discussion of human rights with the claim that it is the duty of all Christians take an "active part in public life."[58] John suggests that to achieve such dutiful Christian participation education must become more integral so that the "divorce between" Christian "faith and practice" can be overcome.[59]

In the end, besides his canonization of Cardijn's method in *Mater et Magistra*, John's retrieval of Jesus' call to read the signs of the times adds much magisterial weight to the turn toward a praxis-based methodology and the interpretation of historical realities as a *locus theologicus*.

Pope John XXIII Turns to the Poor

John's focus on socio-cultural, political, and economic realities, and their effect on the poor, is not new in the tradition of papal social teaching. Holland explains that the postmodern "Johannine

---

55 John XXIII, *Pacem in Terris*, 11n8.

56 John XXIII, *Pacem in Terris*, 12 and 13.

57 To support his claims concerning the right to freedom of movement within states and between states John argues that everyone carries a universal citizenship based on human dignity (no.25). John's argument for the right to migrate is very relevant today in both the United States and Europe.

58 John XXIII, *Pacem in Terris*, 146.

59 John XXIII, *Pacem in Terris*, 152-3.

strategy follows and builds on the earlier Leonine strategy."[60] In fact, John XXIII explains that one of the goals in writing *Mater et Magistra* is to re-contextualize the teachings of Pope Leo XIII's encyclical *Rerum Novarum* in light of changes in scientific, economic, and political conditions.[61]

John specifically wants to renew Leo's teaching and concern for "workers' conditions" as well as the problems of "weak and harassed men."[62] For example, in *Mater et Magistra* John emphasizes the need to protect and care for the most vulnerable and weaker members of society. In addition, John argues that nations "should safeguard the rights of all citizens, especially the weaker, particularly workers, women, and children."[63] Moreover, John claims that the richer sectors of a nation ought to assist those working in poor areas who are not enjoying the fruits of progress.[64]

John also adds a global dimension to his discussion of the relationship between richer and poorer nations.[65] John also calls for "aid to less developed areas" as a requirement of "justice" between "nations differing in economic development."[66] As Marvin Mich notes, the "Church owes much to John XXIII and the social teaching of *Mater et Magistra*" for opening up "the ability to see the need for a preferential option for the poor."[67]

---

60 Joe Holland, *Social Analysis II - End of the Modern World: The Need for a Postmodern Global Ecological Civilization & a Call for a Postmodern Ecological Renaissance* (unpublished manuscript, 2013, obtained in private email exchange with the author), 168.

61 John XXIII, *Mater et Magistra*, 50.

62 John XXIII, *Mater et Magistra*, 7 and 8.

63 John XXIII, *Mater et Magistra*, 16.

64 John XXIII, *Mater et Magistra*, 150-156.

65 John XXIII, *Mater et Magistra*, 157-177.

66 John XXIII, *Mater et Magistra*, 150, 157.

67 Mich, "Commentary," 211n93.

Vatican Council II

On the Feast of the Conversion of St. Paul, January 25, 1959, Pope John XXIII calls an ecumenical council to renew the Church's ways of "thinking, deciding, and acting."[68] Nearly two years later, on Christmas Day 1961, John formally convokes the Council with the Apostolic Constitution *Humanae Salutis* (Of Human Salvation).[69] John XXIII unfortunately dies before the Council end, but another Pope, Paul VI, presides over the final session of the Council. During the final session *Schema XIII* is drafted. *Schema XIII* is the working draft of what becomes *Gaudium et Spes: The Pastoral Constitution on the Church in the Modern World.*

In what follows I argue that key theological advisors at Vatican Council II renew the positions of those who laid the foundations of the turn toward a theological methodology of praxis that interprets historical reality as a *locus theologicus*. To support this claim, I show that Yves Congar resurrects Blondel's ideas at the Council. Second, I show that the committee that drafts *Schema XIII* specifically uses Cardijn's See-Judge-Act method to construct the document.[70]

I also discuss how M-D Chenu states that the methodology of reading the signs of the times becomes key to the drafting process of Schema XIII. Last, I explain that Cardijn argues that the pastoral

---

68 Thomas Hughson S.J., "Interpreting Vatican II: 'A New Pentecost,"*Theological Studies* 69, no.1 (March 2008): 3-37.

69 Giuseppe Alberigo, *A Brief History of Vatican II,* (Orbis: Maryknoll, 2006), 14.

70 *Gaudium et Spes* was not the only Vatican II document to use the phrase "signs of the times." For example, in the Decree on Ecumenism states that Catholics ought "to recognize the signs of the times and to take an active and intelligent part in the work of ecumenism (UR4). Similarly, the Decree on the Ministry and Life of Priests urges priests and laity "to recognize the signs of the times" (PO, 9). For more details on this see Giuseppe Alberigo, *History of Vatican II: Vol. V,* (Maryknoll: Orbis Press, 2006), 637. Also see, Albergio, *A Brief History of Vatican II,* 143n378.

constitution ought to reflect a focus on the unjust reality of global poverty and plight of the poor.

Vatican Council II: Congar Resurrects Blondel

Yves Congar is born on April 13, 1904, in Sedan, France to a family originally from Celtic Brittany.[71] He enters the Dominican Order in France in 1925 and studies at its theological center *Le Saulchoir*, when it is in exile in Belgium.[72] In the midst of Vatican Council II, Congar publishes *The Meaning of Tradition* (1964). In it Congar praises Blondel's description of tradition as historical, calling it "one of the finest descriptions of tradition that exist."[73] In addition, Congar argues that Blondel successfully showed that the Christian tradition has the ever-present experience of historical reality as a source of authentic reference for Christian ethics and history.[74]

Congar finds Blondel's position appealing because he agrees that the interpretation of historical reality holds a privileged position over ideological assertions.[75] In fact, at the Council, Congar renews Blondel's ideas to assert that Christian "tradition" is the "living communication" of God to His people, and, therefore, the "content is inseparable from the act by which one living person hands it on to another."[76] What this means is that Congar affects the Council with his belief that: "Everything is absolutely historical including the person of Jesus Christ. The Gospel is historical; Thomas

---

71 O'Meara, *Scanning*, 43.

72 O'Meara, *Scanning*, 44. *Le Saulchoir* educated not only Yves Congar but also scholars from other provinces such as Edward Schillebeeckx and Gustavo Gutierrez (who was not a Dominican at the time), 22.

73 Yves Congar, *The Meaning of Tradition*. trans., A.N. Woodrow. (San Francisco: Ignatius Press, 1964) 26n13.

74 Congar, *Meaning*, 27.

75 Congar, *Meaning*, 28.

76 Congar, *Meaning*, 24.

Aquinas is historical; Pope Paul VI is historical."[77] Who else influences the final documents that emerge at Vatican II? Re-enter Cardijn and M-D. Chenu.

Gaudium et Spes:
Conciliar Canonization of Cardijn's Method of Praxis

Gigacz explains that "In October 1964, after much criticism of an earlier draft of the Schema, the Central Sub-Commission adopted the See-Judge-Act method to re-draft the final version."[78] In fact, "The Commission instructed: To the maximum extent possible each (drafting) sub-commission should: start from the facts; bring a Christian judgment in the light of the Gospel and Catholic tradition from the Fathers up to contemporary documents of the Magisterium; indicate concrete orientations for action (pastoral aspect)."[79] The Central Sub-Commission also decided: "Sub Commission I will provide a *'conspectus generalis mundi hoderni'* (*signa temporum*)."[80]

---

77 O'Meara, *Scanning*, 55n38.

78 A copy of the original report of the Central Sub-Commission meetings that makes the decision to use the See-Judge-Act method to write *Gaudium et Spes* is available at the Archives of the *Institut catholique de Paris*. And, it can be found at http://www.josephcardijn.com/1964-schema-xiii-adopts-see-judge-act. The original document "Vatican II, Schema XIII, *Réunion Sous Commission Centrale*, is constructed October 17 - 20, 1964.

79 The original states, *"Méthodes de travail :1. L'organisation interne de chaque sous-commission et ses travaux relèvent de l'autorité de son Président,1. Dans toute la mesure du possible, chaque sous-commission devra : partir des faits ; porter un jugement chrétien, à la lumière de l'Evangile et de la tradition catholique, depuis les Pères jusqu'aux documents contemporains du magistère. indiquer des orientations concrètes d'action (aspect pastoral)."* For more see, http://www.josephcardijn.com/1964-schema-xiii-adopts-see-judge-act.

80 Gigacz's translation of this phrase is "general outline of the world situation, signs of the times." http://www.josephcardijn.com/1964-schema-xiii-adopts-see-judge-act.

In other words, those in charge of drafting *Schema XIII* not only explicitly use Cardijn's See-Judge-Act method but also integrate a methodological primacy on reading the signs of the times. This fact is a crucial development in the Church's turn toward a theological methodology of praxis that interprets historical reality as a *locus theologicus*. M-D Chenu echoes this sentiment.

At Vatican Council II Chenu, former regent of studies of the French Dominican school *Le Saulchoir*, serves as the personal theological advisor to Bishop Claude Rolland of Antisirabé (once a student at *Le Saulchoir*) and is asked to help write *Schema XIII*.[81] Chenu explains that from September to October of 1964 the sub-committee conducts an accurate analysis, description and theological interpretation of "signs of the times."[82]

Chenu claims that the subcommittee decided to move away from the abstract study of the nature of man (being) and toward temporal circumstances and signs of the times to focus on the problem of human historicity.[83] Chenu also states that the sub-committee takes a more historical approach because of their belief that history and Spirit are consubstantial.[84] In the end, Chenu claims that the focus on the signs of the times is "the most important aspect of the schema."[85]

---

81 O'Meara, *Scanning*, 19 and 36-38.

82 M-D Chenuu, "Les Signes des Temps," *Nouvelle Revue Théologique* 87/1 (1965) : 29-39.

83 Chenu, "Signes," 29-31.

84 Chenu, "Signes," 30-31.

85 O'Meara, *Scanning*, 38. Also see, Alberigo, *Brief History of Vatican II*, 145n385. And, it is worth noting that Gigacz claims Alphonse Gratry may have been the first to refer to "signs of the times" in the sense it later took in John XXIII's *Pacem in Terris* and thence Vatican II, (unpublished dissertation, no. 3.2n16. refers to Gratry 1864: I, 78).

Cardijn Turns *Guadium et Spes*
toward the Poor

At one of the "interventions" during the debate about *Schema XIII*, Cardinal Cardijn[86] expresses that "In its solicitude for the condition of people today, the Church must have the greatest consideration for the general aspiration of the people of the Third World to equality with the old countries in every domain of human life."[87] Cardijn further argues: "The faithful of the old Christian nations must, by all means, help relieve the suffering, the present misery and anguish of the Third World."

In addition, Cardijn states "The Council, very strongly manifesting its Christian concern, must solemnly implore the old rich nations to unite…all their scientific, technical, economic and political resources…in order to relieve and suppress all the great sufferings, all the great anguishes of the Third World."[88] It is clear therefore that Cardijn strongly urges the Church to confront the reality of the poverty and suffering of people around the world.

After the final draft of *Schema XIII* is brought to the Council, Cardinals and Bishops make speeches for or against different aspects of the document. Gigacz explains, "With the assistance of Fr. Yves Congar, O.P.,"[89] Cardijn prepares a speech to argue that "in this Pastoral Constitution ... it is extremely important that it considers people not in a general manner but as they are concretely in the

---

86 Stefan Gigacz notes that "Cardijn was made a bishop and cardinal by Pope Paul VI at the beginning of 1965. He was thus able to participate as a Council father in the fourth and final session of the Second Vatican Council at the end of that year." For more see, *http://*www.josephcardijn.com/cardijn-vatican-ii. Accessed July 7, 2015.

87 Gigacz, Unpublished dissertation.

88 Gigacz, Unpublished dissertation.

89 Congar's notes concerning his work with Cardijn can be found on the website http://*www.josephcardijn.com/cardijn-vatican-ii.* Accessed July 7, 2015. For more also see: Albergio, *A History of Vatican II: Vol V,* 91n161.

world today."[90] Cardijn also state that the document must speak to "young people, workers, and, the Third World"[91] because Jesus "said: 'The Father sent me to bring good news to the poor.'"[92]

The final version of *Gaudium et Spes* reflects the work of many of the aforementioned interlocutors. The final document makes explicit that the Church "realizes that it is truly and intimately linked with mankind and its history," especially with "The joys and hopes, the griefs and anxieties of the men of this age, especially those who are *poor* or in any way afflicted, these too are the joys and hopes, the griefs and anxieties of the followers of Christ."[93]

Moreover, the authors of the document support their claims about the poor with appeals to New Testament accounts of Jesus' praxis on behalf of the poor. For example, Luke 16:18-31 is invoked to show that the Church believes that "everyone must consider his every neighbor without exception as another self" so as "not to imitate the rich man who had no concern for the poor man Lazarus."[94]

And, the Fathers and Doctors of the Church are invoked to affirm the Church believes: "that men are obliged to come to the relief of the poor and to do so not merely out of their superfluous goods." The document further states: "Since there are so many people prostrate with hunger in the world, this sacred council urges all, both individuals and governments, to remember the aphorism of the

---

90 Gigacz, http://www.josephcardijn.com/cardijn-vatican-ii. 1965 intervention. Also see Albergio, History of Vatican II: Vol. V, 144n381.

91 Gigacz, http://www.josephcardijn.com/cardijn-vatican-ii.

92 For more see: http://www.josephcardijn.com/young-workers-and-the-developing-world. Accessed July 7, 2015.

93 Paul VI, *Gaudium et Spes*, 1. Emphasis added by author.

94 Paul VI, *Gaudium et Spes*, 27n50.

Fathers...Feed the man dying of hunger, because if you have not fed him, you have killed him."[95]

But how is this focus on the poor developed after the Council? The canonical turn toward a theological methodology of praxis and the interpretation of historical reality, especially the reality of the poor, as a *locus theologicus,* is confirmed by Pope Paul VI.

Giovanni Battista Montini:
Pope Paul VI

Giovanni Battista Montini is born "to middle-class parents in Concesio, near Brescia, in northern Italy on September 26, 1898."[96] Montini is ordained a priest on May 29, 1920 and worked in various Vatican offices for more than thirty years until 1954, when he is named Archbishop of Milan. In 1958 Pope John XXIII makes Montini a cardinal and involves him in "preparations for Vatican Council II."[97] After the death of John XXIII, Montini is elected Pope and takes the name Paul VI.

Pope Paul VI issues many documents and encyclicals but an analysis of *Populorum Progessio* (1967)[98] and *Octogesima Adveniens*

---

95 Paul VI, *Gaudium et Spes,* 69n10, n12.

96 Anthony D. Andreassi, "Pope Paul VI," *The Modern Catholic Encyclopedi*a. Glazier, Michael and Monika K. Hellwig, editors. (Collegeville: Liturgical Press, 1994), 652-3.

97 Andreassi, Paul VI, 653. Montini, for example, belonged to the Central Preparatory Committee and the Technical Organizing Committee. In these capacities, he was often consulted by Pope John, who even invited him to reside at the Vatican, a privilege extended to no other Council Father. During the First Session, he is appointed to the Secretariat for Extraordinary Affairs, a post that seems to have been meant precisely to give him the opportunity to play an important role in the decisions that gave overall direction to the Council's work. For more on this issue see Edward O'Connor, C.S.C., *Pope Paul and the Spirit: Charisms and Church Renewal in the Teaching of Paul VI,* (Notre Dame: Ave Maria Press, 1978), 64n4.

98 Paul VI, *Populorum Progressio,* in *Catholic Social Thought: The Documentary Heritage,* edited by David J. O'Brien and Thomas A. Shannon. (Orbis: Maryknoll, 2010)..

(1971)[99] show that he adds canonical weight to his predecessor's use of Cardijn's See-Judge-Act method. [100] To support this claim, I develop an argument in three steps.

- First, I appeal to *Populorum Progressio* and *Octogesima Adveniens* to show that Paul draws from Cardijn's method to interpret historical reality, or "read the signs of the times."

- Second, I appeal to the same two documents to show that Paul's methodological focus on historical reality aligns him with his predecessor, John XXIII.

- Third, I use the same documents to show that Paul VI adds canonical weight to the Church's turn to poverty and the poor as a *locus theologicus*.

Pope Paul VI Draws from Cardijn's See-Judge-Act Method

Pope Paul VI draws from Cardijn's See-Judge-Act method to write *Populorum Progressio* (1967). The document is parceled into three subsections: (1) "The Data of the Problem," (2) "The Church and Development," and, (3) "Action to be Undertaken." In subsection one, the "data" is the historical reality that Paul "sees." In subsection two, Paul explains how the Church "judges" the data by the light of the gospel and wisdom of the Christian tradition. In subsection three, Paul provides a pastoral reflection that advocates change of certain political realities via strategic Christian "action." In other words, as Allan Figueroa Deck explains: "Paul VI follows the lead

---

99 Paul VI, *Octogesima Adveniens*, in *Catholic Social Thought: The Documentary Heritage*, edited by David J. O'Brien and Thomas A. Shannon, Orbis: Maryknoll, 2010).

100 Christine Gudorf, "Commentary on *Octogesima Adveniens*," in *Modern Catholic Social Teaching: Commentaries and Interpretations*, Kenneth R. Himes, O.F.M, editor, (Washington DC: Georgetown University Press: 2005), 318n5.

of his predecessor John XXIII in proposing the 'observe, judge, act' paradigm of pastoral reflection."[101]

Four years later, to honor the eightieth anniversary of the publication of Leo XIII's *Rerum Novarum*, Paul VI issues *Octogesima Adveniens* (1971). In the document Paul VI explicitly draws from Cardijn's See-Judge-Act method of theological praxis. Paul writes: "It is up to the Christian communities to analyze with objectivity the situation which is proper to their own country, to shed light on it of the Gospel's unalterable words and to draw principles of reflection, norms of judgment and directives for action from the social teaching of the church."[102] In other words, Paul uses Cardijn's method to integrate social analysis[103] and theological reflection "to bring about the social, political and economic changes seen in many cases to be urgently needed."[104]

Pope Paul VI Turns to Historical Reality

After becoming pope, Paul VI travels to Latin America in 1960, to Africa in 1962, and, to the Holy Land and India. His travels help him see that many people are "striving to escape" realities of "hunger, misery, endemic diseases, and ignorance."[105] The poverty Paul VI observes in his travels around the world inspires him to confront the political reality of underdevelopment, which he attributes to colonialist politics and *laissez-faire* economics.[106] For example, Paul writes that laissez-faire capitalism "left to itself it works rather to widen the differences in the world's levels of life, not to diminish

---

101 Allan Figueroa Deck, S.J. "Commentary on *Populorum Progressio*," 299.

102 Paul VI, *Octogesima Adveniens*, 4.

103 Gudorf, *"Commentary on Octogesima Adveniens,"* 319.

104 Paul VI, *Octogesima Adveniens*, 4.

105 Paul VI, *Populorum Progressio*, 1 and 4.

106 Deck, "Commentary," 292.

them: rich peoples enjoy rapid growth whereas the poor develop slowly."[107]

In *Octogesima Adveniens* (1971) Paul claims that "flagrant inequalities exist in the economic, cultural, and political development of nations." And, while "Some countries enjoy prosperity," many "others are struggling against starvation."[108] Paul VI states that such realities are caused by "disordered growth" in global economic structures, which forces the weakest members of society to subsist in "dehumanizing living conditions" on the outskirts of cities.[109]

Pope Paul also urges laypeople to confront this "dehumanizing" reality and "take up as their own proper task the renewal of the temporal order."[110] To achieve this goal, Paul argues that "it is not enough to recall principles, state intentions, point to crying injustices, and utter prophetic denunciations; these words will lack real weight unless they are accompanied for each individual by a livelier awareness of personal responsibility and by effective action."[111]

Pope Paul VI Turns to the Poor as a Locus Theologicus

In *Populorum Progressio* Paul discusses underdevelopment and global poverty in light of the teaching and example of Jesus, "who cited the preaching of the Gospel to the poor as a sign of his mission."[112] Not only does Paul VI invoke Jesus as the foundation for his concern for the poor, he also supplements his claim with appeals to various statements from the Christian tradition. To make his case

---

107 Paul VI, *Populorum Progressio*, 8.

108 Paul VI, *Octogesima Adveniens*, 2.

109 Paul VI, *Octogesima Adveniens*, 10-11.

110 Paul VI, *Octogesima Adveniens*, 48.

111 Paul VI, *Octogesima Adveniens*, 48.

112 Paul VI, *Populorum Progressio*, 12n11.

Paul appeals to 1 John 3:17 which states, "If someone who has the riches of this world sees his brother in need and closes his heart to him, how does the love of God abide in him."[113]

To add depth to his argument about the poor, Paul invokes the words of Saint Ambrose: "You are not making a gift of your possessions to the poor person. You are handing over to him what is his. For what has been given in common for the use of all, you have arrogated to yourself. The world is given to all, and not only to the rich."[114]

In addition, Paul explains: "no one is justified in keeping for his exclusive use what he does not need when others lack necessities,"[115] because "today...in whole continents countless men and women are ravaged by hunger," and "countless numbers of children are undernourished."[116] Paul then invokes the Biblical figure of Lazarus and the parable about the rich man in order to make an analogy concerning the relationship between rich and poor nations (LK 16:19-31).[117]

The focus of *Populorum Progressio* is clear - the mission of the Church must be one that enacts a preferential option for the poor. For example, Paul writes: "we must repeat once more that the superfluous wealth of the rich countries should be placed at the service of poor nations."[118] And, that "when so many people are hungry" and there happens to be "public and private squandering of wealth" on such things as "armaments" we must "denounce it."[119]

---

113 Paul VI, *Populorum Progressio*, 23n21.

114 Paul VI, *Populorum Progressio*, 23n22.

115 Paul VI, *Populorum Progressio*, 23.

116 Paul VI, *Populorum Progressio*, 45.

117 Paul Vi, *Populorum Progressio*, 47

118 Paul VI, *Populorum Progressio*, 49.

119 Paul VI, *Populorum Progressio*, 53

Paul adds that "if ever there was a reality whose scope and urgency required the engagement of the highest echelons of government at the level of the state and international bodies it was global poverty."[120] The evidence from *Populorum Progressio* clearly shows that Paul's focus on the reality of poverty is a call for the Church's "charity for the poor in the world" to become "more active."[121]

In *Octogesima Adveniens* Paul continues to develop the gospel theme of a preferential option for the poor.[122] In *Octogesima Adveniens* Paul writes: "In teaching us charity, the Gospel instructs us in the preferential respect due to the poor and the special situation they have in a society: the more fortunate should renounce some of their rights so as to place their goods more generally at the service of others."[123]

Paul also enlarges the theological understanding of the "poor to include the handicapped and the maladjusted, the old, and different groups of those on the fringes of society."[124] Paul includes in his definition of the poor anyone who is "among the victims of situations of injustice" particularly "those who are discriminated against on account of their race, origin, color, culture, sex, or religion."[125] Paul specifies that among victims of injustice are specifically "emigrant workers" who, due to "their real participation in the economic effort of the country that receives them," should receive "decent housing" and the right to "professional advancement."[126]

---

120 Deck, "Commentary," 301. Also see Paul VI, *Populorum Progressio*, 33.

121 Paul VI, *Populorum Progressio*, 76.

122 Gudorf, "Commentary," 323

123 Paul VI, *Octogesima Adveniens*, 23.

124 Paul VI, *Octogesima Adveniens*, 15

125 Paul VI, *Octogesima Adveniens*, 16.

126 Paul VI, *Octogesima Adveniens*, 17.

Populorum Progressio and *Octogesima Adveniens* clearly and prophetically speak out on behalf of the needs of the global poor while calling upon the rich to cooperate in alleviating those needs through focused attention upon the economic and political reality of global poverty and the plight of the poor. And, because Pope Paul VI draws from the See-Judge-Act method he adds considerable canonical weight to the Catholic Church's epoch-defining turn toward a theological methodology of praxis that interprets historical reality, especially the reality of the global poverty, as a *locus theologicus*.

Conclusion

I have argued that in the mid-twentieth century the Catholic Magisterium canonizes Cardijn's See-Judge-Act method with its praxis-based methodology that interprets historical reality as a *locus theologicus*.

To support this claim, I appealed to two encyclicals written by Pope John XXIII, specifically *Mater et Magistra* and *Pacem in Terris*. I also appealed to the work done at Vatican II by Cardinal Cardijn, and theological advisors M-D Chenu and Yves Congar, particularly their contributions of retrieving Blondel as well as the use of Cardijn's method to write *Gaudium et Spes*.

Last, I showed that Pope Paul VI, particularly in *Populorum Progressio* and *Octogesima Adveniens*, confirmed the canonical turn to Cardijn's See-Judge-Act method and the interpretation of historical reality, with an added focus on the interpretation of global poverty as a *locus theologicus*.

PART II

LATIN AMERICAN PRAXIS

3

THE LATIN AMERICAN TURN TO PRAXIS:

GROUNDED IN A PREFERENTIAL OPTION

FOR THE POOR

Overview

B oth the Episcopal Conference of Latin America [*Consejo Epis-copal Latinoamericano*], and Latin American "liberation" theologians, adopt and develop Cardijn's See-Judge-Act method of theological praxis to interpret historical reality as a *locus theologicus*.

To support this claim, I present select material from the documents produced by the bishops at meetings at Medellin, Colombia (1968), Puebla, Mexico (1979), and Aparecida, Brazil (2007). I also analyze the work of Gustavo Gutierrez and Clodovis Boff to show that they offer reflections on method and methodology, praxis, and the interpretation of historical reality as a *locus theologicus*. I also explain that what results from the Latin American turn to methods praxis is a prophetic call for the Catholic Church to reorient its mission toward a preferential option for the poor. First, however, it is important to contextualize the historical reality of Latin America.

Post-Conciliar Latin America:
Historical Context

"One should never speak of Latin America as if it were a single, homogenous region, since in fact the area is exceedingly diverse."[1] Yet, at the same time, "Latin American countries share a common basis in law, language, history, culture, sociology, colonial experience, and overall political patterns."[2]

For example, colonial Latin America is "dominated by a political, social, and economic structure that has its roots not in modernity but in medievalism."[3] What Spain and Portugal "brought to the New World reflected the traditions" of Western European feudal society, including "a rigid, authoritarian political system; a similarly rigid and hierarchical class structure; a feudal, statist, and mercantilist economy; an absolutist church; and a similarly closed and absolutist educational system."[4] And, because "The economy was feudal and exploitative; in accord with the prevailing mercantilism, the wealth of the colonies was drained to benefit the mother countries and was not used for the betterment of the colonies themselves."

According to Wiarda and Kline "the Roman Catholic Church reinforced royal authority and policy in the colonies" because it is similarly absolutist and authoritarian.[5] Its role is to Christianize and

---

1 Howard J. Wiarda and Harvey F. Kline. *An Introduction to Latin American Politics and Development*, (Boulder: Westview Press, 2001), 1.

2 Wiarda and Kline, *Latin American Politics and Development*, 1.

3 Wiarda and Kline, *Latin American Politics and Development*, 13.

4 Wiarda and Kline, *Latin American Politics and Development*, 16.

5 Wiarda and Kline do say that during colonial times "some individual clergy sought to defend the Indians against enslavement and maltreatment," but, in general, "the Church was primarily an arm of the state." The one area the Church was given power to oversee was "intellectual life and education" which "was scholastic, based on rote memorization, deductive reasoning, and unquestioned orthodoxy." 17

pacify the indigenous population and thus serve the "Crown's assimilationist policies." O. Ernesto Valiente also writes that "until the mid-20th century the church honored this alliance and tacitly endorsed the socioeconomic structures that relegated the majority of the population to substandard living conditions."[6]

Speaking about Latin America from a contemporary U.S. theological perspective, Elizabeth Johnson likewise argues: "For centuries the Catholic Church was complicit in creating such historical-sociocultural realities that favored those who ruled."[7] Simply put, the colonial power structure, aided by the hierarchy of the Catholic Church, contributes to the creation of an exploitative colonial economy built on a "gap between the wealthy ruling class and the vast masses of the population."[8]

Wiarda and Kline add that even though "Spanish and Portuguese colonial rule lasted...from the late fifteenth through the early nineteenth century, it was a remarkably stable period with few revolts."[9] In the "late eighteenth century" however, "the first serious cracks began to appear in this monolithic colonial structure. Under the impact of the eighteenth-century Enlightenment, ideas of liberty, freedom, and nationalism began to creep in, and the examples of revolutions in the United States (1776) and France (1789) caused tremors in Latin America."[10]

---

6 O. Ernesto Valiente, "The Reception of Vatican II in Latin America," *Theological Studies* 73 (2012): 797.

7 Elizabeth Johnson, *Quest for the Living God: Mapping Frontiers in the Theology of God.* (New York: Continuum, 2007), 71. Also see O. Ernesto Valiente's discussion of Spanish and Portugese colonial power in Latin America in "The Reception of Vatican II in Latin America," *Theological Studies*, no. 73 (2012): 795-823.

8 José Comblin, *People of God* (Maryknoll: Orbis Books, 2004), 40.

9 Wiarda and Kline, *Latin American Politics and Development*, 17.

10 Wiarda and Kline, *Latin American Politics and Development*, 17-8.

Wiarda and Kline describe how "the independence struggles in Latin America waxed and waned for nearly two decades" before Simon Bolivar and Jose de San Martin are able to defeat the royalist forces in the key battle of Ayacucho in 1824, thus ending Spanish authority in South America."[11] By the mid-1820's almost all Spanish forces and ruling authorities retreat from mainland Latin America. The exceptions are the islands of Cuba and Puerto Rico, which remain Spanish colonies until 1898.[12]

It is not be surprising, therefore, that after independence Latin America enters a chaotic period.[13] Wiarda and Klein state that, "deprived of their Spanish markets but still lacking new ones, many of the countries slipped back to a more primitive barter economy and living standards plummeted...In the absence of political parties, organized interest groups, or well-established institutions of any kind, the Latin American countries sank into either dictatorship or anarchy." Hence, the immediate post-independence period, from the mid-1820s until the the mid-1850s, is, in most countries, a time of turbulence and decline.[14]

Wiarda and Kline add that, "By the 1850s a degree of stability had begun to appear in many Latin American countries."[15] Along with increasing stability comes foreign investment and greater productivity. "British capital was invested in the area, providing a major stimulus to growth. New lands were opened to cultivation and new exports such as sugar, coffee, tobacco, beef, and wool began to restore national coffers."[16] These changes accelerate "in the

11 Wiarda and Kline, *Latin American Politics and Development*, 19.

12 Wiarda and Kline, *Latin American Politics and Development*, 19.

13 Wiarda and Kline, *Latin American Politics and Development*, 20.

14 Wiarda and Kline, *Latin American Politics and Development*, 21.

15 Wiarda and Kline, *Latin American Politics and Development*, 21.

16 Wiarda and Kline, *Latin American Politics and Development*, 21.

1870s and 1880s" and represent "the first stirrings of modernization in Latin America."[17]

Moreover, "economic growth" at this time "also increased political stability, although not in all countries."[18] Wiarda and Kline argue that "three patterns may be observed."[19] The first, present in Argentina, Brazil, Chile, and Peru "involved the consolidation of power by an export-oriented landed oligarchy where "power changed only among the elites."[20] The second pattern, evident in Mexico, Venezuela, and the Dominican Republic, involves the seizure of power by strong authoritarian dictators while a third pattern emerged slightly later in the first decades of the twentieth century, in the smaller, weaker, and resource-poor countries of Central America and the Caribbean.[21] In Haiti, Cuba, the Dominican Republic, Nicaragua, and Panama a pattern emerges that involved "U.S. military intervention and occupation, with the Marines carrying out many of the same policies as the...oligarchs and dictators."[22]

By the 1930's "large-scale industrialization began in most Latin American countries. But, most of the heavy industries - steel, electricity, petroleum, manufacturing - were established as state-owned industries."[23] Wiarda and Kline describe this system as "state capitalism" to distinguish it from the "laissez-faire or free market capitalism" that emerged in Western Europe. However, after "the market crashed in the United States in 1929 and Europe the following year, the bottom dropped out of the market for Latin American

17 Wiarda and Kline, *Latin American Politics and Development*, 22.

18 Wiarda and Kline, *Latin American Politics and Development*, 22.

19 Wiarda and Kline, *Latin American Politics and Development*, 22.

20 Wiarda and Kline, *Latin American Politics and Development*, 22.

21 Wiarda and Kline, *Latin American Politics and Development*, 22.

22 Wiarda and Kline, *Latin American Politics and Development*, 22.

23 Wiarda and Kline, *Latin American Politics and Development*, 8.

exports, sending the region's economies into a tailspin and under-mining their political systems as well."[24]

Between 1930 and 1935 governments are overthrown in four-teen of the twenty Latin American countries. Thus, "the chasm be-tween traditional powerholders and the new social and political forces clamoring for change had grown wider; the new forces were demanding reform and democratization."[25] And, "some countries, after a brief interruption and instability in the early 1930s, reverted to oligarchic rule. In other countries, new, military dictatorships came into power, such as those of Fulgencio Batista in Cuba, Ana-stasio Somoza in Nicaragua, Rafael Trujillo in the Dominican Re-public, and Jorge Ubico in Guatemala."[26]

Wiarda and Kline explain that "During World War II and the postwar period, Latin America developed rapidly on the basis of what was called the import-substitution industrialization (ISI) model."[27] However, "instead of decreasing the need to export pri-mary goods, ISI increased that need, since exports were needed to pay for machinery for the new industries, which had to be im-ported."[28] In addition, "growing demands for new social programs outstripped many countries' ability to pay for them."

The demands for social programs led to volatility in politics. According to Wiarda and Kline, "Politically, the 1960s was a period when workers, peasants, and left-wing guerrillas were all mobiliz-ing: the traditional elites, feeling threatened by the mass mobiliza-tion, thus turned to the military to keep lower classes in check. This is called "bureaucratic authoritarianism" - or rule by institutional

---

24 Wiarda and Kline, *Latin American Politics and Development*, 23.

25 Wiarda and Kline, *Latin American Politics and Development*, 23.

26 Wiarda and Kline, *Latin American Politics and Development*, 24.

27 Wiarda and Kline, *Latin American Politics and Development*, 8-9.

28 Wiarda and Kline, *Latin American Politics and Development*, 9.

armed forces and their civilian supporters."[29] While "There was a brief democratic interlude in the late 1950s and early 1960s in Argentina, Brazil, the Dominican Republic, and Honduras...by the late 1960s and through the 1970s Latin American had succumbed to a new wave of militarism. By the mid-1970s, fourteen of the twenty countries were again under military-authoritarian rule."[30] And, "Only Colombia, Costa Rica, and Venezuela were democracies, and even they were elite-directed regimes."[31]

Robert Lasalle-Klein notes that what is crucial to understand about this time in Latin America is that twentieth century struggles to end military rule and oppression by local elites is led by a spirit of decolonialization that mobilized literally millions of people in Latin American civil society behind demands for elections and economic reform.[32]

For example, "Frequently chaotic, driven by nationalistic concerns, and sometimes backed by armed rebellions," these political movements eventually "succeeded in bringing an end to military rule in Argentina in 1983, Bolivia in 1982, Brazil in 1985, Chile in 1990, El Salvador in 1984, Guatemala in 1986, Haiti in 1990 and 1994, Honduras in 1982, Nicaragua in 1979, Panama in 1989, Paraguay in 1993, Peru in 1980, and Uruguay in 1985."[33] In the end, a difficult and bloody struggle waged by popular mass mobilizations against the military and traditional elites is what caused the military dictatorships to be no longer viable.

Another crucial aspect of the political reality is that the Latin American bishops did not initially support the leftist political

---

29 Wiarda and Kline, *Latin American Politics and Development*, 26.

30 Wiarda and Kline, *Latin American Politics and Development*, 26.

31 Wiarda and Kline, *Latin American Politics and Development*, 26.

32 Lassalle-Klein, *Blood and Ink*, 14.

33 Lassalle-Klein, *Blood and Ink*, 14.

movements that were mobilizing civil society in massive numbers against the military dictatorships in order to promote democratic socialism. According to Jaime Vidaurrazaga the initial seeds of change in Latin America stem from a "budding historical movement of social, economic, and political transformation in which the poor themselves were the historical subjects fighting for their own rigths and for a new society."[34]

Vidaurrazaga adds that the "irruption of the poor" in "Latin American society had not been orchestrated or engineered by church activists, but Vatican II-minded church leaders could not let the opportunity to effect meaningful change in favor of the poor pass by during such an upsurge of activism."[35] As Thomas Kelly notes, "the church had always been political," the political movements simply opened up an opportunity for the Church to make a real shift and side with the poor.[36]

As the political clashes turned violent, many of the Latin American bishops begin to question why reality is marked by economic inequality, sociopolitical and religious injustice, and decide to make the question of poverty and its causes, along with poor people themselves, the central theological *locus* of their teaching.[37] The choice of poverty as the primary *locus* stems from their belief that poverty is a contradiction of Christian existence.[38] Why do they

---

34 Jaime Vidaurrazaga, "Appropriating the Bible as 'Memory of the Poor," in *The Bible and Catholic Theological Ethics*. Edited by Yiu Sing Lúcás Chan, James F. Keenan, and Ronaldo Zacharias, (Maryknoll: NY, Orbis Books, 2017), 185.

35 Vidaurrazaga, "Appropriating the Bible," 185. Vidaurrazaga borrows the phrase "irruption of the poor" from Gustavo Gutierrez. For more, see Gustavo Gutierrez, *A Theology of Liberation: History, Politics, and Salvation*, trans. And ed. Sister Caridad Inda and John Eagleson (Maryknoll, NY: Orbis Books, 1988), xx-xxi.

36 Thomas M. Kelly, *When the Gospel Grows Feet: Rutilio Grande, SJ, and the Church in El Salvdor, An Ecclesiology in Context*, (Collegeville: MN, Liturgical Press, 2013), 151.

37 Johnson, *Quest*, 71.

38 Johnson, *Quest*, 71.

believe this? Because lack of food and drinkable water, lack of housing, education, health care, and lack of employment not only add up to short lives of misery but are also an affront to Christian notions of the human, the good life, and the Kingdom of God.[39] Where is this belief first affirmed by the bishops?

Medellin, Colombia (1968)

Valiente explains that even before Pope Paul VI delivers "the concluding address of Vatican II on December 8, 1965, preparations had already begun for the Second Episcopal Conference of Latin American Bishops."[40] In fact, "Chilean bishop Manuel Larrain, president of CELAM at the time, and his vice-president, Brazilian bishop Helder Camara, decided that an assembly of Latin American bishops" is "needed to examine the continent's situation in light of Vatican II."[41]

The Second General Conference of Latin American Bishops eventually takes place between August 24 and September 6, 1968, in Medellin, Colombia. The bishops produce several documents at this meeting. The *Justice, Peace,* and *Poverty* documents clearly put into practice Cardijn's See-Judge-Act method with its praxis-based methodology. The documents provide a good example of how the bishops appropriate Cardijn's method to make a theological interpretation of Latin American political and economic reality, which led to their prophetic call for a preferential option for the poor.

---

39 Johnson, *Quest*, 71.

40 Valiente, "Reception," 801.

41 Valiente, "Reception," 801.

The Bishops Turn to
Cardijn's See-Judge-Act Method

All three documents are divided into three sections: I. Pertinent Facts; II. Doctrinal Basis; and III. Projection for Social Pastoral Planning, which follow the formula of See-Judge-Act. In "Part I" of the *Justice* document the bishops present "pertinent facts" that describe Latin America as a place where misery "besets large masses of human beings in all of our countries."[42] In Section II, the bishops use Jesus' eschatological vision to argue that any reality characterized by abject poverty is an affront to Jesus' claim that the Kingdom of God is at hand (MK 1:15).[43] In section III the bishops assert that the Church's "pastoral mission" must include educative programs that inspire changes in personal and social action.[44]

The *Poverty* document, like the *Justice* document, is parceled into three sections. Section I describes "the Latin American scene" as one of "tremendous social injustices...which keep the majority of our peoples in dismal poverty, which in many cases becomes inhuman wretchedness."[45] In section II, "Doctrinal Motivation," the bishops assert that "it will be necessary to reemphasize strongly that the example and teaching of Jesus...place before the Latin American Church a challenge and a mission that she cannot sidestep and to which she must respond with a speed and boldness

---

42 Second General Conference of Latin American Bishops, *Medellin, Justice Document*, 1; quoted in *Renewing the Earth: Catholic Documents on Peace, Justice and Liberation*. Edited by David J. O'Brien and Thomas A. Shannon, (Garden City: NY, Image Books, 1977), 549.

43 Medellin, *Justice*, 3-5.

44 Medellin, *Justice*, 6.

45 Medellin, *Poverty*, 1.

adequate to the urgency of the times."[46] In Section III, "Pastoral Orientations," the bishops argue:

> *We ought to sharpen the awareness of our duty of solidarity with the poor, to which charity leads us. This solidarity means that we make ours their problems and their struggles, that we know how to speak with them. This has to be concretized in criticism of injustice and oppression, in the struggle against the intolerable situation which a poor person often has to tolerate, in the willingness to dialogue with the groups responsible for that situation in order to make them understand their obligations.*[47]

In their statement, "Message to the Peoples of Latin America," the bishops state that "We believe that we are in a new historical era. This era requires clarity in order to see, lucidity in order to diagnose, and solidarity in order to act."[48] Cardijn's See-Judge-Act formula is clearly present in the statement.

The Bishops Turn to Historical Reality
and an Option for the Poor

Part I of the *Peace* document focuses on historical reality, again using Cardijn's See-Judge-Act method and a praxis-based methodology. The bishops describe how they see economic underdevelopment in Latin America as an obstacle to peace,[49] adding that economic underdevelopment in Latin America creates "extreme inequality among social classes in Latin America" resulting in a "socioeconomic, cultural, political, racial, and religious...bi-classism" in

---

46 Medellin, *Poverty*, 7.

47 Medellin, *Poverty*, 10.

48 Medellin, *Message to the Peoples of Latin America*, quoted in *Renewing the Earth: Catholic Documents on Peace, Justice and Liberation*. Edited by David J. O'Brien and Thomas A. Shannon, (Garden City: NY, Image Books, 1977), 574.

49 Medellin, *Peace*, 1.

both urban and rural areas.[50] They argue that this extreme inequality is partially due to power unjustly exercised by the historically dominant sectors, who create an economic gap and social poverty that represent not only a class divide between rich and poor in Latin America but real structural sin and "institutionalized violence."[51]

In part II of the document the bishops offer a theological reflection on reality, asserting that the establishment of peace must take place through the transformation of powerful groups who are responsible for social, political, economic, and cultural oppression that result in mass inequality.[52] The bishops add that such inequalities and structural deficiencies are evident in whole towns that "lack necessities" that "hinders all initiative in social and political life, thus violating fundamental rights."[53] The bishops then assert that these structural deficiencies will only change through a transformation of attitudes and conversion of hearts.[54]

In part III the bishops argue that the unjust realities in Latin America call Christians to create a more just society through action, particularly educative action,[55] oriented toward defending the rights of the poor and oppressed in light of the Gospel.[56] To defend the rights of the poor the bishops explain that Catholic "schools, seminaries, and universities" should nurture a critical and prophetic sense of excessive inequalities between the poor and rich and the weak and powerful.[57] Thus, the Medellin documents show that the Latin American bishops make a prophetic turn to the historical

---

50 Medellin, *Peace*, 2-3.

51 Medellin, *Peace*, 6 and 16.

52 Medellin, *Peace*, 14.

53 Medellin, *Peace*, 16n26.

54 Medellin, *Peace*, 14.

55 Medellin, *Peace*, 20.

56 Medellin, *Peace*, 22.

57 Medellin, *Peace*, 23-25.

reality of poverty using Cardijn's See-Judge-Act method and a praxis-based methodology.[58] While "preferential option for the poor" is implicit in texts produced at Medellin, the phrase does not become explicit until the 1979 CELAM meeting in Puebla, Mexico.[59]

Puebla, Mexico (1979)

The Third General Conference of Latin American bishops takes place at Puebla, Mexico. The *Puebla* document, like the Medellin documents, turns toward the interpretation of historical reality by utilizing Cardijn's See-Judge-Act method.[60] The document begins with a graphic "description of the situation," moves on to "an examination of its causes," and concludes with a "judgment in faith that all of this merits."[61] Gutierrez explains that by placing theological judgment second, the bishops are able to generate a prophetic denouncement of structural realities that oppress the poor in Latin America.[62] Gutierrez also asserts that, like Medellin, "Puebla's conviction is the fruit of praxis."[63]

The Bishops Return to
Cardijn's See-Judge-Act Method

In Part One, the bishops describe facts and signs from their own cultural context.[64] In other words, using Cardijn's method, the

58 Jon Sobrino, *Puebla and Beyond: Documentation and Commentary*, eds. John Eagleson and Philip Scharper, (Maryknoll: Orbis, 1979), 290.

59 Hollenbach, *Commentary*, 287n32.

60 Valiente, "The Reception of Vatican II in Latin America," 812. Valiente claims that Puebla endorsed the "see, judge, act" methodology of *Gaudium et Spes* and Medellin.

61 Gustavo Gutierrez, *The Power of the Poor in History*, (Maryknoll: Orbis, 2010), 132.

62 Gutierrez, *Power of the Poor*, 136

63 Gutierrez, *Power of the Poor*, 151.

64 McGrath, *Puebla and Beyond: Documentation and Commentary*, John Eagleson and Philip Scharper, ed. (Maryknoll: Orbis, 1979), 90.

bishops read the signs of the times.[65] In Part II the bishops reflect theologically on the "signs of the times" and interpret their historical reality in the light of the gospel.[66] In McGrath's language, the second part of the Puebla document is where the Bishops "gospelize" reality.[67] McGrath, like Gutierrez, claims that by placing theological reflection second, after social analysis, Catholic social teaching is able to adapt to changing circumstances of time and place, yet always remain in fidelity to the Gospel.[68]

Parts III, IV, and V detail a pastoral strategy to initiate change in Latin America.[69] While much could be said about these chapters, the key for our purposes is the bishops' use of Cardijn's See-Judge-Act method to interpret Latin American historical reality, judge it according to the Gospel, and propose strategies for ecclesial action. But, what is the outcome from our perspective of the bishops turn to historical reality via Cardijn's method of theological praxis?

The Bishops Canonical Turn
Toward for a Preferential Option for the Poor

At Puebla, the bishops build on the prophetic position of Medellin.[70] The bishops write: "We place ourselves within the dynamic thrust of the Medellin Conference" and adopt its vision of reality.[71] The focus is therefore on the "preferential but not exclusive love for

---

65 McGrath, *Puebla and Beyond*, 91.

66 McGrath, *Puebla and Beyond*, 94-7.

67 McGrath, *Puebla and Beyond*, 96.

68 McGrath, *Puebla and Beyond*, 100.

69 Third General Conference of the Bishops of the Latin American Episcopate, *Final Document: Puebla de Los Angeles, Mexico*, No. 1299.

70 Gutierrez, *Power of the Poor*, 126-127.

71 Third General Conference of the Bishops of the Latin American Episcopate, *Puebla*, No. 25.

the poor"[72] who suffer from "inhuman poverty in which millions of Latin Americans live."[73]

The bishops explain that poverty in Latin America finds expression in things such as a "high rate of infant mortality, lack of adequate housing, health problems, starvation wages, unemployment and underemployment, malnutrition, job uncertainty, compulsory mass migrations, etc."[74] And, they assert that what makes poverty most visible are "concrete faces in real life" that ought to prompt us "to recognize the suffering features of Christ the Lord, who questions and challenges us."[75] It follows, therefore, that Christians should see the suffering features of the crucified Jesus in:

> *the faces of young children, struck down by poverty before they are born; the faces of young people, who are disoriented because they cannot find their place in society, and who are frustrated by the lack of opportunity to obtain training and work; the faces of the indigenous peoples, and frequently the Afro-Americans as well; living marginalized lives in inhuman situations, they can be considered the poorest of the poor; the faces of the peasants, in exile almost everywhere on our continent ... the faces of laborers, who frequently are ill-paid and who have difficulty in defending their rights...the faces of the underemployed and the unemployed, the faces of the marginalized and overcrowded urban dwellers, whose lack of material goods is matched by the ostentatious display of wealth by other segments of society; the faces of old*

---

72 Gutierrez, *Power of the Poor*, 131.

73 Third General Conference of the Bishops of the Latin American Episcopate, *Puebla*, 29.

74 Third General Conference of the Bishops of the Latin American Episcopate, *Puebla*, 29.

75 Third General Conference of the Bishops of the Latin American Episcopate, *Puebla*, 31.

people ... frequently marginalized that disregards people not engaged in production.[76]

Building on Medellin, the bishops add that these faces reveal not only social sin but a reality that demands a "conversion on the part of the whole church to a preferential option for the poor."[77] In the end, the bishops advocate prophetic "action by the church...so that the displaced and marginalized people of our time do not become permanent second-class citizens."[78]

While Jon Sobrino acknowledges that the spirit of Medellin is present at Puebla, he claims there are differences between the final documents.[79] Sobrino explains that the Medellin document cites a number of biblical and conciliar sources whereas the Puebla document draws more from Pope Paul VI's *Evangelii Nuntiandi* and discourses of Pope John Paul II.[80] Sobrino also claims that, in contrast to Medellin, the bishops at Puebla present an interpretation that is more culturalist, doctrinaire, and in accord with Western habits of thought.[81]

Sobrino does affirm that at Puebla the bishops succeed in helping the church continue to respond to the economic poverty, social marginalization, and political repression in Latin American that only worsens in the ten years after Medellin.[82] And he concludes

---

76 Third General Conference of the Bishops of the Latin American Episcopate, *Puebla*, 32-39.

77 Third General Conference of the Bishops of the Latin American Episcopate, *Puebla*, 1134.

78 Third General Conference of the Bishops of the Latin American Episcopate, *Puebla*, 1291. The bishops appeal to Luke 7:21-23 and Luke 4:18-21 to support their claims about a preferential option for the poor.

79 Sobrino, *Puebla and Beyond*, 302.

80 Sobrino, *Puebla and Beyond*, 300.

81 Sobrino, *Puebla and Beyond*, 291.

82 Sobrino, *Puebla and Beyond*, 302.

that the bishops' advocacy of a preferential option for the poor is crucial in the development of a theological ethic that aims to shape history in accord with Jesus's notion of the kingdom of God.[83] His argument, then, is that the Latin American option for the poor emerges from a prophetic theological ethic, which seeks to eliminate poverty as scandalous to Jesus' good news about the Kingdom of God being at hand (MK 1:15).[84]

From Santo Domingo (1992)
to Aparecida (2007)

In October 1992, the Fourth General Conference of Latin American Bishops convene in Santo Domingo, in the Dominican Republic.[85] The final document of the Conference yielded a different product from those of previous conferences at Medellin and Puebla. Valiente explains, "It does not begin with an analysis of reality, or a discernment of the signs of the times."[86] Rather than adopting Cardijn's See, Judge, Act method, the bishops "point of departure" is an "ahistorical Christological reflection."[87]

Valiente adds that, despite this shortcoming, the "preferential option for the poor" is reaffirmed.[88] In the end, according to Valiente, the Santo Domingo document lacks the "prophetic energy of Medellin" and the "theological density" of Puebla.[89] However, the

---

83 Sobrino, *Puebla and Beyond*, 307.

84 Sobrino, *Puebla and Beyond*, 307.

85 Valiente, "Reception," 815.

86 Valiente, "Reception," 816.

87 Valiente, "Reception," 816.

88 Valiente, "Reception," 817. He notes references to a preferential option for the poor in the *Puebla Final Document*:. 50, 179, 180, 275, 296, 302.

89 Valiente, "Reception," 818n92, which cites Gustavo Gutierrez.

bishops return to Cardijn's method at the Fifth General Conference at Aparecida, Brazil in 2007.

Before the 2007 meeting, twenty-two national episcopal conferences critique the preparatory document that ignores Cardijn's method in favor of its ahistorical Christology.[90] In response, a task force from CELAM is created, which crafts a working "synthesis document" that integrates the See-Judge-Act method. By using Cardijn's method the bishops are able to refocus their efforts on reading the signs of the times (historical reality) and to sustain their commitment to the prophetic denunciation of poverty as an affront to God's kingdom.[91] A brief analysis of the Bishops' final document from Aparecida supports this claim.

The Bishops Return to
Cardijn's See-Judge-Act Method

In Part I, "The Life of Our People Today," the bishops write that "in continuity with previous general conferences of Latin American bishops, this document utilizes the see-judge-act method."[92] The bishops state that with Cardijn's method the Church is able to see Latin America reality, judge it according to Jesus Christ and the tradition of the church in order to enact the spreading of the kingdom of God.[93] In other words, they use Cardijn's method to critique reality using the criterion of Christian wisdom to discern Christian missionary action.[94]

---

90 Valiente, "Reception," 819.

91 Valiente, "Reception," 819.

92 General Conference of the Bishops of Latin America and Caribbean. *The Aparecida Document: V.* (Lexington, 2014) 27.

93 General Conference of Bishops of Latin America and Caribbean, *Aparecida*, 27.

94 General Conference of Bishops of Latin America and Caribbean, *Aparecida*, 27.

The Bishops Focus Historical Reality and
a Preferential Option for the Poor

The bishops' focus on the historical reality of poverty at Aparecida demonstrates continuity with Medellin and Puebla.[95] Like previous conferences, the Aparecida conference focuses on how people face exclusion and live in dire poverty because of their race and economic condition, including women, young people, poor people, the unemployed, migrants, displaced, landless peasants, boys and girls subject to child prostitution, and victims of abortion.[96] The bishops explain that the Church must continue to denounce these realities as structures of death, violence and injustice.[97]

The bishops argue that the root cause of Latin American misery and oppression is the influence of Western culture, insofar as it is driven by idols of power, wealth, monetary pleasure and an overvaluation of individual subjectivity.[98] In addition, the bishops claim that the cultural colonialization of Latin America by western empires imposes a notion of the human person grounded in narcissistic individualism and hedonistic self-satisfaction.[99] The bishops denounce this form of culture for its focus on the individual at the expense of indifference toward the poor and most vulnerable.[100]

After presenting a socio-analytic description of what they perceive to be the root causes of poverty in Latin America, the bishops provide a critical theological reflection using the bible to show that the poor give us an opportunity to encounter Christ himself (Matt.

---

95 General Conference of Bishops of Latin America and Caribbean, *Aparecida*, 38.

96 General Conference of Bishops of Latin America and Caribbean, *Aparecida*, 38.

97 General Conference of Bishops of Latin America and Caribbean, *Aparecida*, 45.

98 General Conference of Bishops of Latin America and Caribbean, *Aparecida*, 24; 34.

99 General Conference of Bishops of Latin America and Caribbean, *Aparecida*, 34-35.

100 General Conference of Bishops of Latin America and Caribbean, *Aparecida*, 34-35.

25:37-40).[101] The bishops explain that contemplation of Jesus' suffering face in the marginated, and the encounter with Him in the afflicted and outcast, is the root of their advocacy for a preferential option for the poor.[102] The bishops state: "The suffering faces of the poor" and the "suffering face of Christ" are connected because as Jesus said: "whatever you did for one of these least brothers of mine, you did for me." (Matt 25:40).[103]

The bishops suggest, therefore, that the Gospel of Matthew, chapter 25, reveals how "the poor and those who suffer actually evangelize us" because their suffering represents Jesus' suffering on the cross.[104] In other words, the suffering faces of street people in large cities, migrants, sick people, addicts, and the imprisoned become the face of Jesus on the Cross.[105]

The bishops conclude that because intolerable social and economic inequalities exist in Latin America the Church must be an "advocate of justice and of the poor."[106] To meet such goals the bishops argue that a preferential option for the poor must permeate all Catholic structures and priorities, including Catholic professionals and politicians who are responsible for the finances of nations, the employment of people, and the economic development of countries.[107] The bishops' also warn that the option for the poor cannot remain at the level of theoretical claims. Rather, the bishops suggest

---

101 General Conference of Bishops of Latin America and Caribbean, *Aparecida*, 88.

102 General Conference of Bishops of Latin America and Caribbean, *Aparecida*, 88n148

103 General Conference of Bishops of Latin America and Caribbean, *Aparecida*, 125n178.

104 General Conference of Bishops of Latin America and Caribbean, *Aparecida*, 88.

105 General Conference of Bishops of Latin America and Caribbean, *Aparecida*, 126, 129-132.

106 General Conference of Bishops of Latin America and Caribbean, *Aparecida*, 125n, 223n224.

107 General Conference of Bishops of Latin America and Caribbean, *Aparecida*, 125.

that devoting time to the poor, providing them with attention, listening to them with interest, standing by them, and striving to transform their situation from within their midst is what Jesus himself proposes: "when you hold a banquet, invite the poor, the crippled, the lame, the blind (Lk 14:13).[108] In addition to the work done by many Latin American bishops, one priest achieves perhaps more than anyone else in raising awareness about poverty as a *locus theologicus*.

Gustavo Gutierrez

On June 8, 1928, Gustavo Gutierrez is born into genuine poverty and a loving mestizo family (part Hispanic and Quechua Indian) in Lima, Peru. Gutierrez spends his early years bedridden by osteomyelitis from age twelve to eighteen. Later, after three years as a medical student at the University of San Marcos, Gutierrez enters the local seminary. After studies in philosophy and psychology at the Catholic University of Louvain in Belgium, as well as theology at the University of Lyon in France and the Gregorian University in Rome (1951-9), Gutierrez is ordained a priest by the Archdiocese of Lima in 1959.[109]

In 1965 Gutierrez attends the fourth and final session of Vatican II (1962-1965) as theological assistant to Bishop Manuel Larrain of Chile.[110] In July 1968, taking inspiration from the Council, Gutierrez offers "what many consider the first proposal for a 'theology of liberation' at a gathering of priests and lay people in Chimbote, Peru, one month before Medellin."[111] Three years later Gutierrez publishes *A Theology of Liberation* (1971) where he describes his work as

---

108 General Conference of Bishops of Latin America and Caribbean, *Aparecida*, 126.

109 Lassalle-Klein, *Blood and Ink*, 19.

110 Lassalle-Klein, *Blood and Ink*, 20.

111 Lassalle-Klein, *Blood and Ink*, 20.

theological reflection born of the experience of unjust realities.[112] Gutierrez's definition draws from the well of Cardijn's See-Judge-Act method and a praxis-based methodology, as well as the Magisterium's focus on interpreting historical reality, or reading the signs of the times. To support this claim, I appeal to several of Gutierrez's writings.

Gutierrez's Turn to Theological Praxis

Gutierrez describes contemporary theology as critical reflection on praxis, which requires an examination of human activity in the world.[113] Later, when his notion of theology as a second act leads Clodovis Boff and others to misunderstand theology as a subsequent event to praxis (thereby separating theology from praxis), he clarifies his definition of theology in *The Power of the Poor in History* as referring to "critical reflection *in, and on*, faith as liberation praxis" (my emphasis).[114]

Invoking Yves Congar, Gutierrez claims: "Seen as a whole, the direction of theological thinking has been characterized by a transference away from attention to the being of supernatural realities (metaphysics and ontology), and toward attention to the relationship with man, with the world, and with the problems of all those who for us represent the Others."[115] Gutierrez adds that the Magisterium canonizes this turn toward historical reality at Vatican II

---

112 Gutierrez, Gutierrez, *A Theology of Liberation: History, Politics, and Salvation,* (Maryknoll: Orbis, 1988), xiii.

113 Gutierrez, *Liberation,* 6. Gutierrez also claims a praxis approach is implicit in Ignatian methods of theological discernment.

114 Gutierrez, *The Power of the Poor,* 60.

115 Gutierrez, *Liberation,* 6n25.

where the activity of the Church in the world becomes understood as the starting point for theological reflection.[116]

This point is crucial, for Gutierrez insists, with Vatican II, that theology begins with the activity of the Church in the world. In other words, the theologian serves the Church in reflecting on its lived faith (as Anselm insists) and collaborating with God's action in the world, especially in carrying on the mission of Jesus to announce and initiate the Kingdom of God in history as good news for the poor. Gutierrez' position is not derived from epistemological or philosophical warrants (like that of Clodovis Boff who we discuss next), but starts from the historical reality of God's action as experienced and recounted by the people Israel and followers of Jesus in the bible and in Church teaching.

Gutierrez says that, besides the work of the Magisterium at Vatican II, another important forerunner in the Catholic shift toward historical reality and praxis is Maurice Blondel and his theory about human action, serving as the starting point for all philosophical speculation.[117] Gutierrez explains that yet another factor in the turn to historical reality and praxis is the development of the eschatological dimension of biblical teaching.

Gutierrez points out that historical research on the bible shows a strong eschatological perspective that focuses on the importance of concrete behavior, deeds, action, and praxis in the Christian life.[118] Gutierrez argues that these developments, along with others, leads to the understanding that theological methodology begins with critical reflection on humankind in the world, particularly on

---

116 Gutierrez, *Liberation*, 7.

117 Gutierrez, *Liberation*, 7-8n30.

118 Gutierrez, *Liberation*, 8n34.

economic and socio-cultural issues.[119] For Gutierrez, theology is the second step.[120]

But, here it is important to recall our earlier discussion of Blondel in order to understand that Gutierrez means to say the the Church's praxis of faith is the primary object of theology. And, theology, like all thinking, is primary action-oriented. But it is not that thinking takes place later, after action is done. The point is that theology operates in a hermeneutical circle or constantly unfolding spiral with the praxis of faith.

In other words, Gutierrez suggests that, as a second step, theology uses social analysis as a critical hermeneutic reflection on historical reality in contrast to the vision of reality present in the Christian tradition. Thus, Gutierrez's definition of theological praxis frames a methodology that moves from "history to faith and from faith to history."[121] Here, it is important to repeat that the key point is that the historical reality of God's action in history and the praxis of faith has priority in the ongoing spiral, not necessarily that reflection is always a later moment in a action-reflection sequence.

In the end, Gutierrez's key claim is that "if the church wishes to deal with the real questions of the modern world and to attempt to respond to them, it must open a new chapter of theologico-pastoral epistemology."[122] Instead of using only revelation and tradition as starting points, as classical theology has generally done, Gutierrez argues the Church "must start with facts and questions derived from the world and from history."[123]

---

119 Gutierrez, *Liberation*, 9.

120 Gutierrez, *Liberation*, 9n39.

121 Gutierrez, *Power of the Poor*, 15 and 61.

122 Gutierrez, *Liberation*, 9.

123 Gutierrez, *Liberation*, 9-10n42.

Gutierrez's Turn toward
a Preferential Option for the Poor

Gutierrez credits Pope John XXIII for initiating the Church's return to the biblical theme of a preferential option for the poor. Gutierrez notes that, when preparing for the Second Vatican Council, John XXIII makes an important claim: "in dealing with the underdeveloped countries, the Church presents herself as she is and as she wants to be -- as the Church of all men and especially the Church of the poor."[124] Gutierrez also credits Pope Paul VI for adding vitality to John's idea of a "Church of the poor" with the publication of *Populorum Progressio*.[125]

In his own writings, Gutierrez focuses on material poverty in Latin America in order to describe the lack of access to basic economic goods necessary for a human life.[126] For example, Gutierrez explains that material poverty in Latin America means more than to live in subhuman conditions, it is to be illiterate, to be exploited by others and to not know that you are a person.[127]

Gutierrez adds that poverty in Latin America also means death, death due to hunger and sickness.[128] And, death, being a symptom of poverty, reveals a shocking reality that is contrary to the reign of life that Jesus Christ proclaims possible with his announcement that the Kingdom of God is at hand.[129] In other words, for Gutierrez, hunger, inadequate healthcare, and lack of material resources like water, are signs of the times by means of which Jesus' announce-

---

124 Gutierrez, *Liberation*,162.

125 Gutierrez, *Liberation*, 162.

126 Gutierrez, *Liberation*, 163.

127 Gutierrez, *Liberation*, 164.

128 Gutierrez, *We Drink from Our Own Wells*, 9.

129 Gutierrez, *We Drink from Our Own Wells*, 17.

ment of the Kingdom of God challenges Christians to love God in our neighbors who live in poverty.[130]

Gutierrez also provides a detailed account of biblical references to show how material poverty is a central concern in both the Old and New Testaments. He highlights how Old Testament prophets condemn every form of keeping the poor in poverty, and of creating new poor through: fraudulent commerce and exploitation (Hos. 12:8, Amos 8:5; Mic. 6::10-11; Isa.3:14; Jer.5:27; 6:12), the hoarding of lands (Mic.2:1-3; Ezek.22:29; Hab.2:5-6), dishonest courts (Amos 5:7, Jer. 22:13-17, Mic.3:9-11, Isa.5:23, 10:1-2), the violence of the ruling classes (2 Kings 23:30, 35; Amos 4:1; Mic.3:1-2; 6:12, Jer.22:13-17), slavery (Neh.5:1-5; Amos 2:6,8:6), and unjust taxes (Amos 4:1; 5:11-12).[131]

Gutierrez adds to his list a selection of New Testament passages from the Gospel of Luke (6:24-25, 12:13-21, 16:19-31, 18:18-26) and the Letter of James (2:5-9, 4:13-17, 5:16) to show that oppression of the poor by the rich is condemned. He highlights Jesus' statement, "Blessed are you poor," (Lk 6:20) to claim that the first beatitude is about material poverty,[132] arguing that Luke discusses material poverty because he is sensitive to social realities, especially those characterized by a real lack of goods.[133]

He explains that, "Blessed are you poor for yours is the Kingdom of God," does not mean, "accept your poverty because later this injustice will be compensated for in the Kingdom of God."[134] Rather, he argues that "if we believe that the Kingdom of God is

---

130 Gutierrez, *We Drink from Our Own Wells*, xix-xxi.

131 Gutierrez, *Liberation*, 167n23.

132 Gutierrez, *Liberation*, 170

133 Gutierrez, *Liberation*, 170.

134 Gutierrez, *Liberation*, 170.

received in history, that it is at hand (Mark 1:15), then the reestab-
lishment of justice in this world is implied."[135]

Gutierrez explains that "The other line of thinking regarding
poverty in the Bible is related to an openness to God."[136] Gutierrez
claims that the poverty that is "blessed" in Mark 5:1 (Blessed are the
poor in spirit) has been understood since the time of Zephaniah to
mean: totally at the disposition of the Lord.[137] Gutierrez claims that
when Matthew says blessed are the poor in spirit, he is referring to
spiritual openness to God.[138] What is most important about spiritual
openness, for Gutierrez, is to be open to God through the love of
neighbor because solidarity with the neighbor manifests a style of
life oriented to loving God in others.

In the end, Gutierrez's argument is that Christians must "remember the poor" (Gal 2:10) because the overwhelming majority of
the global population experiences hunger and exploitation, inadequate health care and lack of suitable housing, difficulty in obtain-
ing an education, inadequate wages and unemployment, struggles
for their rights, and repression.[139] And, that we must remember the
poor because they are indeed "the concrete locus of our encounter
with the Father of Jesus Christ."[140]

---

135 Gutierrez, *Liberation*, 171.

136 Gutierrez, *Liberation*, 169.

137 Gutierrez, *Liberation*, 169. Such an open disposition calls to mind Rahner's
reworking of Heidegger's notion of *vorgriff*.

138 Gutierrez, *Liberation*, 170.

139 Gutierrez, *We Drink From Our Own Wells*, 124-125.

140 Gutierrez, *Power of the Poor*, 20.

Clodovis Boff

In 1976 Clodovis Boff publishes his dissertation, *Theology and Praxis: Epistemological Foundations*. [141] Boff's primary claim is that theological methodology must necessarily account for socio-analytic mediation if it takes its point of departure from material praxis. To show how Boff prioritizes the socio-analytic mediation of historical reality in his account of theological praxis I appeal to several of Boff's texts.

Boff Draws from Cardijn's Method

Boff claims that a shift toward a praxis-based methodology can overcome the failures of the classic epistemological approach of theology, especially moral theology. Boff adds that the speculative and idealistic focus of the classic approach is insufficient for the clarification of praxis.[142] Boff argues instead that theology, as a theoretical practice, ought to transform socio-cultural analysis, or "raw material," in order to generate a "theology of" immigration, poverty, war, racism, the environment, etc.[143] In other words, Boff draws from Cardijn's method to argue that theological praxis functions to transform raw material (1st generality) into a determinate product (3rd generality) by the operation of principles found in the articles of faith (2nd generality).[144]

Boff reiterates his description of theological methodology, albeit in different language, in *Introducing Liberation Theology*[145]

---

141 Clodovis Boff, *Theology and Praxis: Epistemological Foundations*, trans., Robert R. Barr, reprint edition (Eugene: Wipf & Stock, 1987), 221.

142 Boff, *Theology and Praxis*, 221.

143 Boff, *Theology and Praxis*, 225.

144 Boff, *Theology and Praxis*, 225.

145 Clodovis Boff and Leonardo Boff. *Introducing Liberation Theology*. trans., Paul Burns. (Maryknoll: Orbis, 1987).

(1986/1987), which was co-written with his brother, Leonardo. The Boffs write that the first step of an adequate methodology of theological praxis begins with dialogical action wherein the oppressed come together to discuss their situation and the causes of their oppression.[146] In the second step the community reflects theologically on the situation of oppression.[147] Here, the community judges realities experienced by their neighbor, especially the poor, in light of the life, deeds, and death of Christ, who makes the poor a focus of his praxis.[148] The third step is where action takes place with the aim of liberation from an oppressive situation.[149] This final step moves theological methodology beyond a merely intellectual moment that is content with purely theoretical pursuits that include reading articles, attending conferences, and skimming through books.[150]

The Boffs explain that their three-step approach embodies a tripartite structure of socio-analytical mediation, hermeneutical mediation, and practical mediation.[151] Thus, "The socioanalytic mediation contemplates the world of the oppressed. It seeks to understand why the oppressed are oppressed." Second, "the hermeneutic mediation contemplates the word of God. It attempts to see what the divine plan is with regard to the poor." Third, "the practical mediation contemplates the aspect of activity and seeks to discover the appropriate lines of operation for overcoming oppression in conformity with God's plan."[152]

---

146 Boff and Boff. *Introducing Liberation Theology*, 5.

147 Boff and Boff, *Introducing Liberation Theology*, 7.

148 Boff and Boff, *Introducing Liberation Theology*, 7.

149 Boff and Boff, *Introducing Liberation Theology*, 9.

150 Boff and Boff, *Introducing Liberation Theology*, 9.

151 Boff and Boff, *Introducing Liberation Theology*, 24. Also see, Clodovis Boff, *Mysterium Liberationis: Fundamental Concepts of Liberation Theology*, 74.

152 Clodovis Boff, *Mysterium Liberationis*, 74.

The Boffs explain that their three-step method can be formulated differently according to context. First, the professional method: socio-analytical, hermeneutical, and theoretico-practical. Second, the pastoral method: See, Judge, Act. And, third, the popular method: the confrontation between gospel and life.[153] The Boff's make clear that two things unite all three types. First, is the crucial pre-theological step, which includes personal contact with an oppressive reality.[154] The second is an axial faith that seeks to transform history through critique and action inspired by the Gospel itself.[155] What this means for Boff is that theology is a second act (*actus secudus*) where the articles of faith operative in the second generality, function as a hermeneutic that is able to theologize raw material.[156]

For example, Boff claims that theological praxis ought to utilize scripture as the "*norma normans*" (norm of norms) and the "*norma normata*" (norming norm), to create an interpreting interpretation (*norma normans ut normata*), that judges situations according to the Spirit of Christ.[157] Boff's most powerful claim, is, therefore, that the *norma normans ut normata* of theological hermeneutic reasoning (second generality) must become embodied in concrete life (third generality) where hermeneutics flowers into ethics.[158] While Boff's contribution is important, he diverges from Gutierrez. Where the Peruvian priest focuses on the primacy of the praxis of faith for

---

153 Boff and Boff, *Introducing Liberation Theology*, 13 & 24. Also see Clodovis Boff, "Epistemology and Method of the Theology of Liberation," in *Mysterium Liberationis*, 68. This same schema is present in the content of *Salvation and Liberation: In Search of a Balance between Faith and Politics* (1979).

154 Boff and Boff, *Introducing Liberation Theology*, 22-24.

155 Boff and Boff, *Introducing Liberation Theology*, 14-17.

156 Boff, *Theology and Praxis*, 132.

157 Boff, *Theology and Praxis*, 140.

158 Boff, *Theology and Praxis*, 137-8.

theology, Boff's Kantian epistemology creates a theory-praxis problem that Gutierrez avoids and Ignacio Ellacuria will critique.

Boff's Turn Toward
a Preferential Option for the Poor

Boff claims that the radical originality of the Latin American methodological turn to praxis is the insertion of the theologian into the real life of the poor.[159] In other words, Latin American theological method is novel because it begins with "living contact with the struggle of the poor," not "abstract topics or general ideas."[160] The first moment, the encounter with the poor, is therefore pre-theological.[161] Boff writes that by shifting the methodological starting point to praxis the "raw, naked reality of oppression" can be analyzed as a *locus theologicus*.[162] Why is this claim so significant?

The "pre-theological moment means a concrete conversion of life, including a class conversion, in the sense of actual solidarity with the poor and a commitment to their liberation."[163] To experience conversion, or to have a *metanoia*, is significant because it challenges the theologian to recognize that something is "not right" or "unjust" about the historical reality at hand. Thus, theological methodology that begins from the side of the oppressed empowers the theologian to offer a prophetic critique of the reality that is "seen" and judged through "socioanalytic mediation" of "life."[164] Why is this type of approach important for Boff?

---

159 Boff, *Mysterium Liberationis*, 66

160 Boff, *Mysterium Liberationis*, 64.

161 Boff, *Mysterium Liberationis*, 66 and 73.

162 Boff, *Mysterium Liberationis*, 59-62.

163 Boff, *Mysterium Liberationis*, 74.

164 Boff, *Mysterium Liberationis*, 70.

The merit of an approach that begins from the perspective of masses of the poor opens a way for the bible to be used as a tool to judge, with criticity, the reality of the poverty in Latin America.[165] Such an approach also respects the suggestion of Paul VI who, in *Evangeli Nuntiandi*, notes that the relationship between the reality of the poor and the word of God creates a "hermeneutical circle" of "mutual appeal" between sources of knowledge.[166]

This means that the Word of God retains primacy of value and critique even though it loses primacy in methodology.[167] In sum, Boff argues that theologizing with this version of the hermeneutical circle "prioritizes the moment of application over that of explanation" as it seeks to "activate the transforming energy of the biblical texts" to transform persons and history.[168] The key is that the logic of action moves interpretive theories into practice.[169]

Despite the virtues of Boff's work, his use of Kantian epistemological categories creates problems regarding the relationship of theology and praxis that do not appear in the work of Gutierrez and Ellacuria. Lassalle-Klein notes that Boff speaks of "the (practical) 'leap' to span the gulf dividing theory and praxis corresponding to the (epistemological) 'leap' in the opposite direction, from praxis to theory."[170]

In *Theology and Praxis*, Boff describes theology as theoretical, speculative thinking, and praxis as committed, experientially situated thinking. Lassalle-Klein asserts, "Following Kant, Boff argues

---

165 Boff, *Mysterium Liberationis*, 63.

166 Boff, *Mysterium Liberationis*, 80. Also, Paul VI, *Evangeelli Nuntiandi*, accessed January 15, 2015, Vatican.va, 29.

167 Boff and Boff, *Introducing Liberation Theology*, 33.

168 Boff, *Mysterium Liberationis*, 80.

169 Boff and Boff, *Introducing Liberation Theology*, 24.

170 Boff, *Theology and Praxis*, 213. Cited in Robert Lassalle-Klein, "The Jesuit Martyrs," 257.

that theological reason constructs its object, beginning with 'the concept (*Begriff*) [which] seizes its object only theoretically that is in its ideal form.' Like Kant, he both asserts and denies access to "the 'real,' the concrete," or the 'thing in itself.'"[171] For Gutierrez and Ellacuria, however, theology starts with the real.

Lassalle-Klein's point is that Boff finds himself caught on the horns of the dilemma posed by Kantian idealism and epistemology. On the one hand, for Boff, "Praxis is...subsumed within theology as the material of its labor, the material 'upon which' it works." On the other, theological and scientific theory imposes its concepts, synthesizing the partially organized data of praxis under formal concepts.

His says this produces intelligible objects for scientific or theological thought, in such a way "that [praxis'] manner of presence in theological space is that of theoretical form, which is the only form that can take up that space." Consequently, theological reason is given the job of the Kantian "epistemological vigilance in order to avoid an oblique relationship of terms ... pertaining to two distinct orders...(theological) theory and (social) praxis."[172]

Lassalle-Klein says that Ignacio Ellacuria rejects this approach as an example of reductionist idealism and its nominalist tendency to confuse concepts with reality. Lassalle-Klein cites a little known unpublished 1985 schema in which Ellacuria explicitly critiques Boff's 1978 work, asserting (among other critiques),

> *The correct theological praxis not only "permits" (C. Boff) a corresponding theological discourse [to emerge] "in regards to the theoretical object" or simply "to the extent that the (real) problems of praxis are assumed by theory in the form of (theoretical) questions." Instead, theological praxis "provokes" a*

---

171 Boff, *Theology and Praxis*, 71. Cited in Lassalle-Klein, "The Jesuit Martyrs," 257.

172 Boff, *Theology and Praxis*, 208. Cited in Lassalle-Klein, "The Jesuit Martyrs," 257.

theological discourse that is not purely formal, and it theoretically "strengthens" that discourse from the level of the primordial apprehensions that are the beginning and end of human intellection.[173]

Lassalle-Klein explains that this assertion is grounded in Ellacuria's insistence, following the Spanish philosopher Xavier Zubiri, that "the structural unity of intellection and sensing" form two dimensions of a single act of sentient intelligence. Zubiri writes,

It is not only that human sensing and intellection are not in opposition. Rather, their intrinsic and formal unity constitutes a single and distinct act of apprehension. As sentient, the act is an impression. As an intellection, the act is an apprehension of reality. In this way, the distinct and unified act of sentient intellection is an impression of reality. Intellection is a way of sensing. And, in human persons, sensing is a mode of intellection.[174]

Lassalle-Klein argues that this comprises "an explicit rejection of Kantian idealist percept-concept epistemology wherein, on the one hand, sensibility is receptivity to sense data under the forms of space and time, while on the other, understanding is the faculty of synthesizing this data into experiential knowledge of objects and reason is the faculty of synthesizing knowledge of objects into systems (which have no direct reference to the thing-in-itself or logical validity beyond their regulative function)."[175]

---

173 Ignacio Ellacuria, "Relacion teoria y praxis en la teologia de la liberacion," in Ignacio Ellacuria, *Escritos teologicos I* (UCA Editores, 2000), 236-237. Cited in Robert Lassalle-Klein, personal correspondence with Robert Pennington (June 3, 2017). Transcript in personal files of the author.

174 Zubiri, *Inteligencia sentiente*, 13; cited in Lassalle-Klein, *Blood and Ink*, 213.

175 Lassalle-Klein, personal correspondence (June 3, 2017).

Lassalle-Klein explains that Zubiri and Ellacuría use the term intellection to emphasize that intelligence must be understood as an action (that of apprehending and knowing) rather than as a thing produced by using a faculty (understanding or reason). Intellection is therefore conceptualized as the sensible and intellectual apprehension of whatever we encounter as real. As a result, sensible and intellectual apprehension are not understood as separate moments in a sequence, but rather as aspects or dimensions of a single action or process.

Accordingly, theology must not be understood as a second act, in the sense of a later theoretical moment in a sequence that begins with the sensible apprehension of the object in praxis. Theology is secondary only in the sense that intellection begins with the apprehension of whatever we perceive as real.

Contra Boff, therefore, Ellacuria asserts that, "Although theological theory and theological praxis are not the same, their relations are necessary and mutually codetermining," so that every theory must be understood "as a moment of a unitary praxis," and "some form of theory is inevitable in any human praxis." As a result, when speaking of Christian theology and praxis, "it is necessary to continue vigilantly insisting on the codetermination and coherence ... of theological theory and theological praxis."[176]

Conclusion

At post-conciliar meetings at Medellin in Columbia, Puebla in Mexico, and Aparecida in Brazil, the Latin American bishops and theologians adopt and develop Cardijn's See-Judge-Act method as a model of theological praxis, which they use to critique historical reality and advocate for a preferential option for the poor. I

---

176 Ellacuria, "Relacion teoria y praxis," 236. Cited in Lassalle-Klein, personal correspondence.

provided warrants for this claim from the final documents produced at Medellin, Puebla, and Aparecida, as well as the writings of Peruvian priest and theologian Gustavo Gutierrez and the Brazilian priest and theologian, Clodovis Boff.

In the next chapter, I will examine the work of Jesuit priest, Ignacio Ellacuria, who provides powerful philosophical arguments for the turn to historical reality and methods of theological praxis outlined above. As we will see, Ellacuria was martyred for his efforts to support the struggle of the people of El Salvador to transform their reality from one of oppression to liberation.

4

IGNACIO ELLACURIA'S PRAXIS
& TURN TO THE CRUCIFIED POOR:
BUILDING ON RAHNER, ZUBIRI, & ROMERO,
ALONGSIDE SOBRINO

Overview

I gnacio Ellacuria, Basque Jesuit theologian, and nationalized citizen of El Salvador, is martyred for prophetically embodying the canonical turn toward the interpretation of the historical reality of the poor as the primary *locus theologicus* for followers of Jesus.

The foundations of Ellacuria's praxis are rooted in his interpretation of the Church's preferential option for the poor expressed at Medellin and Puebla, Jesus' preaching of the Reign of God, Karl Rahner's transcendental and historical methodology, Xavier Zubiri's focus on the primacy of reality, and Archbishop Oscar Romero's praxis and preferential option for the poor as the leader of the Church of El Salvador. Ellacuria integrates these sources in a praxis that provides the Catholic Church with a moral exemplar of how a theological methodology can facilitate the taking down of crucified people from their cross.[1]

To support these claims, I will first describe the contributions of three key figures to Ellacuria's intellectual and spiritual formation: Karl Rahner, Xavier Zubiri, and Archbishop Romero. Second, I will examine Ellacuria's concept of the crucified people, his claims about philosophical and theological praxis, and the implications of those claims for ecclesiology. Third, I will conclude with a brief discussion of how the writings of Jon Sobrino reflects key aspects of the work of his confrere Ellacuria.

The Pastoral Formation of
Ignacio Ellacuria S.J.

Ignacio Ellacuria is born November 9, 1930, in Portugalete, the heart of the Basque country, on the North Atlantic Coast of Spain. In 1940 he begins his studies at the Jesuit high school in Tudela, Spain.[2] Later, Ellacuria enters the Jesuit novitiate at Loyola, and, in September of 1949, he takes vows in the Society of Jesus.[3] Shortly thereafter he begins undergraduate studies in Quito at the *Universidad Catolica del Ecuador*.[4] In Quito, Ellacuria studies Transcendental Thomism and learns to synthesize Thomas Aquinas' work with the modern philosophies of Kant, Husserl, and

---

1 Ignacio Ellacuría, "El pueblo crucificado, ensayo de soteriología histórica," *Escritos teológicos*, II (San Salvador: UCA Editores, 2000), 137-70; "The Crucified People: An Essay in Historical Soteriology," in Michael Lee, ed., *Ignacio Ellacuría: Essays on History, Liberation, and Salvation* (Maryknoll, NY: Orbis Books, 2013), 196.

2 Robert Lassalle-Klein, "Introduction," in *Love That Produces Hope: The Thought of Ignacio Ellacuria*. Ed. Kevin Burke. (Collegeville: Michael Glazier/Liturgical Press, Spring 2006), xvn13,14.

3 Lassalle-Klein, "Introduction," xv-xvi.

4 Lassalle-Klein, "Introduction," xvi.

Heidegger.[5] During his time in Quito Ellacuria becomes dissatisfied "with scholasticism as a disembodied and intellectualist form of thought," and begins to see "the need to humanize and reorient it toward the existential and vital problematic of concrete human beings."[6]

In 1955 Ellacuria returns to El Salvador where he is assigned to teach Thomistic philosophy at San Salvador seminary.[7] In 1958 he departs San Salvador to pursue a master's degree in theology with the Jesuit faculty at Innsbruck, Austria.[8] During his time in Innsbruck, Ellacuria says that: "the only thing that made the theologate worthwhile was the opportunity to study with Rahner."[9] In fact, Ellacuria begins to see his own work as a development of Rahner's.[10]

For example, the English forward to Ellacuria's first book describes the author as a "former student of Karl Rahner," whose work represents "a synthesis" that tries "to combine the insights of Rahner with those of the Theology of Liberation."[11] What is paramount to understand about Ellacuria's reinterpretation of Rahner's Transcendental Thomism is that turning to a praxis-based methodology, Ellacuria seeks to overcome the abstract nature of Rahner's methodology. But, to understand how Ellacuria moves beyond his teacher let us first look at Rahner's work on method and methodology.

---

5 Lassalle-Klein, "Introduction," xvi.

6 Lassalle-Klein, "Introduction," xvii, n40.

7 Lassalle-Klein, "Introduction," xx.

8 Lassalle-Klein, "Introduction," xx.

9 Lassalle-Klein, "Introduction," xxi, n69.

10 Lassalle-Klein, "Introduction," xxi.

11 Lassalle-Klein, "Introduction," xxii, n74.

Karl Rahner:
A Jesuit Locus of Ellacuria's Formation

Karl Rahner is born March 5, 1904, in Freiburg in southwest Germany.[12] He enters the Society of Jesus in 1922 and is ordained a priest in 1932. In 1934, Rahner is a student at the University of Freiburg where, along with traditional Thomist studies, he participates in Martin Heidegger's seminars.[13] And, as *peritus* for Cardinal Franz Konig of Vienna, Rahner becomes one of the most influential theological advisors at Vatican II.[14] Before he dies March 30, 1984, Rahner publishes more than four thousand works,[15] several of which show that his theological methodology involves a turn to "the world" or historical reality as a *locus theologicus*.

Rahner's Theological Method:
Transcendental & Historical

According to Leo O'Donovan, Rahner claims that in order "to treat a theological question adequately one must approach it from both a transcendental and a historical perspective."[16] In other words, Rahner's methodology is based on the "reciprocal interdependence of transcendental and historical reflection in

---

12 Anne Carr, "Karl Rahner," in *A Handbook of Christian Theologians*, Martin E. Marty and Dean G. Peerman, eds. (Nashville: Abignon Press, 1965), 519.

13 Carr, "Rahner," 519. Also see Phillip Endean, *Karl Rahner: Spiritual Writings*, (Maryknoll: Orbis, 2004), 10-11. For a full account of the Rahner's experience with Heidegger see Peter Joseph Fritz, *Karl Rahner's Theological Aesthetics*, (Washington, D.C.: The Catholic University of America Press, 2014)

14 Carr, "Rahner," 519.

15 Carr, "Rahner," 519.

16 Leo J. O'Donovan, "Orthopraxis and Theological Method in Karl Rahner," in *Proceedings of the Thirty-Fifth Annual Convention: The Catholic Theological Society of America* 35 (1980), 49.

theology."[17] Such an approach reflects an Ignatian spirituality that locates "God in all things." According to O'Donovan, Rahner's pursuit of finding God in all things is what prompts him to use a "dialectic" method of "historical transcendence."[18] Let us now turn to one of Rahner's most important texts, which shows how he uses a dialectic method of historical transcendence to explain the "doctrine of the Trinity."[19]

Rahner's Turn to the World
as a Locus Theologicus

In 1967, two years after the end of Vatican Council II, Rahner publishes *The Trinity*, which provides insight into his understanding of the dynamic, reciprocal interdependence of the transcendence of God and the historical world. Here, Rahner develops the axiom that: "The 'economic' Trinity is the 'immanent' Trinity and the 'immanent' Trinity is the 'economic' Trinity."[20] A key aspect of Rahner's axiom is that "The Trinity" is something that is not only "expressed as a doctrine,"[21] but is also "experienced precisely in this reality."[22] But, how, according to Rahner, is the Trinity experienced in reality?

Rahner writes that because "the Spirit proceeds from the Father through the Son,"[23]... "God's self-communication consists precisely in the fact that God...really enters into man's situation"

---

17 O'Donovan, "Orthopraxis," 49-50.

18 O'Donovan, "Orthopraxis," 61.

19 O'Donovan, "Orthopraxis," 51.

20 Karl Rahner, *The Trinity*, trans. Joseph Donceel, (London: Herder and Herder, 1970), 22.

21 Rahner, *Trinity*, 39.

22 Rahner, *Trinity*, 47.

23 Rahner, *Trinity*, 66-67.

in the historical Jesus.[24] Rahner's methodology is therefore based on his theory that "if there occurs a self-communication of God to historical man...it can occur only in this unifying duality of history and transcendence."[25] In sum, Rahner believes that "divine self-communication occurs in unity and distinction in history (of the truth) and in the spirit (of love)."[26] Both condition one another. And, it is likely that he arrives at this conclusion through his Thomistic reinterpretion of Heidegger's concept of *dasein*, or being-in-the-world, so that, "God may be extended to relate to history, if one concedes the point that history reveals God as the transcendent ground of the world, which is discovered primarily by human apprehension of it."[27]

Xavier Zubiri:
A Basque Locus for Ellacuria's Formation

Ellacuria's appropriation of Rahner is deeply influenced by the Spanish philosopher, Xavier Zubiri. In 1961, shortly after he is ordained a priest, Ellacuria visits family in Bilbao, Spain, when he seeks out the famous Spanish philosopher Xavier Zubiri.[28] At their first meeting Ellacuria tells Zubiri that he wants to write a doctoral dissertation with him and about him.[29] Ellacuria presents the formal outline to Zubiri in October 1963 and defends *La Principalidad*

---

24 Rahner, *Trinity*, 89.

25 Rahner, *Trinity*, 92.

26 Rahner, *Trinity*, 99.

27 Fritz, *Rahner*, 207-208.

28 Lassalle-Klein, "Introduction," xxiii. Both Zubiri and Ellacuria share a predilection for the theology of Karl Rahner. xxiv.

29 Lassalle-Klein, "Introduction," xxiii.

de la esencia en Xavier Zubiri at the University of Complutense, in Madrid, in 1965.[30]

Ellacuria's efforts to historicize Rahner's work are grounded in his decision to focus on Zubiri's category of "historical reality" as the proper object of philosophy and theology.[31] Ellacuria's focus on the historical reality of El Salvador led him to see the "crucified people" as the "principle....sign of the times," which ought to orient the "universal historical mission" of the church in the world today.[32] Before discussing Ellacuria's work on the "crucified people," let us examine the foundations of his turn to historical reality in the work of Xavier Zubiri.

Xavier Zubiri is born December 4, 1898 in Donostia-San Sebastian, Gipuzkoa, Spain. Between 1915 and 1919 he studies philosophy and theology in the *Seminario de Madrid*.[33] Later in 1919, at the *Universidad Central de Madrid*, he meets philosopher Jose Ortega y Gasset who opens his "mind to the value of Edmund Husserl's *Logical Investigations*."[34] In 1920, Zubiri earns his doctorate in theology at the University of Rome and is ordained a priest a year later.[35]

Between 1920 and 1921 he studies philosophy at the *Institut Superieur de Philosohie* at the University of Louvain and earns a master's degree after submitting a study on Husserl.[36] In 1921, Zubiri receives a doctorate in philosophy at the *Universidad*

---

30 Lassalle-Klein, "Introduction," xxiii.

31 Lassalle-Klein, "Introduction," Love, xxiv-xxv, n97.

32 Lassalle-Klein, "Introduction," love, xxv,n102.

33 Orringer, "Introduction," *Dynamic Structure of Reality*, ix.

34 Orringer, "Introduction," *Dynamic Structure of Reality*, ix-x.

35 Orringer, "Introduction," *Dynamic Structure of Reality*, xi.

36 Orringer, "Introduction," *Dynamic Structure of Reality*, x.

Central de Madrid with a thesis on Husserl.[37] After he publishes the dissertation in 1923, Zubiri spends three years in Germany for postdoctoral philosophical studies with Edmund Husserl and Martin Heidegger.[38]

While Zubiri praises Husserl's *"epoche,"* he also critiques Husserl and Heidegger for what he describes as their idealist logification of intelligence.[39] Zubiri insists that, rather than "Husserl's pure consciousness, or Heidegger's understanding of *dasein*, the primogenital location of intellection is actually sensation itself."[40] Zubiri focuses on "sentient intelligence" in order to overcome what he calls Husserl's and Heidegger's "entification of reality," which Lassalle-Klein describes as "the reduction of ... reality to a form or subcategory of being."[41] Zubiri claims that, due to the entification of reality, the larger category of being (*ser*) has improperly displaced reality in Western philosophy.[42] In sum, Zubiri argues that the entification of reality damages modern philosophy because it leads people away from the exigencies of reality and toward the illusions of being.[43] How does Zubiri make his case?

In *Dynamic Structure of Reality* (*Estructura dinámica de la realidad*, 1968), Zubiri argues that "reality is prior to being" and "grounds being."[44] To support his claim, Zubiri develops Heidegger's concept of *dasein*, the theory that a being is always "there," or, thrown into a spatiotemporal place. Zubiri uses

---

37 Orringer, "Introduction," *Dynamic Structure of Reality*, x.

38 Orringer, "Introduction," *Dynamic Structure of Reality*, x.

39 Lassalle-Klein, *Love*, 91.

40 Lassalle-Klein, *Love*, 92n26,27.

41 Lassalle-Klein, *Love*, 93.

42 Lassalle-Klein, *Love*, 94.

43 Lassalle-Klein, *Love*, 97n51.

44 Orringer, *Dynamic Structure of Reality*, xiii.

Heidegger's concept to question Aristotle's claim that the primary character of reality is being, *being subjectum*.[45] Contra Aristotle, Zubiri claims "reality is radically and primarily...not a subject [*subjetualidad*] but a structure."[46] In other words, Zubiri believes "reality" is "something in its own right" because it is "radically structural."[47] But, why is Zubiri's claim that "reality" is structural important to his work as a whole, as well as to the work of Ellacuria? A brief exposition of Zubiri's theory of physical "respectivity" will provide insights necessary to address this question.

Zubiri describes "respectivity" not as conceptual, mental, or abstract in character.[48] Rather, "Respectivity is a physical dimension of things" that "relates to the constitution of each thing."[49] "Respectivity" is understood therefore as "absolutely physical.... It is a strictly physical moment in the traditional and philosophical sense of the word. It is real with the physical reality of something [and] ... has a formally physical character."[50] Despite being a "dynamic structure," however, respectivity does not cause change in the formal sense, but, rather, fosters becoming...not in itself but in another.[51] In other words, "the one who becomes" can do so only "in [interaction with] the other."[52] Or, with a slight variation of language: "in the other, that is where becoming is, not in the one itself."[53]

45 Zubiri, *Reality*, 21-2.

46 Zubiri, *Reality*, 25.

47 Zubiri, *Reality*, 25-6

48 Zubiri, *Reality*, 38-9.

49 Zubiri, *Reality*, 37-9.

50 Zubiri, *Reality*, 39.

51 Zubiri, *Reality*, 40-1.

52 Zubiri, *Reality*, 41.

53 Zubiri, *Reality*, 41.

Zubiri's description of "respectivity" as a "physical" giving of oneself, emphasizes that living beings are always conditioned by a "position," "a locus, a [place]," and "a situation."[54] Zubiri writes: "The *locus*...and the *situs*...define and constitute the placement of a living being in reality." What is absolutely central to Zubiri's claim is that the *locus* and *situs* "are not simply the surroundings of a living being...but something completely different: they are a medium for the living being."[55]

Thus, "Not only does the medium have this spatiotemporal character for each living being, but if we take many living beings together, then the medium has a different character, an ecological one: it is precisely their (*oikos*), the house where each lives."[56] In other words: "No living being develops its activity...unless it is immersed in a medium," where the living being is conditioned to perform actions that are not spontaneous but provoked, or forced, by the medium.[57]

What this means for Zubiri is that the dynamic activity of each living being promotes "the persistence of substantive structures,"[58] or a human "habitude-respect structure,[59] that becomes the site for the arousal of actions,"[60] which "are in one form or another aroused by something that is not the living being itself."[61]

---

54 Zubiri, *Reality*, 104 and 110.

55 Zubiri, *Reality*, 111.

56 Zubiri, *Reality*, 111-112.

57 Zubiri, *Reality* 128.

58 Zubiri, *Reality*, 112.

59 Zubiri, *Reality*, 114.

60 Zubiri, *Reality*, 118.

61 Zubiri, *Reality*, 123n26.

Zubiri concludes therefore that "the activities of a living being are immanent in contrast with all the other actions happening in the universe, which are transcendent."[62] He describes immanent actions of living beings as responses to the outer transcendent medium, and each response is, in a way, a change.[63] As Zubiri states: "the range of adequate responses that the living being continues to give at every instant modifies it."[64] Paradoxically this means "the living being is always itself but never the same."[65]

The key idea is that living beings are not simply subjective beings but are actually respective structural realities that are always giving themselves in some location within the *oikos* that constitutes the transcendental medium in which they are the center.[66] Now, with Zubiri's notion of respectivity in place, we can explore how Ellacuria grounds his philosophical and theological work on Zubiri's achievement.

Ellacuria Develops Zubiri's Turn to Reality

Robert Lassalle-Klein explains that Ellacuria adopts Zubiri's critique of what he sees as the tendency of Western philosophy to reduce reality to a form or subcategory of being (the entification of reality) and to subsume the other aspects of intellection into what the mind, acting as "logos," affirms, proposes, or predicates about its objects (the logification of intelligence).[67] Ellacuria argues that this tendency is responsible for the crippling inability of

---

62 Zubiri, *Reality*, 123.

63 Zubiri, *Reality*, 131.

64 Zubiri, *Reality*, 131.

65 Zubiri, *Reality*, 132.

66 Zubiri, *Reality*, 133.

67 Lassalle-Klein, *Blood and Ink,* 206 and 210.

Latin American academic and political writers to adequately address the 'brute reality' of the continent. To overcome the problems of logification and entification, Ellacuria builds on Zubiri's claim that: "knowing and reality are in their very root strictly and rigorously related. There is no priority of one over the other."[68]

Lassalle-Klein notes that Ellacuria adopts Zubiri's claim that "intellection begins with...the sentient or primordial apprehension of a thing as being something 'in and of itself' (*en y poor si mismo*) or "of its own" (*de suyo*)."[69] As noted in our earlier discussion of Ellacuria's critique of Clodovis Boff, Ellacuria follows Zubiri to insist that "sensible and intellectual apprehension cannot be separate moments in a sequence, but must be aspects of a single action or process."[70]

This concept of sentient intelligence provides the epistemological foundation for Ellacuria's appropriation of Zubiri's concept of respectivity that sentient beings are "not only open to reality and located in reality, but we are bound to reality" in such a way that our "unavoidable relationship with the 'power of the real'" forces us to face a steady flux "of choices regarding whether and how to appropriate ourselves in relation to the realities we encounter."[71]

---

68 Robert Lassalle-Klein, *Blood and Ink*, 212-216. What is important to note is that Joe Bracken points out that Zubiri's work mirrors Thomas Aquinas' assertion found in his *Summa Theologica*, I, Q.85, art. 2, ad 2. For example, Aquinas argues that the intellect in act and the thing understood in act are one and the same reality under different formalities. For more see, Joseph A. Bracken, "Structures, Systems and Whiteheadian Societies: The Quest for Objectivity" in *The Xavier Zubiri Review Review*, 12 (2010-2012) : 21.

69 Lassalle-Klein, *Blood and Ink*, 214n71.

70 Lassalle-Klein, *Blood and Ink*, 213.

71 Lassalle-Klein, *Blood and Ink*, 218n91-219.

Lassalle-Klein explains that, for Ellacuria, sentient intelligence implies a threefold process of human self-definition (historicization) driven by our bondedness to the power of reality.[72] First, everything that we encounter "is already given as a reality," which means that "I am forced" to "become aware of it," "to realize about it [*hacerse cargo de ella*] as a reality,"[73] or to grasp "what is at stake" in the reality I encounter [*hacerse cargo la realidad*]. Second, becoming aware of a reality imposes an ethical demand to 'assume responsibility for' it, to "do something about" it, and/or to respond to it in some way [*cargar con la realidad*]. Third, assuming responsibility for a reality pushes us to formulate a praxis that aims 'to take charge of" of changing or transforming it [*encargarse de la realidad*].[74]

Ellacuria argues that every aspect of the process of human self-definition (historicization) must necessarily pass through these three steps. This follows from his definition of the term historicization (a more limited term in Zubiri's writing), which Lassalle-Klein says has two meanings in Ellacuria's work.[75] The first, more general meaning, refers to the incorporative and transformative power that human praxis exerts over the historical and natural dimensions of reality.[76] Here, "the historicization of nature consists . . . in the fact that humanity makes history from nature and with nature."[44]

And in a second, more narrow meaning, Ellacuría says, "Demonstrating the impact of certain concepts within a particular context

72 Lassalle-Klein, *Blood and Ink*, 221n105.

73 Lassalle-Klein, *Blood and Ink*, 221n103 and 104.

74 Lassalle-Klein, *Blood and Ink*, 221n106.

75 Lassalle-Klein, *Blood and Ink*, 197.

76 Ellacuría, *Filosofía de la realidad histórica*, 169.

is [also] . . . understood here as their historicization."[77] Here historicization refers to a procedure for testing and validating truth claims associated with a concept.

This is derived from the idea that if the truth of a historicized concept lies in its "becoming reality," then it follows that the concept's "truth can be measured in [its] results."[46] Since human activity is essentially the incorporative and transformative power that human praxis exerts over historical and natural dimensions of reality, it follows therefore that it must pass through the aforementioned steps.[78]

Ellacuria's development of Zubiri's work ultimately rejects "pernicious philosophical influences," which identify transcendence with separateness and teach that "historical transcendence is separate from history."[79]

Ellacuria argues instead that transcendence is "something that transcends in and not as something that transcends away from [history]; as something that physically impels to more, but not by taking out of; as something that pushes forward, but at the same time retains."[80]

From whom, other than Zubiri, does Ellacuria develop his ideas about the historicization of transcendence? Enter Archbishop of El Salvador, Oscar Romero.

---

77 Ignacio Ellacuría, "La historización del concepto de propiedad como principio de desideologización," *ECA* 31, nos. 335-336 (1976): 425-50; translated as "The Historicization of the Concept of Property," in John Hassett and Hugh Lacey, eds., *Towards a Society That Serves Its People* (Washington, DC: Georgetown University Press, 1991), 109.

78 Lassalle-Klein, *Blood and Ink*, 221n107&108.

79 Lassalle-Klein, *Blood and Ink*, 222n114.

80 Lassalle-Klein, *Blood and Ink*, 223.

Oscar Romero:
A Salvadoran Locus for Ellacuria's Formation

Oscar Romero is born to a rural family in Ciudad Barrios, San Miguel, in El Salvador on August 15, 1917.[81] Romero enters seminary studies and is later ordained in Rome, April 4, 1942. However, World War II forces Romero to abandon his doctoral studies and return to El Salvador.[82]

In 1967 Romero becomes secretary-general of the Salvadoran Bishops Conference. Soon after, Romero is named executive secretary of the Central American Bishops Conference and auxiliary bishop of San Salvador.[83] In 1974 Romero is named bishop of Santiago de Maria in Usulutan.[84] At this time the government and military is involved in a brutal repression of the rural poor.[85] By February 1977, when Romero is installed as Archbishop of San Salvador, paramilitary and military groups launch a full-scale attack on members of the Catholic church because of their support for land reform, including the rights of peasants and workers.[86]

A few weeks after he becomes Archbishop, Romero's friend Rutilio Grande S.J. is assassinated.[87] The assassination of Grande

---

81 Marie Dennis, Renny Golden, Scott Wright. *Oscar Romero: Reflections on His Life and Writings.* (Maryknoll: Orbis, 2000), 7. Another insightful text about Romero and conversion is Damian Zynda, *Archbishop Oscar Romero: A Disciple Who Revealed the Glory of God.* (Scranton, PA: Scranton University Press, 2010).

82 Dennis, Golden, Wright. *Oscar Romero,* 8.

83 Dennis, Golden, Wright. *Oscar Romero,* 8.

84 Dennis, Golden, Wright. *Oscar Romero,* 8.

85 Dennis, Golden, Wright. *Oscar Romero,* 8.

86 Dennis, Golden, Wright. *Oscar Romero,* 9.

87 Dennis, Golden, Wright. *Oscar Romero,* 9. For more on Grande see Thomas M. Kelly, *When the Gospel Grows Feet: Rutilio Grande, SJ, and the Church in El Salvdor, An Ecclesiology in Context,* (Collegeville: MN, Liturgical Press, 2013), 110. What is

changes Romero, and provokes what Robert Lassalle-Klein describes as the political dimension of Romero's conversion to Medellin's preferential option for the poor.[88] Romero himself asserts that "Father Grande's death and the death of other priests after his impelled me to take an energetic attitude before the government."[89] He says, "I remember that because of Father Grande's death I made a statement that I would not attend any official acts until this situation [of who had killed Grande] was clarified." As a result, "A rupture was produced, not by me with the government but [by] the government itself because of its attitude."

Lassalle-Klein argues "it was only after the death of Fr. Rutilio Grande that Romero began to take full responsibility as archbishop for the systematic and ongoing violations of human rights by the government and others through public denouncements of this ongoing pattern that defined the situation in the country through the end of his life."[90] Indeed, Romero began to live out Grande's mission of evangelizing the poor and encouraging them to historicize the gospel.[91] Romero ultimately wants "to be the voice of those

---

key to note about Grande for the purposes of this research is that he offered "workshops on analyzing one's own reality through the method of 'see, judge, act.'" For more on Grande see Thomas M. Kelly, *Rutilio Grande, SJ: Homilies and Writings*. (Collegeville: MN, Liturgical Press; 2015).

88 Ignacio Ellacuria, "Monsenor Romero: One Sent by God to Save His People" in *Ignacio Ellacuría: Essays on History, Liberation, and Salvation*, ed. Michael E. Lee. (Orbis: Maryknoll, 2013), 285 - 292.

89 Interview of Archbishop Oscar Romero with Tommie Sue Montgomery, December 14, 1979; cited in Tommie Sue Montgomery, *Revolution in El Salvador: From Civil Strife to Civil Peace* (Boulder, CO: Westview Press, 1995), 95. Cited in Lassalle-Klein, *Blood and Ink*, 244.

90 Lassalle-Klein, *Blood and Ink*, 111.

91 Ellacuria, "Monsenor Romero," 288.

who have no voice,"[92] because "in the voiceless people" he sees "the very voice of God."[93]

On March 24, 1980, as he cerebrates the Eucharist in the chapel of the Divine Providence hospital, Romero is shot and dies.[94] Six days later at Romero's funeral Mass 150,000 people crowd into the square in front of the cathedral despite the risk of military assault. As Cardinal Corripio of Mexico eulogizes Romero, Salvadoran soldiers fire into the crowd from the roof of the Presidential Palace while bombs explode killing dozens and sending people into pandemonium.[95] The military's "lesson" at the funeral Mass is that those who keep alive the spirit of Romero will find the same fate as the Archbishop.

Romero's Historicization of the Gospel

Eight months after Romero is killed Ellacuria honors him in an essay that describes the Archbishop as an eminent example of how to historicize the force of the gospel.[96] Ellacuria explains that the foundation of Romero's historicization of the Gospel is "two pillars: a historic pillar...and a transcendent pillar."[97] Romero's position, one that embraces God's presence (transcendence) within history, stems not only from his historical encounter with the suffering and oppressed people of El Salvador, but, also from

92 Oscar Romero, *The Violence of Love*. (Maryknoll: Orbis Books, 2004), 151. Original homily, July 29, 1979.

93 Ellacuria, "Monsenor Romero:" 289-90.

94 Dennis, Golden, Wright. *Oscar Romero*, 11.

95 Dennis, Golden, Wright, *Oscar Romero*, 104.

96 Ignacio Ellacuria, "Monsenor Romero: One Sent by God to Save His People" in *Ignacio Ellacuría: Essays on History, Liberation, and Salvation*, ed. Michael E. Lee. (Maryknoll: New York, Orbis Books, 2013), 286-7.

97 Dennis, Golden, Wright. *Oscar Romero*, 117n6

his experience at the bishops' conferences at Medellin and Pue-bla.[98] Romero's experience there opens his ability to see Jesus Christ in the poor.[99] For example, Romero states:

> *each time we look upon the poor, on the farmworkers who harvest the coffee, the sugarcane, or the cotton, or the farmer who joins the caravan of workers looking to earn their savings for the year...re-member, there is the face of Christ...The face of Christ is among the sacks and baskets of the farmworker; the face of Christ is among those who are tortured and mistreated in the prisons; the face of Chris is dying of hunger in the children who have nothing to eat; the face of Christ is the poor who ask the church for their voice to be heard.[100]*

Romero also states that the face of Jesus can also be seen in:

> *the real faces of the poor...farmworkers without land and without steady employment, without running water or electricity in their homes, without medical assistance when mothers give birth, and without schools for their children....factory workers who have no labor rights...human beings who are at the mercy of cold economic calculations, shantytown dwellers whose wretchedness defies imagination, suffering the permanent mockery of the mansions nearby.[101]*

---

98 Ellacuría, "Monseñor Romero," 285.

99 Romero, *The Violence of Love*, 116. "The pastoral and evangelical teaching of Vatican Council II, which in 1968 became also the pastoral policy for Latin America...continues to raise questions for us now at the dawn of a new Medellin to take place at Puebla. This teaching declares that...God's reign must be established now on earth." (Original homily, January 7,1979).

100 Dennis, Golden, Wright. *Oscar Romero*, 35n29.

101 Dennis, Golden, Wright. *Oscar Romero*, 44n2.

The Archbishop's claim about encountering Jesus in the faces of the poor is based on his conviction that "each person's life, each one's history is the meeting place God comes to."[102]

Romero's Gospel hermeneutic ultimately transforms his ecclesiology and his missiology. He insists, for example, that the Church ought to come to the aid of those who suffer, those who reveal the face of Jesus Christ, because "Christian faith does not cut us off from the world but immerses us in it." In other words, Romero suggests there is a "political dimension of the Christian faith."[103] In fact, it is the political dimension of Romero's conversion to the option for the poor that ultimately leads to his assassination, which Ellacuria says "is without question the most important event in modern Salvadoran history," because "with Monsenor Romero, God passed through El Salvador.[104]

Gustavo Gutierrez, to a similar effect, argues that "we could say, without exaggeration, that the life and death of Monsignor Romero divides the recent history of the Latin American church into a before and after."[105] In the end, like Romero, Ellacuria sought to historicize the gospel by grasping what is at stake in, assuming responsibility for, and doing something to change, the unjust historical reality of poverty and military repression that defined the daily lives of the crucified the people of El Salvador.

Ignacio Ellacuria: A Martyr's Method of Praxis

In *Freedom Made Flesh: The Mission of Christ and His Church* (1976), originally published in Spanish in 1973, Ellacuria seeks to

---

102 Dennis, Golden, Wright. *Oscar Romero*, 73n12.

103 Dennis, Golden, Wright. *Oscar Romero*, 16-17n8.

104 Ignacio Ellacuría, *"Monsenor Romero,"* 285.

105 Dennis, Golden, Wright. *Oscar Romero*, 105n42.

undermine the "prejudice that salvation is ahistorical," which he says leads to a style of theological interpretation of social realities wherein the "unity of man, world, and history" are broken up into an "abstract scheme" that limits a truly theological approach to history.[106] In order to overcome this problem, Ellacuria suggests that theology should become "real in the strongest sense of the term." To achieve such realism "the Christian and the theologian must turn their attention to the history that is being made by human beings."[107] And, specifically, the Latin American Church must turn to the historical reality "of the poor" as the "proper locale" for theologizing because "in a real sense the poor are what Latin America is: poor in health, poor in education, poor in living standard, poor in having a say in their own destiny."[108]

Ellacuria's focus on the poor as a christological *locus theologicus* leads him to argue that the poor, the "vast portion of humankind," are "crucified people," who ought to be considered the principal sign of the times "by whose light the others should be discerned and interpreted."[109] In other words, Ellacuria believes that the fundamental reality "that should serve as a starting point for theological reflection" is "the excruciating reality" of the "crucified people."[110] And, to do this, theology will need to develop a methodological approach grounded in the historical reality of the

---

106 Ignacio Ellacuria, *Freedom Made Flesh: The Mission of Christ and His Church (1976)*, 11-12.

107 Ellacuria, *Freedom Made Flesh*, 14.

108 Ellacuria, *Freedom Made Flesh*, 146.

109 Robert Lassalle-Klein, "Marina,' in *Jesus of Galilee: Contextual Christology for the 21st Century*, ed. Robert Lassalle-Klein. (Orbis: Maryknoll, 2011.), 107n14.

110 Ignacio Ellacuria, "The Crucified People: An Essay in Historical Soteriology" in *Ignacio Ellacuría: Essays on History, Liberation, and Salvation*, ed. Michael E. Lee. (Orbis: Maryknoll, 2013), 209.

poor, which "has been scandalously ignored by those who theorize from the geographical world of oppressors."[111]

Ellacuria's Philosophical & Theological Method of Praxis

Ellacuria outlines such an approach in a 1975 plenary address to an international conference on methods of theological reflection in Mexico City. Here, Ellacuria outlines the foundations of his praxis-based methodology when he asserts that historical reality is the proper object of philosophy and theology, building on his assertion (elsewhere) that "historical reality, dynamically and concretely considered, has the character of praxis."[112]

As noted earlier, Lassalle-Klein explains[113] that Ellacuria follows Zubiri's claim that historical reality emerges through the appropriation and transformation of the historical and natural (i.e., the material, biological, and sentient) dimensions of reality and that the process of historicization (or human self-definition) is driven by the fact that when something "is already given as a reality . . . I am forced to become aware of it" or "to realize about it [*hacerse cargo de ella*] as a reality."[114]

But Ellacuria moves beyond Zubiri when he argues that the process of "facing up to real things as real has a triple dimension,"[115] which he asserts involves not only (1) "becoming aware of," "realizing about," or "grasping what is at stake in reality" (*hacerse cargo de*

111 Ellacuria, "The Crucified People," 209.

112 Ellacuría, *Filosofía de la realidad histórica*, 599.

113 Lassalle-Klein, *Blood and Ink*, 221.

114 Ellacuría describing Zubiri in "La historicidad del hombre in Xavier Zubiri," 526. See Zubiri, *Sobre la esencia*, 447. Translation by Robert Lassalle-Klein.

115 Ellacuría, "Hacia una fundamentación," 208. Translation by Robert Lassalle-Klein.

la realidad), but also (2) an ethical demand "to pick up" or "assume responsibility for reality" (*cargar con la realidad*), and (3) a praxis-related demand to change or "to take charge of reality" (*encargarse de la realidad*).[116] Ellacuria describes these as the "noetic, ethical, and praxical" dimensions of human intellection.[117]

Kevin Burke says that Ellacuría describes the "noetic dimesion" as the moment practitioners realize the weight of reality [*el hacerse cargo de la realidad*], the "ethical dimension" as the moment where practitioners learn to shoulder the weight of reality [*el cargar con la realidad*], and the "praxis-oriented dimension," as the moment where practitioners learn to take charge of the weight of reality [*el 'encargarse' de la 'realidad'*]."[118]

Ellacuria argues that theological method must follow this tripartite structure in order to overcome the tendency of theologies and other forms of discourse shaped by reductionist idealism to avoid "real questions of content and praxis."[119] Unlike classic western idealism, Ellacuria's praxis-based methodology begins with a socio-cultural reading of the historical context in order to disclose the structural and systematic character of political and economic injustice.

---

116 Robert Lassalle-Klein's translation of Ellacuría's three famously difficult phrases generally follow those of Jon Sobrino, in Jon Sobrino, "Jesus of Galilee from the Salvadoran Context: Compassion, Hope, and Following the Light of the Cross," in "The Galilean Jesus," *Theological Studies* 70, no. 2 (2009): 449 (special issue; ed. Robert Lassalle-Klein).

117 Ellacuria, "Laying the Philosophical Foundations of Latin American Theological Method (1975)," in *Ignacio Ellacuría: Essays on History, Liberation, and Salvation*, ed. Michael E. Lee, (Orbis: Maryknoll, 2013), 63.

118 Kevin Burke, *The Ground Beneath the Cross: The Theology of Ignacio Ellacría*, (Washington, D.C.: Georgetown University Press, 2000), 127.

119 Ellacuria, "Latin American Theological Method," 64.

However, while Ellacuria follows Gutierrez in his focus on the primacy of the praxis of faith for theology, he rejects Boff's Kantian epistemology, replacing it with Zubiri's insistence on the primacy of reality and the unity of sentient intelligence, within theology. Thus, theology and praxis must be understood as "mutually codetermining," just as every theory must be understood "as a moment of a unitary praxis."[120] In this sense, then, theology is not a second act, but rather simply the "ideological moment"[121] of the praxis of faith.

This brings us, then, to Ellacuria's historicized understanding of the hermeneutical circle. Ellacuria asserts that "the circularity to which Latin American theological method ought to attend" is a "circularity that is real, historical, and social."[122] He says this "fundamental circularity, which happens in every human knowing…is not the circularity of a theoretical horizon."[123] Rather, he insists, "we are talking about the circularity of a historical-practical horizon and some structural, socio-historical realities that flow from that horizon and also reconfigure it."[124]

Thus, Ellacuria's theological methodology leads him to focus on the hermeneutical circle between Jesus' crucifixion and that of the "crucified people," who, as the "majority of humanity," owe "its situation of crucifixion" to a sinful social order organized and

---

120 Ellacuria, "Relacion teoria y praxis," 236. Cited in Lassalle-Klein, personal correspondence.

121 Ignacio Ellacuría, "Latin American Theological Method," 78. For more see, "Theology as the Ideological Moment of Ecclesial Praxis," in *Ignacio Ellacuría: Essays on History, Liberation, and Salvation*, ed. Michael E. Lee, (Orbis: Maryknoll, 2013), 262.

122 Ellacuria, "Latin American Theological Method," 87.

123 Ellacuria, "Latin American Theological Method," 87.

124 Ellacuria, "Latin American Theological Method," 87.

maintained by a minority that exercises its dominion through a series of factors.[125]

Echoing Zubiri's claims about respectivity, Ellacuria argues that the hermeneutical circle must focus on the physical aspect of intellection because physicality is where all comprehension and activity starts. He says, "The circularity is physical: it is physical in the point at which all comprehension and all activity starts."[126] And he argues that "human intelligence can only act from the senses and in reference to the senses because they are…biological functions."[127] Thus, the formal structure and differentiating function of intelligence is not a structure of comprehending being, but rather the structure of apprehending reality and engaging it [*enfrentarse con ella*; 'confronting oneself with it'].[128]

In the end, Ellacuria's most important insight in regard to methodology is that "This active dimension of knowledge is not purely praxic, as Aristotle wanted, but must be strictly **poeisis-based** (my own emphasis), in the sense that it has to objectify itself in exterior realities beyond the active immanence of one's own interiority and subjective intentionality.[129] Ellacuria's claim about the relationship between knowledge and *poeisis*, besides being underdeveloped in theological circles, carries immense power if considered in regard to the intersection of Christian Ethics and pedagogy. If theories and practices of teaching aim to focus on students' *poeisis* then the *telos*, or goal, of theological pedagogy would shift toward a focus on practical action that aims to "find God in

---

125 Ellacuria, "Latin American Theological Method," 208.

126 Ellacuria, "Latin American Theological Method," 87.

127 Ellacuria, "Latin American Theological Method," 79n7.

128 Ellacuria, "Latin American Theological Method," 80.

129 Ellacuria, "Latin American Theological Method," 83.

all things by laboring in the midst of all things."[130] What this signifies is that labor, either in the production of artifacts, such as a house in an economic sense; the extraction of natural resources in a business sense; or policies that limit migration or health care in a political sense, must also be understood as part and parcel of the professional labor that either realizes the Kingdom of God or the "anti-kingdom" of God. What, though, is the ethical ideal that informs Ellacuria's claim about historicizing theoretical knowledge so that it becomes not only praxis but ecclesial *poeisis*?

Ellacuria's Eschatological Ethic as Integral to Ecclesial Praxis and Poeisis

Ellacuria argues "If the fundamental object of the mission of Jesus was the Reign of God, it should also be the object of ecclesial praxis and the ideological moment of that praxis."[131] What Ellacuria suggests, then, is "all other theological subjects should arise (not only in theoretical interpretation but also in projects and actions) within the framework of the Reign of God and in its historical realization."[132]

Ellacuria's claim about the Reign of God is central to his understanding of theological methodology, the hermeneutical circle, and praxis. Ellacuria writes "a hermeneutical circle, which moves from the Reign to praxis but returns from praxis to the Reign," focuses on the "fundamental object of theology: the Reign of God" as a "reality and concept that is both historical and structural."[133]

---

130 Lassalle-Klein, *Blood and Ink*, 199n58, 59, 60, 61.

131 Ignacio Ellacuria, "Theology as the Ideological Moment of Ecclesial Praxis (1978)," in *Ignacio Ellacuria: Essays on History, Liberation, and Salvation*, ed. Michael E. Lee. Orbis: Maryknoll, 2013), 265.

132 Ellacuria, "Theology as the Ideological Moment," 265.

133 Ellacuria, "Theology as the Ideological Moment," 266-7.

Ellacuria adds that because the concept of the Reign of God is dynamic on a historical and transhistorical level, theological reflection has to concern itself directly with what constitutes the realization of the Reign of God.[134] Plus, for Ellacuria, " the church of the poor is...the privileged place for theological reflection and for the realization of the Reign of God."[135]

Ellacuria ultimately embraces what biblical scholars call the "eschatological reserve" of what Jesus names the Reign (Kingdom) of God, which draws his attention to specific ways that the Kingdom is being realized in history, and ways in which it is not as a result of sin.[136] Ellacuria wants Christian communities to historicize eschatological judgments in such a way that *poiesis*, or objectified action, facilitates the realization of the Kingdom of God on earth.[137]

For example, Ellacuria is concerned about the relationship between theoretical knowledge, praxis, *poeisis*, and objectified action, because, as noted earlier, this relationship has the power to turn the *telos*, or goal, of theological pedagogy toward practical action in a way that aims to "find God in all things by laboring in the midst of all things."[138] What this means is that labor, the creation of products and policies, especially in a business or governmental context, must also carry the aim of realizing the Kingdom of God on earth. In the end, Ellacuria is shot and killed for historicizing his political and civic commitment to God's plan to realize the Kingdom of God in El Salvador. Fortunately, one of his closest

---

134 Ellacuria, "Theology as the Ideological Moment," 267.

135 Ellacuria, "Theology as the Ideological Moment," 272.

136 Lassalle-Klein, *Blood and Ink*, 223.

137 Lassalle-Klein, *Blood and Ink*, 223.

138 Lassalle-Klein, *Blood and Ink*, 199n58, 59, 60, 61.

friends, Jon Sobrino S.J., continues to reflect on, and build upon, the legacy left by Ellacuria, Romero, and Rutilio Grande.

Jon Sobrino:
Salvadoran Praxis in Jesus' Kingdom of God

Like the Latin American bishops, Gutierrez, Boff, and Ellacuria, Jon Sobrino's theological methodology privileges historical reality as a *locus theologicus* wherein the hermeneutical circle places "logical priority" on "present reality over past reality."[139] Sobrino therefore gives methodological primacy to the world of the poor as the proper place for theology.[140]

One of Sobrino's most significant achievements is his development of Ellacuria's claim that the reality of the poor is the defining sign of the times that confronts and calls us to take the "innocent victims" of our world "down from the cross."[141] Building on Ellacuria's hermeneutical focus on the relationship between the suffering experienced by the crucified Christ and the crucified people of El Salvador, Sobrino adds Christological depth to the Christian eschatological ethic. In the following subsection I will briefly examine articles Sobrino authors between 1978-1984, which are compiled in *Jesus in Latin America*[142] and *Spirituality of*

---

139 Dean Brackley, "Theology and Solidarity: Learning From Sobrino's Method" in *Hope & Solidarity*, Stephen J. Pope, ed. (Maryknoll: Orbis, 2008), 12n25.

140 Like Dean Brackley, Rafael Luciani writes that Sobrino thinks that wherever it is "practiced empirically, theology should be affected in-depth by the reality of the poor." For more see *Hope & Solidarity: Jon Sobrino's Challenge to Christian Theology*, edited by Stephen J. Pope (Maryknoll: Orbis, 2008), 9; 107.

141 Rafael Luciani, "Hermeneutics and Theology in Sobrino's Christology," in *Hope & Solidarity*, Stephen J. Pope, ed. (Maryknoll: Orbis, 2008), 109n27.

142 Jon Sobrino, *Jesus in Latin America* (Maryknoll, NY: Orbis Books, 1982), xv. The book is a compilation of a number of articles written between 1978-1982.

Liberation: Toward Political Holiness.[143] The section will conclude with a focus on his Christological eschatology.

Sobrino's Turn to Historical Reality as the Basis of Theological Praxis

Sobrino takes an *a posteriori* methodological "point of departure" from within the "historical reality" of "poverty,"[144] which he places in a hermeneutical circle with Jesus' ministry to the poor, particularly "sinners, publicans, prostitutes (Mark 2:6; MT 11:19, 21:32; LK 15:1), the simple (MT 11:25), the little (MK 9:2; MT 10:42, 18:10, 14), and the least (MT 25:40-45)."[145] Sobrino's methodology therefore begins with his experience of historical reality and moves to what is most central to the Christian tradition, Jesus' concern for the poor, "those lesser than others" and "those who suffer need, the hungry and thirsty, the naked, the foreigners, the sick and imprisoned, those who weep, those weighed down by a burden."[146]

Sobrino's claim is based on his assertion that "The gospel narratives clearly show that a basic characteristic of Jesus' praxis is that he surrounds himself with sinners, publicans, the sick, lepers, Samaritans, pagans, and women through his life."[147] Thus, Sobrino's Christology is grounded in the idea that, if the goal of Christian ethics is to bring about the Kingdom of God in history, then we must necessarily look at, and imitate, the interactions

---

143 Jon Sobrino, *Spirituality of Liberation: Toward Political Holiness* (Maryknoll, NY: Orbis Books, 1985) is a compilation of a number of articles written on spirituality from 1980 to 1984.

144 Sobrino, *Spirituality of Liberation*, 157-8

145 Sobrino, *Jesus in Latin America*, 89.

146 Sobrino, *Jesus in Latin America* 90

147 Sobrino, *Jesus in Latin America*, 140.

between Jesus and the poor and outcast as the *bonum morale* (ethical virtue) to be embodied in Christian praxis.[148]

Sobrino also insists that the quantitative reality of poverty carries a qualitative responsibility,[149] a call to take down from the cross those who "in the human race today...are crucified."[150] Sobrino's interest in the world of the crucified is therefore not esoteric.[151] He argues that each day millions of people in the world die in ways that are analogous to how Jesus died at the hands of idolaters of national security or wealth.[152] Men and women are crucified, murdered, tortured to death, or 'disappeared' while other millions die a slow crucifixion caused by structural injustice.[153]

Sobrino's argument is actually simple: when one's death is the product of injustice, then an analogy obtains with the life and death of Jesus.[154] In other words, the "crucified of history" provide an analog to understand "Jesus' reality as the crucified one."[155] Sobrino's methodology therefore moves "from a point of departure in the poor" into dialogue with the gospel of Matthew 25, which functions as a hermeneutic for theological reflection.[156] By using Matthew 25 as a lens to see "the crucified in history" it becomes possible to see the wounds of Jesus in the poor.[157] In the end,

---

148 Sobrino, *Jesus in Latin America,* 140-141; 144-145

149 Sobrino, *Jesus in Latin America,* 141.

150 Sobrino, *Jesus in Latin America,* 148.

151 Sobrino, *Jesus in Latin America,* 151.

152 Sobrino, *Jesus in Latin America,* 151.

153 Sobrino, *Jesus in Latin America,* 151-152.

154 Sobrino, *Jesus in Latin America,* 152.

155 Sobrino, *Jesus in Latin America,* 148.

156 Sobrino, *Jesus in Latin America,* 11.

157 Sobrino, *Jesus in Latin America,* 157.

Sobrino argues that a moral Christian life is historicized in giving life to the crucified.[158] For Sobrino, to work for the kingdom is to help transform the world and history into closer conformity with God's will and therefore to incarnate, give form to, and render verifiable, the ethos of a follower of Jesus Christ.[159]

Historicizing Jesus' Eschatological Praxis

Sobrino advances Ellacuria's turn to the historical reality of the crucified people through his analysis of Jesus' praxis, using the kingdom of God, which he announced, as a critical-analogical hermeneutic. Taking Sobrino's insight as a point of departure, I would argue that Jesus' praxis should be understood as a kind of eschatopraxis (a model of a praxis associated with the historicization of the Kingdom of God as the ultimate "social imaginary" that provides the "end" or "*telos*" of Jesus' mission and activity). But what warrants can we provide for this claim? How can we know if Jesus' led a life of eschatopraxis?

Sobrino argues that Christology is integrally linked with historical eschatology because without Jesus' notion of the kingdom of God "there is no radical force to transform and project the present."[160] Thus, Sobrino's Christological eschatology, like Ellacuria's, aims 'to see transcendence as something that transcends in and not something that transcends from" or beyond the world.[161] In other words, "finding God in history does not mean abandoning what is human,"[162] and "social conditions become an object of

---

158 Sobrino, *Jesus in Latin America*, 156.

159 Sobrino, *Jesus in Latin America*, 156; 162.

160 Palazzi, *Hope & Solidarity*, 132n2.

161 Palazzi, *Hope & Solidarity*, 132-3n5.

162 Palazzi, *Hope & Solidarity*, 133.

transformation as the place of the historical realization of the kingdom of God."[163] What this means for Sobrino is that the kingdom of God makes a fraternal demand on the disciples and followers of Jesus Christ who are "called blessed, happy, because by giving food to the hungry, water to the thirsty, by clothing the naked and visiting those who are in prison, by means of concrete gestures, they give life" as they see, judge, and act within the kingdom.[164] Happiness (blessedness), therefore, is a consequence of the labor it takes to build the kingdom in our present historical reality.

But, if historicizing the eschatological praxis of Jesus leads to a happy life, how, then, is it historicized? Sobrino says that the praxis of Jesus consistently denounces the anti-kingdom idols of his time.[165] The same applies to the idols of indifference, selfishness, and greed today. Followers of Jesus must take seriously these idols and devote themselves to the marginal and neglected of the world, the victims whose lives are snatched away by the political, economic, and religious idolatry of our time.[166]

Eschatological praxis is, therefore, a way to see, judge, and act with criticity in regard to the political and economic conditions created by sin.[167] In short, eschatological praxis aims to issue a radical judgment of "certainly not!" against the structures that create victims and sufferers, and that deceive people with political ideologies that distort and disguise reality, especially the reality of the poor.[168] By acting against that which crucifies the "crucified peoples" of our world, a sense of happiness (blessedness) emerges.

---

163 Palazzi, *Hope & Solidarity*, 134.

164 Palazzi *Hope & Solidarity*, 134n11.

165 Palazzi, *Hope & Solidarity*, 139.

166 Palazzi, *Hope & Solidarity*, 139.

167 Palazzi, *Hope & Solidarity*, 139.

168 Palazzi, *Hope & Solidarity*, 140.

Conclusion

In the end, Ignacio Ellacuria, Basque Jesuit theologian, and nationalized citizen of El Salvador, is martyred for historicizing the canonical turn to methods and methodologies of theological praxis that focused on the interpretation of historical reality (especially the historical reality of what he called the "crucified peoples," the poor majorities of the planet) as a primary *locus theologicus*.

The conceptual foundations of Ellacuria's intellectual and practical accomplishments are rooted in the work of his teachers, Karl Rahner and Xavier Zubiri, while his understanding of the mission of Archbishop Oscar Romero to the people of El Salvador shapes his praxis. Guided by his interpretation of what Jesus names the Reign of God, Rahner's transcendental and historical methodology, Zubiri's focus on reality, and Romero's option for the poor and his ability to find Christ in them, Ellacuria's lifetime of work provides Catholic theology and philosophy with a moral exemplar of theological praxis that is dedicated to taking crucified people down from their cross.[169]

To provide warrants for these claims the first three subsections of this chapter examined the influence of Ellacuria's teachers, Karl Rahner and Xavier Zubiri, and his friendship with Archbishop Romero. After contextualizing Ellacuria's intellectual and spiritual formation I appealed to his writings on the crucified people and theological method. I then concluded with a brief exposition of some aspects of Sobrino's Christology and treatment of the

---

169 Ignacio Ellacuría, "El pueblo crucificado, ensayo de soteriología histórica," *Escritos teológicos*, II (San Salvador: UCA Editores, 2000), 137-70; quoted in "The Crucified People: An Essay in Historical Soteriology," in Michael Lee, ed., *Ignacio Ellacuría: Essays on History, Liberation, and Salvation* (Maryknoll, NY: Orbis Books, 2013), 196.

Kingdom of God as developments of Ellacuria's focus on the historical reality of the crucified people.

In the next chapter I will argue that it is plausible to say that the magisterial, philosophical, and theological developments I have chronicled in the first four chapters; the canonical turn to Cardijn's method, praxis-based methodologies, and the interpretation of historical reality, especially of the poor, as a *locus theologicus*, has turned the Catholic Church toward a form of practical theology.

PART III

FROM PRAXIS TO PRACTICAL THEOLOGY

5

CONTEMPORARY
CATHOLIC PRACTICAL THEOLOGY:
FROM WESTERN EUROPE TO THE UNITED STATES
& AT THE VATICAN

Overview

Practical theology is a growing field within Catholic theology in the twenty-first century.[1] It can be described as theology done with a praxis-based methodology that focuses on the interpretation of historical reality as a *locus theologicus*. What makes practical theology unique, therefore, is its methodology, which typically consists of at least three, but, as many as six steps or movements. Before the first movement, a questionable ethical and/or moral practice is identified.

---

1 Claire E. Wolfteich, ed. *Invitation to Practical Theology: Catholic Voices and Visions* (New York: Paulist Press, 2014). Also see, Kathleen A. Cahalan and Gordon Mikoski, eds. *Opening the Field of Practical Theology: An Introduction*, (Landham: MD, Rowan and Littlefield Publishers, 2014). Also see, Bonnie J. Miller-McLemore, ed. *The Wiley-Blackwell Companion to Practical Theology* (Wiley-Blackwell: Oxford, 2012). Also see, Kathleen Cahalan, "Locating Practical Theology in Catholic Theological Discourse and Practice," in *International Journal of Practical Theology*, 15no.1, 2011, p. 1-21.

- The first movement, taking the questionable practice as a point of departure, involves the collection of empirical data, either qualitative or quantitative,[2] through focus groups, case studies,[3] congregational studies,[4] participatory action research,[5] and ethnography.[6]

- The second movement integrates social analysis where theoretical data from social and/or physical sciences is used to clarify and explain the empirical data gathered in the first movement.

- The third movement draws from sources from the Christian tradition and places them into a dialectical relationship with the data from movement one and two.

What is key at this stage of the process is that the wisdom from the Christian tradition is used to critique, or counterpoint, the data gathered in movement one and two. After critical theological reflection, the fourth, fifth, and/or sixth movement involves creating a strategy that aims to actively transform the practice in question.

---

2 Hans Schilderman, "Quantitative Method," in *The Wiley-Blackwell Companino to Practical Theology*, ed. Bonnie J. Miller-McLemore (Wiley-Blackwell: Oxford, 2012), 123-132. Also see Johannes van der Ven *Practical Theology: An Empirical Approach* (Leuven, Belgium: Peeters Publishers, 1998).

3 Daniel S. Schipani, "Case Study Method," in *The Wiley-Blackwell Companino to Practical Theology*, ed. Bonnie J. Miller-McLemore (Wiley-Blackwell: Oxford, 2012), 91-101.

4 James R. Nieman, "Congregational Studies," in *The Wiley-Blackwell Companino to Practical Theology*, ed. Bonnie J. Miller-McLemore (Wiley-Blackwell: Oxford, 2012), 133-142.

5 Elizabeth Conde-Frazier, "Participatory Action Research," in *The Wiley-Blackwell Companino to Practical Theology*, ed. Bonnie J. Miller-McLemore (Wiley-Blackwell: Oxford, 2012), 234-243.

6 Mary Clark Moschella, "Ethnography," in *The Wiley-Blackwell Companino to Practical Theology*, ed. Bonnie J. Miller-McLemore (Wiley-Blackwell: Oxford, 2012), 224-233. Also see *Ethnography as Christian Theology and Ethics*, ed. Christian Schaaren and Aana Marie Vigen (New York: Continuum International Publishing Group, 2011).

Taking this understanding of practical theological methodology as my point of departure I will argue that in the twentieth century the Catholic Church makes a canonical pastoral-theological, philosophical, and magisterial turn to methods and methodologies of praxis that interpret historical reality as a *locus theologicus*.

To provide warrants for this claim I first appeal to the work of figures from Western Europe, specifically Karl Rahner and Johann Baptist Metz. I then appeal to the work of figures from the United States, particularly David Tracy, Joe Holland and Peter Henriot, and Thomas Groome. And, I conclude by showing that the first Latin American Pope, Francis, also uses a methodology of theological praxis to interpret historical reality as a *locus theologicus*, thereby confirming the Catholic Church's canonical turn toward practical theology.

Karl Rahner Opens the Discussion
of Catholic Practical Theology

Karl Rahner is a foundational figure in the discussion of Catholic practical theology. In lectures between 1965 and 1967 he describes practical theology as a "theological discipline which is concerned with the Church's self-actualization here and now - both that which is and that which ought to be."[7] But, what does Rahner mean when he claims practical theology is concerned not only with "that which is" but also "that which ought to be?"

In regard to "that which is" Rahner explains: "Practical theology's subject matter is everyone and everything in the Church."[8] In

---

7 Karl Rahner, *Theological Investigations: Vol. IX. Writings of 1965-67*, (New York: Herder and Herder, 1972), 102.

8 Rahner, *Theological Investigations: Vol. IX*, 104. Two paragraphs after his first reference to practical theology having everyone and everything as its subject matter Rahner again states: "Everything is its subject matter." Rahner also discusses

other words, if the subject matter of practical theology is everyone and everything connected with the church then economic practices, political practices, environmental practices, healthcare practices, and business practices can be interpreted in a theological way.[9] But, what about "that which ought to be?"[10] Rahner's work on eschatological hermeneutics provides a potential response to this aspect of his claim.

According to Peter Phan, Rahner believes that "All Christian theology is in a very genuine sense eschatology, since for him Christian eschatology is nothing but Christian anthropology read in the future tense, and Christian anthropology in turn is necessarily Christian theology."[11] Moreover, Rahner believes: "Eschatology...gives expression...to man as Christianity understands him: as a being who exists from out of his present 'now' towards the future."[12] So, accounting for Rahners' interpretation of eschatological hermeneutics, it is possible to claim that the "scientific organization" of a Rahnerian practical theological method must be one that moves from an anthropological "that which is" to reflection on an eschatological "that which ought to be" in order to question the ethics and morality of real practices in places where the Church pursues its mission.

In the end, Rahner's work is of inestimable value when considering why practical theology is considered a rigorous scientific discipline in Catholic circles. However, it is Rahner's student, Johann

---

practical theology in *Theological Investigations Vol. X* with little difference from what he writes in *Vol. IX*.

9 Rahner, *Theological Investigations: Vol. IX*, 105.

10 Rahner, *Theological Investigations: Vol. IX*, 102.

11 Peter Phan, *Eternity in Time: A Study of Karl Rahner's Eschatology*, (Selinsgrove: Susquehanna University Press, 1988), 23n34, n35.

12 Phan, *Eternity in Time*, 43. Also see Karl Rahner, *Foundations of Christian Faith: An Introduction To The Idea of Christianity*, (New York: Crossroad Publishing Company, 2010), 431-447.

Baptist Metz, who, through critique of his teacher's inattention to praxis, enriches the discourse about Catholic practical theology.[13]

Johann Baptist Metz:
Questioning Rahner's Inattention to Praxis

Johann Baptist Metz advances the discussion of Catholic practical theology by questioning whether Rahner's transcendental anthropology (which is always eschatological) properly accounted for the fact that man's existence is always concrete and historical.[14] In other words, Metz critiques Rahner's transcendental theological methodology for not having the structure of historical experience.[15] To move beyond Rahner's approach Metz suggests that practical theology should not consider theory and praxis in the classic order of priority, in which praxis is regarded as the concrete application of a previously defined theory.[16] Primacy, according to Metz, is instead placed on the theological intelligibility of praxis.[17]

To make his case about praxis, Metz draws from the work of Immanuel Kant to argue that when history is made it is due to the primacy of practical reason.[18] And, building on the work of Karl Marx, Metz claims that the dialectic of theory and praxis shows that individual moral praxis is not, and cannot, in any sense be socially and politically innocent.[19] Metz then combines Kant and Marx to craft the argument that theology ought to use a dialectical praxis-

---

13 Phan claims that Metz's criticism is the only one Rahner took seriously. For more see, *Eternity in Time*, 31n15.

14 Johann Baptist Metz, *Faith in History and Society: Toward a Practical Fundamental Theology.* (New York: Crossroad, 1980), 65n2.

15 Metz, *Faith in History*, 65.

16 Metz, *Faith in History*, 50.

17 Metz, *Faith in History*, 50.

18 Metz, *Faith in History*, 53n7.

19 Metz, *Faith in History*, 53-54.

based methodology that begins with practical hermeneutics, and then integrates past and present moral praxis as forms of ethical instruction, to create a movement that can facilitate social change.[20]

In other words, Metz argues that a methodology grounded in praxis prevents theology from being abstract, and, instead, will be practical in the form of a critical and dialectical hermeneutic.[21] In the end, by critiquing Rahner's transcendental methodology as lacking historical praxis, and building an argument out of the work of Kant and Marx, Metz advances the discourse on Catholic practical theology. The achievements of both Rahner and Metz have been resourced and developed by many practical theologians in the United States.

David Tracy:
Catholic Practical Theology in the United States

David Tracy is recognized as one of the first Catholic theologians in the United States to develop a practical theology. What is important to note is that Tracy actually claims that there are three types of theology "fundamental, systematic," and "practical," yet, in what follows, I will only examine Tracy's writings on practical theology.[22]

In a chapter of Don Browning's 1983 publication *Practical Theology*, Tracy defines practical theology as a discipline whose methodology facilitates mutually critical correlations between the meaning of an interpretation of the Christian tradition and the meaning

---

20 Metz, *Faith in History*, 54.

21 Metz, *Faith in History*, 56.

22 For more on Tracy's descriptions of the "three disciplines of theology; fundamental, systematic, and practical" see, David Tracy, *The Analogical Imagination: Christian Theology and the Culture of Pluralism*, (New York: Crossroad, 1986), 54-59.

of an interpretation of the contemporary situation.[23] Tracy explains that the first methodological movement begins with models of human transformation provided by psychology, social science, historical studies, cultural anthropology, philosophy, ecological theories, religious studies and theology.[24] The second movement usually involves an analysis of these claims against concrete ideals for the future, whether humanist, utopian, or eschatological.[25] The third movement employs critical hermeneutic theories to clarify ambiguity in movements one and two.[26]

Tracy asserts that, in movement three, the major task of critical theory is to unmask the systematic distortions in the personal, social, cultural historical and religious models of human transformation.[27] Tracy explains that the fourth movement must therefore be concerned with ethical reflection, which he defines as critical theoretical reflection on moral praxis.[28]

Tracy adds that because of its focus on ethical-political situations practical theology necessarily appeals to Christianity's prophetic, eschatological, and ethical function.[29] By framing ethics as critical reflection on moral praxis, Tracy is able to turn from an ethics and politics that relies on metaphysical theories toward an understanding of ethics and politics as critical reflection with a

---

23 David Tracy, "The Foundations of Practical Theology," in *Practical Theology*, ed. Don Browning, (New York: Harper and Row, 1983), 62.

24 Tracy, "Foundations of Practical Theology," 76.

25 Tracy, "Foundations of Practical Theology," 77.

26 Tracy, "Foundations of Practical Theology," 78.

27 Tracy, "Foundations of Practical Theology," 78

28 Tracy, "Foundations of Practical Theology," 78.

29 Tracy, "Foundations of Practical Theology," 75-6.

tradition of practical wisdom (*phronesis*) that aims to make prudent decisions as to what is to be done in variable situations.[30]

At the foundation of Tracy's approach is Aristotle's notion of praxis, which is based on the idea that moral agents are always guided by some goal of the good and virtuous life, and, therefore, actions are always conditioned by contact with various traditions of practical wisdom (*phronesis*).[31] However, in *Analogical Imagination* (1981) Tracy builds on his methodological position with the claim that the historical realities of our common human experience are a theological locus for Christian reflection and self-understanding.[32]

Tracy, like Metz, therefore describes practical theology as a paradigm of praxis that aims to analyze some radical situation of ethical-religious import (sexism, racism, classism, elitism, anti-Semitism, economic exploitation, environmental crisis, etc) in some philosophical, social-scientific, culturally analytic or religiously prophetic (eschatological) manner in order to transform reality.[33] Tracy ultimately prioritizes praxis over theory in regard to philosophical and theological methodology because he claims that theory is dependent on praxis as its own originating and self-correcting foundation.[34]

What is key to Tracy's methodology is that he follows many of the Catholic political and liberation theologians who use praxis in relation to some form of Christian eschatology, or Marxist ideology-critique, to set up a critique of church, academic, and social

---

30 Tracy, "Foundations of Practical Theology," 73.

31 Tracy, "Foundations of Practical Theology," 75.

32 David Tracy, *The Analogical Imagination: Christian Theology and the Culture of Pluralism*, (New York: Crossroad, 1986.), 49n13.

33 Tracy, *Analogical Imagination*, 57-58.

34 Tracy, *Analogical Imagination*, 58.

structures.[35] For example, Tracy points to Metz's political theology as an example of how praxis and a prophetic eschatology can be integrated to critique real moral and ethical crisis as opposed to an intellectual analysis of cognitive claims related to Christian doctrine.[36]

In 2009 Tracy changes his definition of practical theology. Tracy explains that his earlier definition ought to have emphasized the need for a theological correlation with the aesthetic, the contemplative metaphysical, and spiritual traditions of Christianity.[37] Tracy claims that such a focus is necessary because aesthetics is intrinsically related to ethics.[38] According to Tracy, practical theological ethics is, however, more of a teleological ethics of apperception rather than a Kantian ethics of obligation.[39]

Tracy sums-up his new formulation of practical theology by stating that all theology should be practical (praxis-determined) as both ethical-political (prophetic) and aesthetic, even mystical.[40] And, Tracy adds that ethical and politically focused practical theologies (e.g., liberation, feminist, postcolonial, gay, and political theologies) will necessarily emphasize justice, like many of the Jewish and Christian prophets, including Jesus (especially the Lukan

---

35 Tracy, *Analogical Imagination*, 72n98.

36 Tracy, *Analogical Imagination*, 78.

37 David Tracy, "A Correlational Model of Practical Theology Revisited," in *Invitation to Practical Theology: Catholic Voices and Visions*, Claire E. Wolfteich, ed. (New York: Paulist Press, 2014), 71. Originally published in David Tracy, *Plurality and Ambiguity: Hermeneutics, Religion, and Hope.* (Harper & Row: San Francisco, 1987).

38 Tracy, "A Correlational Model," 72.

39 Tracy, "A Correlational Model," 72.

40 Tracy, "A Correlational Model," 73. Tracy follows Rahner who claimed that to be a Christian in the 21st century you will have to be a mystic or not Christian at all.

Jesus) while the aesthetic, metaphysical, wisdom and mystical theologies will emphasize love or loving wisdom-in-action.[41]

Beyond Tracy the discipline of practical theology flourished in fields of Catholic higher education in the United States from 1970 onward. One of David Tracy's students, Joe Holland, a social ethicist, and his cohort Peter Henriot S.J., developed the now famous Pastoral Circle method which is described in *Social Analysis: Linking Faith and Justice*.

Joe Holland & Peter Henriot S.J.:
Praxis & the Pastoral Circle Method

Joe Holland and Peter Henriot create the pastoral circle method to overcome what they believe is a flaw in theological and philosophical methodology of Tracy, particularly the lack of intimate contact of the researcher with the community or people being investigated.[42] Holland and Henriot's pastoral circle method does not, however, only seek to build on Tracy's methodology, it is also rooted in Cardinal Cardijn's See-Judge-Act method.[43]

Unlike Cardijn's three steps, the Pastoral Circle method is comprised of four movements.[44] Movement one begins with insertion, a methodological movement not present in Tracy's methodology. By positioning "insertion" first in their pastoral circle method, Holland and Henriot are able to emphasize immersion in a community

---

41 Tracy, "A Correlational Model," 72.

42 Joe Holland and Peter Henriot. *Social Analysis: Linking Faith and Justice*, revised and enlarged edition. (Dove Communications and Orbis books in collaboration with The Center of Concern. Mary knoll NY, 1988).

43 Holland and Henriot, *Social Analysis*, 10.

44 Holland and Henriot, *Social Analysis*, 95.

so that people can be asked questions about their sociopolitical and economic reality.[45]

Commenting on the pastoral circle, Rodrigo Mejia states: "To ask real questions, that touch real life, at the beginning of the process, opens a new theological epistemology."[46] Instead of starting only from the data of revelation and tradition, as classical theology has usually done, insertion into a community prompts theologians to start from the data and problems coming from historical reality.[47] Historical reality, in other words, becomes a *locus theologicus*.

In the second movement of the pastoral circle method social analysis is used to examine causes, probe consequences, delineate linkages, and identify actors related to key questions and issues under investigation in the community.[48] In other words, social analysis is used to explore reality in light of historical (time) and structural (space) relationships.[49] The second movement is therefore able to integrate theories from sociology, anthropology, psychology, history, political science, and economics.[50]

In the third movement, sociopolitical and economic questions, issues, and theories are reflected on theologically with resources from Christian tradition including scripture and church social

---

45 Holland and Henriot, *Social Analysis*, 8.

46 Rodrigo Mejia, "The Impact of the Pastoral Circle in Teaching Pastoral Theology," in *The Pastoral Circle Revisited: A Critical Quest for Truth and Transformation*, Frans Wijsen, Peter Henriot, and Rodrigo Mejia, eds. (Maryknoll: Orbis, 2005), 128.

47 Mejia, "The Impact of the Pastoral Circle," 129.

48 Holland and Henriot, *Social Analysis*, 89.

49 Holland and Henriot, *Social Analysis*, 14.

50 Holland and Henriot explain "Social analysis can include political analysis of such issues as healthcare and immigration. Economic analysis can include structural analysis such as banking policies, microfinance, IMF loans. Social analysis also involves historical and cultural analysis to understand the changes of systems and structures throughout time and space," 14.

teaching.[51] In the fourth movement, pastoral planning designs a strategy for action in light of the critical correlation of data from movements one, two, and three.[52] In sum, the four movements form a "spiral of praxis" because the methodology emphasizes the on-going, ever turning relationship between action and reflection.[53]

S. Madge Karecki, Assistant National Director of the Pontifical Mission Societies in the United States, explains that, while Holland and Henriot did not conceive the pastoral circle method as a teaching tool, it has proven effective in enabling students to "do rather than simply to study missiology."[54]

Karecki adds that the pastoral circle method provides students with a way of "doing missiology that begins in their immediate context and their own historical setting."[55] Karecki argues that what is key about the first step, insertion, is that students' experiences of their particular sociocultural context are acknowledged as a *locus theologicus* which empowers them with a sense of agency as they begin to critically reflect on the world around them.[56]

In other words, students begin to see mission as a theological enterprise that is rooted in their own lives rather than something that happens in another place with other people.[57] The value of such a

---

51 Holland and Henriot, *Social Analysis*, 9.

52 Holland and Henriot, *Social Analysis*, 7.

53 Holland and Henriot, *Social Analysis*, 8. The pastoral circle is like the hermeneutical circle in that it is a method of interpretation that asks new questions continuously to challenge older theories against new situations.

54 Madge Karecki, "Teaching Missiology in Context: Adaptations of the Pastoral Circle" in *The Pastoral Circle Revisited: A Critical Quest for Truth and Transformation*, Frans Wijsen, Peter Henriot, and Rodrigo Mejia, eds. (Maryknoll: Orbis, 2005), 137.

55 Karecki, "Teaching Missiology in Context," 138-140.

56 Karecki, "Teaching Missiology in Context," 140.

57 Karecki, "Teaching Missiology in Context," 140.

methodological process helps students better understand the problems and needs of their reality through critical reflection.[58]

Karecki adds that the structure of Holland and Henriot's method fulfills "The pedagogical task of theology" which "is to affirm the deeper dimensions of the human person in relationship to ultimate reality."[59] Karecki also suggests that the pastoral circle method forces students to learn how to become active subjects, not passive objects.[60] In other words, the pastoral circle method encourages a form of "learning" that "becomes transformative as students grapple" with their experiences through "a process of critical theological reflection on their own faith history rooted in a particular context."[61]

In other words, Holland and Henriot's methodology helps overcome "the effects of an educational system that has not equipped them with the necessary skills to engage in learning that requires critical thinking and creativity.[62] And, the methodology facilitates "Perspective transformation" which "is the process of becoming critically aware of how and why our assumptions have come to constrain the way we perceive, understand, and feel about our world; changing these structures of habitual expectation make possible a more inclusive, discriminating and integrating perspective; which, helps, inform how to make choices or act upon new insights."[63]

In the end, Holland and Henriot's pastoral circle is one the most well-known U.S. pieces of literature that contribute to the Catholic

---

58 Karecki, "Teaching Missiology in Context," 141.

59 Karecki, "Teaching Missiology in Context," 138.

60 Karecki, "Teaching Missiology in Context," 138.

61 Karecki, "Teaching Missiology in Context," 138.

62 Karecki, "Teaching Missiology in Context," 140.

63 Karecki, "Teaching Missiology in Context," 141.

Church's canonical turn toward praxis and practical theological methods and methodologies that interpret historical reality as a *locus theologicus*. Another key figure in the development of practical theological methods and methodologies of praxis is Thomas Groome.

Thomas Groome:
Praxis in Context of Religious Education

As a young professor at Boston College, Tom Groome enrolls in a course taught by visiting professor Johann Baptist Metz.[64] Groome explains that Metz's course converts his thinking from being mired in an idealistic transcendental theology toward a narrative based form of practical theology.[65] In the wake of his time with Metz, Groome develops a practical theological approach to religious education that has become a standard in Catholic circles. Below I appeal to several of Groome's texts to show how his work contributes to the Church's turn toward practical theology via a praxis-based methodology that interprets historical reality as a *locus theologicus*.

Groome's Method of Shared Praxis

Groome argues that: "there is a profound problem with how theology is typically taught."[66] The problem is that "the current theory to practice approach presumes that the primary purpose of theology is theoretical investigation and clarity of a very ahistorical

---

64 Thomas Groome, "Practices of Teaching: A Pedagogy for Practical Theology," in *Invitation to Practical Theology: Catholic Voices and Visions*, Claire E. Wolfteich, ed. (New York: Paulist Press, 2014), 277.

65 Groome, "Practices of Teaching," 277.

66 Thomas H. Groome, "Theology on Our Feet: A Revisionist Pedagogy for Healing the Gapbetween Academia and Ecclesia," in *Formation and Reflection: The Promise of Practical Theology*, edited by Lewis S. Mudge and James N. Poling (Fortress Press: Philadelphia, 1987), 55.

and metaphysical kind."[67] Groome suggests that the implication for people being trained for ministry by such an ahistorical mode of theological education is that they are more likely to end up knowing about theology in a theoretical sense than being able to do theology in a pastoral context.[68]

Instead of an ahistorical or metaphysical focus Groome claims "the primary locus for theology" should be "human history as it unfolds in the world. Why? Because human history is the locus of God's activity in time, and, is, therefore, always the first source of God's self-disclosure at any time."[69] In other words, because the world is the arena of God's saving activity, human history must be the primary *locus*, the point of departure and arrival for rational discourse about God.[70] Groome's claim that historical reality is a *locus theologicus* suggests that human praxis, on personal, interpersonal, and social levels, become the primary starting point for doing theology.[71]

Groome adds that teaching students practical theological methods that respect praxis as the primary starting way for doing theology honors three basic pedagogical imperatives. First, it honors God as active in the world and human history thereby forcing participants to attend to their own historical praxis in the world.[72] Second, it honors the story and vision of the Christian faith community.[73] Groome adds that because these two sources, present historical praxis and the Christian story/vision, are placed in a dialectical hermeneutic with each other people come to honor God's coming

---

67 Groome, "Theology on Our Feet," 57.

68 Groome, "Theology on Our Feet," 57.

69 Groome, "Theology on Our Feet," 61.

70 Groome, "Theology on Our Feet," 61.

71 Groome, "Theology on Our Feet," 62.

72 Groome, "Theology on Our Feet," 69.

73 Groome, "Theology on Our Feet," 69. .

reign through lived Christian response within history that is transforming for self, for church, and for society.[74] In this way, the Christian notion of God is both practical and political.[75]

Groome ultimately describes his method of shared praxis as a
movement from "life to faith to life."[76] Groome structures his methodology with this movement as a way to invite people to name and
critically reflect on present praxis and move that reflection into a
dialectical encounter with Christian story and vision, to encourage
a lived Christian faith for the common good.[77] Instead of Cardijn's
three step See-Judge-Act method, and Holland and Herniot's four
step pastoral circle method, Groome describes a five step movement.

The first step is naming present praxis, which consists of ex-
pressing feelings about what is going on in the world and what others are doing. Step two is critical reflection on life from a position
of faith. Depending on the issue, critical reflection can be personal
or sociocultural and can engage reason, memory, imagination, or a
combination of them. Step three involves assessing the wisdom of
the Christian story and vision apropos of the generative theme experienced in step one and reflected on in step two. Step four is the
dialectical hermeneutic that emerges between present praxis and
the Christian story and vision. Step five involves making a decision,
whether it be cognitive, affective, or behavioral.[78]

Groome argues that this five step methodology reclaims a
praxis way of knowing by beginning with reflection on life experiences, which then moves that knowledge into dialogue with the

74 Groome, "Theology on Our Feet," 69.

75 Groome, "Theology on Our Feet," 62n15n16.

76 Groome, "Practices of Teaching," 292.

77 Groome, "Practices of Teaching," 292.

78 Groome, "Practices of Teaching," 294-296.

best available theory (*phronesis*) with the aim of disposing people to do what ought to be done.[79] Groome claims that his method of theological praxis places him in concert with a large swath of practical theologians who favor a methodology that moves from praxis to theory to praxis.[80]

In sum, Groome argues that a praxis way of knowing (epistemology) is an effective pedagogy because it offers a way of knowing that is theoretical (*theoria*), practical (*phronesis*), and productive (*poiesis*).[81] What is key to Groome's method of theological praxis is that the practical wisdom (*phronesis*) of the Christian tradition functions as the critical, ethical hermeneutic perspective.[82] Groome believes the eschatological wisdom of the Christian tradition (which derives from what Jesus named the Kingdom of God) provides a good story and vision to use as the critical hermeneutic perspective.

Tom Beaudoin explains that Groome connects knowing subjects capacity for ideology critique to what Jesus named the Kingdom of God to help people imaginatively search out socioeconomic arrangements that limit or distort human potential.[83] But, how does Groome develop what Jesus named the Kingdom of God into a viable tool of ideology critique?

Groome Turns to Eschatology as Critical Aspect of Praxis

In 1980 Groome wrote *Christian Religious Education* and, in it, explained that Jesus' notion of the Kingdom of God should be the

---

79 Groome, "Practices of Teaching," 281.

80 Groome, "Practices of Teaching," 287.

81 Groome, "Practices of Teaching," 282.

82 Groome, "Practices of Teaching," 282.

83 Beaudoin, "Theological Anthropology," 135.

ultimate purpose, or *telos*, of Christian education.[84] Why does Groome place such a strong emphasis on the Kingdom of God in terms of Christian education? Like Metz and Tracy, Groome claims that Jesus' purpose in life was to preach the gospel of the Kingdom of God.[85] Thus, Groome argues that Christian religious education must necessarily provide Christians with a methodology that is capable of enacting the values associated with Jesus' Kingdom of God.[86]

To provide warrants for his claims about the importance of Jesus' Kingdom of God in religious education, Groome first appeals to the fact that a majority of scripture scholars agree that the Kingdom of God is the "central theme of the gospels."[87] Groome then appeals to the gospel of Mark 1:15, to highlight that when Jesus first appears in Galilee he said: "The reign of God is at hand! Reform your lives and believe in the gospel."[88] Groome claims this statement by Jesus' provides the foundation, constant reference, and central theme of Jesus life.[89] But, if this claim is true then the question in need of an answer is: what did Jesus mean when he said "kingdom of God"?

Groome explains what Jesus meant by "the kingdom of God" with an allusion to Jesus' Jewish heritage. Groome describes how: "For the Israelites the Kingdom of God is a symbol which refers to the concrete activity of God in history."[90] Groome asserts that what is key in this tradition is that Jesus radicalized the Hebrew notion

---

84 Groome, *Religious Education*, 33-34.

85 Groome, *Religious Education*, 35.

86 Groome, *Religious Education*, 36n4.

87 Groome, *Religious Education*, 36.

88 Groome, *Religious Education*, 38.

89 Groome, *Religious Education*, 39.

90 Groome, *Religious Education*, 36.

of the Kingdom in relation to "the Wisdom literature."[91] Groome claims that Jesus radicalized the Hebrew notion of neighbor by removing all limits to the question who is 'my neighbor.'[92] Groome explains that what makes Jesus unique is that he reinterprets "the Jewish tradition" where "neighbor tended to mean fellow-Jew" and "expanded neighbor to mean all people, even one's enemies."[93] What is key to Jesus' radical "proclamation of the Kingdom" is that it offers a new vision and story "of how human life ought to be lived."[94]

Groome reiterates that because the Kingdom of God was crucial to Jesus radical life and mission, Christian moral life ought to be lived in reference to the "vision of the completed kingdom." In other words, Groome thinks that by looking at present sociocultural realities from the point of view of the completed kingdom, where "there shall be no more death or mourning, wailing or pain" (Rev. 21:4), students can learn to be critical of present realities that do not meet the criteria of Jesus' understanding of the Kingdom. Groome, like Rahner, therefore suggests that the vision of the kingdom of God, with an eye to the future, carries "an imperative claim upon the present" one that must measure "all reality…against, the promised future, the fully realized kingdom."[95]

In conclusion, Groome's argument is that if the kingdom of God is seen as in-breaking, and as being worked out by God with human cooperation within history, and not just as a spiritual symbol referring only to an otherworldly reality, then it can function as a critical judgment upon our social, political, and economic structures and

---

91 Groome, *Religious Education*, 41n28.

92 Groome, *Religious Education*, 41.

93 Groome, *Religious Education*, 41n29. See the parable of the Good Samaritan.

94 Groome, *Religious Education*, 41.

95 Groome, *Religious Education*, 46n47.

cultural arrangements.[96] In his own words, Groome states: "while there are signs of the Kingdom already among us, there are social, political, economic, and cultural realities that actively prevent the values of the Kingdom from being promoted. Racism, sexism, oppression, uncontrolled capitalism; rampant consumerism, all stand condemned in light of the Kingdom of God."[97] Who else epitomizes the turn toward a methodology grounded by practical theological praxis? Enter Pope Francis!

Pope Francis' Canonical Turn to Cardijn's See-Judge-Act Method of Praxis

In continuity with the methodological preferences of Pope John XXIII and Pope Paul VI, Pope Francis appropriates the See-Judge-Act method for theological reflection on, and interpretation of, historical reality with a goal of transformative action that creates social justice. The See-Judge-Act method, first developed by Rev. Joseph Cardijn (who later became Cardinal), is used not only to construct *Schema XIII*, the draft of *Gaudium et Spes*, it is also integral to the final documents produced by Latin American bishops and liberation theologians at episcopal meetings at Medellin, Puebla, and Aparecida (the last of which Archbishop Jorge Bergoglio, now Pope Francis, was the primary author). Taking this history as a point of departure I will use this final section to show that Pope Francis uses Cardijn's praxis-based theological methodology to canonize the Church's turn toward practical theology.

In *Laudato Si*, Pope Francis clearly uses the See, Judge, Act method to explain he will review (see) the best scientific research today, then consider (judge) principles from Judeo-Christian tradition, and, in light of this theological consideration (judgment),

---

96 Groome, *Religious Education*, 48.

97 Groome, *Religious Education*, 48.

advance proposals for dialogue and action (act), both on an local and global level.[98] In other words, Francis' methodological process in *Laudato Si* represents Cardijn's method that prioritizes an empirical assessment of reality (step 1) in order to change reality (step 3) through critical theological reflection as a mediatory step (step 2). Francis justifies this methodological approach by invoking a phrase he has uttered more than once: "realities are more important than ideas."[99]

In addition to his use of Cardijn's method in *Laudato Si*, Pope Francis relied on the See-Judge-Act method when he authored the final draft of the Latin American bishops Aparecida document. In the Aparecida document he writes, "in continuity with previous general conferences of Latin American bishops, this document utilizes the see-judge-act method."[100] The document further states that with the method the Church is able to see Latin America reality, judge it according to Jesus Christ and the tradition of the church in order to enact the spreading of the kingdom of God.[101] In sum, the document makes use of Cardijn's method to critique reality using the criterion of Christian wisdom to discern Christian missionary action.[102] There are two crucial insights I would like to discuss regarding Francis' (Bergoglio's) use of Cardijn's method of theological praxis.

---

98 Pope Francis, *Laudato Si*, 15. Accessed January 15, 2015, Vatican.va.

99 Pope Francis, *Laudato Si*, No. 110 and 201, a point he first made in *Evangelii Gaudium* 231. With this statement Francis shows he is much more aligned with an Aristotelian approach as opposed to the Platonic approach favored by his predecessor, Benedict XVI. Later, in number 116 Francis states "the time has come to pay renewed attention to reality."

100 General Conference of the Bishops of Latin America and the Caribbean. *The Aparecida Document: V.* (Lexington, 2014) 27.

101 General Conference of the Bishops of Latin America and the Caribbean, *Aparecida*, 27.

102 General Conference of the Bishops of Latin America and the Caribbean, *Aparecida*, 27.

First, what is crucial about Francis' adaptation of Cardijn's See-Judge-Act method of praxis is that he champions an inter-disciplinary approach that begins with listening.[103] Francis claims that an interdisciplinary methodological approach requires a form of listening to "farmers, consumers, civil authorities, scientists, seed producers, people living near fumigated fields, and others." Since his first encyclical *Evangelii Gaudium*, Francis' has urged Christians to listen to others, especially young people and the elderly.[104] Francis claims that listening to others includes those who gather empirical data and generate science in fields such as anthropology, sociology, and economics, among others.[105]

What this suggests is that the skill of listening to the wisdom and practical reasoning of others, a technique that is part and parcel of ethnographic approaches, is an integral part of Pope Francis appropriation of Cardijn's method of theological praxis.

A second crucial aspect of Pope Francis' appropriation of Cardijn's See-Judge-Act method is that his theological reflection demonstrates a practical theological realism focused by an analogical Christology rooted in the gospel of Matthew 25. As Francis makes clear in the final Aparecida document, the poor give us an opportunity to encounter Christ himself (Matt. 25:37-40).[106]

For example: "The suffering faces of the poor" and the "suffering face of Christ" are connected because as Jesus said: "whatever you did for one of these least brothers of mine, you did for me."

---

103 Pope Francis, *Address of the Holy Father, Tauron Area, Kraków, Sunday, 31 July 2016*. http://w2.vatican.va/content/francesco/en/speeches/2016/july/documents/papafranc esco_20160731_polonia-volontari-gmg.html.

104 Pope Francis, *Evangelii Gaudium*, accessed January 15, 2015, Vatican.va, 84.

105 Pope Francis, *Evangelii Gaudium*, 100n110, 101n111.

106 General Conference of the Bishops of Latin America and the Caribbean, *Aparecida*, 88.

(Matt 25:40).[107] And, "the poor and those who suffer actually evangelize us" because their suffering represents Jesus' suffering on the cross.[108] In other words, the suffering faces of street people in large cities, migrants, sick people, addicts, and the imprisoned become the face of Jesus on the Cross.[109]

Jon Sobrino explains this analogical approach with a rigorous methodological insight. Sobrino claims that an *a posteriori* methodological "point of departure" from within the historical reality of "poverty,"[110] ought to be the place where one enters into the hermeneutical circle in order to think analogically about Jesus' ministry to the poor, particularly "sinners, publicans, prostitutes (Mark 2:6; MT 11:19, 21:32; LK 15:1), the simple (MT 11:25), the little (MK 9:2; MT 10:42, 18:10, 14), and the least (MT 25:40-45)."[111]

Like Pope Francis, Sobrino's theological methodology begins with an experience of historical reality of poverty and moves toward what is most central to the Christian tradition, Jesus' practice of mercy for the poor, "those lesser than others" and "those who suffer need, the hungry and thirsty, the naked, the foreigners, the sick and imprisoned, those who weep, those weighed down by a burden."[112] Sobrino explains that the ethical value of such a methodological perspective is that it empowers people to mercifully respond to the call to take down from the cross those who "in the

---

107 General Conference of the Bishops of Latin America and the Caribbean, *Aparecida*, 125n178.

108 General Conference of the Bishops of Latin America and the Caribbean, *Aparecida*, 88.

109 General Conference of the Bishops of Latin America and the Caribbean, *Aparecida*, 126, 129-132.

110 Sobrino, *Spirituality of Liberation*, 157-8

111 Sobrino, *Jesus in Latin America*, 89.

112 Sobrino, *Jesus in Latin America* 90

human race today...are crucified."[113] In other words, such a methodological perspective empowers Christians to understand the fact that each day millions of people in the world die in ways that are analogous to how Jesus died at the hands of idolaters of national security or wealth.[114]

By using theological reflection to consider how the "crucified of history" provide an analog to understand "Jesus' reality as the crucified one,"[115] a methodology grounded in praxis is able to provide people with a lens to see "the crucified in history" as a place where the practice of mercy, the *bonum morale* (ethical virtue) of the Christian tradition, is made real in Christian praxis.[116]

In *Evangelii Gaudium*, Francis develops this practical theological realism throughout the document. For example, Francis argues: "When we read the Gospel we find a clear indication" we should aid "not so much our friends and wealthy neighbors, but above all the poor and the sick, those who are usually despised and overlooked, 'those who cannot repay you.'" (LK 14:14).[117] Francis provides additional warrants for his claim about the Church's ethical option for mercy toward the poor with examples from various Doctors, Saints, and the Magisterium of the Church. Francis invokes the words of John Chrysostom to remind Christians in the present that early Christians believed: "Not to share one's wealth with the poor is to steal from them and to take away their livelihood."[118]

---

113 Sobrino, *Jesus in Latin America*, 148.

114 Sobrino, *Jesus in Latin America*, 151.

115 Sobrino, *Jesus in Latin America*, 148.

116 Sobrino, *Jesus in Latin America*, 140-141; 144-145, 156.

117 Pope Francis, *Evangelii Gaudium*, 42.

118 Pope Francis, *Evangelii Gaudium*, 50n55.

Francis also invokes the work of Pope John XIII who emphasized the human rights of the poor.[119] And, Francis calls attention to the bishops of Brazil who listened to the cry of the poor and responded by proclaiming:

> *We wish to take up daily the joys and hopes, the difficulties and sorrows of the Brazilian people, especially of those living in the barrios and the countryside - landless, homeless, lacking food and health care - to the detriment of their rights. Seeing their poverty, hearing their cries and knowing their sufferings, we are scandalized because we know there is enough food for everyone and that hunger is the result of a poor distribution of goods and income.*[120]

Francis does not end with verbal posturing and quotations of documents from the bible, fathers, doctors, bishops, or past popes of the Church. No, Francis invokes his own lived experience and encounter with the poor. Francis says: "I can say that the most beautiful and natural expression of joy which I have seen in my life were in poor people who had little to hold on to."[121] Speaking from my own personal experience as a mission worker in the Dominican Republic, I concur with Francis' statement that the poor embody an ineffable beauty and joy. Like Francis, I believe that the poor have much to teach us, and, therefore, we need to listen to poor and embrace the wisdom that God wishes to communicate through them.[122] Such learning entails appreciating the poor in their goodness, listening to their experience of life, their culture, and their ways of living the faith.[123]

---

119 Pope Francis, *Evangelii Gaudium*. 140n154.

120 Pope Francis, *Evangelii Gaudium*, 141n158.

121 Pope Francis, *Evangelii Gaudium*, 14.

122 Pope Francis, *Evangelii Gaudium*, 145.

123 Pope Francis, *Evangelii Gaudium*, 146.

What is most significant about Francis' ethical concern for the poor is that it shows his' approach to theologizing, his method and methodology, is defined by a practical theological realism that sees the church not only existing in history but as a church that aims, in a concrete way, to change historical reality.[124] For Pope Francis the foundation of this realism is found in the gospel,[125] which helps Christians see that reality is the place where people are crucified, and, therefore, must be the place where Christians put theory into practice in order to take people down from their cross.[126]

Conclusion

Practical theology occupies a growing space within Catholic theology in the twenty-first century. Yet, because many are unsure as to what practical theology is, I described practical theology as a paradigm that interprets historical reality as a *locus theologicus* via a praxis-based theological methodology. To show the how this paradigm developed in the Catholic Church I appealed to the works of Karl Rahner, Johann Baptist Metz, David Tracy, Joe Holland and Peter Henriot, and Thomas Groome.

Not only do these theologians and educators focus on historical reality as a *locus theologicus,* it is clear that Pope Francis canonizes the turn toward a practical theological methodology rooted in praxis that aims to transform historical realities and practices that do not feed the hungry, give drink to the thirsty, welcome the stranger, care for the ill, or visit the prisoner.

---

124 Pope Francis, *Evangelii Gaudium,* 86-88.

125 Pope Francis, *Evangelii Gaudium,* 71.

126 Pope Francis, *Evangelii Gaudium,* 163.

6

A PRACTICAL THEOLOGICAL PEDAGOGY:

TEACHING THEOLOGICAL ETHICS

AS ESCHATOPRAXIS

Overview

This sixth and final chapter describes my theological ethics pedagogy. I ground my pedagogical approach upon three claims. First, that teaching ethics requires a discussion of "method—how theology should approach social questions."[1] Second, that "U.S. student culture," in the context of contemporary higher education, can be described as entrance into a "liminal communal space."[2] Third, that "Eschatology is a discourse on liminality, marginality, on that which is different in an ontological, ethical and also epistemological sense."[3]

To move from these insights toward a fuller explanation of my pedagogy I will explain how I teach ethics courses with a practical

---

1 Charles Curran, "Social Ethics: Agenda for the Future," in *Toward Vatican III: The Work that Needs to Be Done*, David Tracy with Hans Kung and Johann Baptist Metz, eds., (New York: The Seabury Press, 1978), 147.

2 Philip Bergman, *Catholic Social Learning: Educating the Faith that Does Justice*, (New York: Fordham University Press, 2011), 100 n20.

3 Vitor Westhelle, *Eschatology and Space: The Lost Dimension in Theology Past and Present*, (New York: Palgrave MacMillan, 2012), 73.

theological methodology. My methodology integrates a focus on praxis and eschatology in order to invite students to think about what it means to have a liminal experience, to cross a threshold, and, to have a *metanoia*, a conversion to seeing and judging reality with an "eschatological imaginary."

A crucial aspect of my practical theological focus on eschatology is that I do not locate the Kingdom of God in some triumphant "End of History" where a second coming of Jesus Christ is postponed till some future date.[4] Instead of a classic eschatological hermeneutic, my method integrates what Ignacio Ellacuria would perhaps describe as a historicized eschatological imaginary. Such an approach helps students learn to learn how to read and judge "signs of places,"[5] in order to discern whether these signs reveal actions of the kingdom of God or the unkingdom.[6] But, how do I put my theory into practice?

Theory & Practice of Teaching Eschatopraxis

To teach students how to practice theological ethics with a method of "eschatopraxis"[7] I introduce a process of interdis-ciplinary learning that is comprised of six movements.

---

4 Richard Kearney, "Epiphanies of the Everyday: Toward a Micro-Eschatology," in *After God: Richard Kearney and the Religious Turn in Continental Philosophy*. Edited by John Panteleimon Manoussakis, (New York: Fordham University Press, 2006), 11.

5 Pedro Casaldáliga, *Creio na Justiça e na Esperança*, (Rio de Janiero: Civilização Brasileira, 1978), 211. For example, students are taught to examine business practices and governmental policies such as mountain-top removal, hydraulic fracturing, immigration policies, and wall street regulatory practices as signs that reveal unjust social structures. Students are also taught to question whether these signs of the anti-kingdom call people to become living signs of the Kingdom of God in service of those who are hungry, thirsty, naked, ill, strangers, and are in prison (MT 25:40).

6 Mark Van Steenwyk, *The Unkingdom of God: Embracing the Subversive Power of Repentance*, (Downers Grove: IVP Press, 2013).

7 As noted earlier, I borrowed the phrase "Eschatopraxis" from Carl Braaten.

- *First movement*: Students read about the epoch-defining twentieth century Catholic turn to methods and methodologies of theological praxis, the interpretation of historical reality as a *locus theologicus*, the preferential option for the poor, and practical theology.

- *Second movement:* I provide a handout to students that outlines an integrated model of two methods of theological praxis: Cardinal Joseph Cardijn's See-Judge-Act method and Holland and Henriot's pastoral circle method. I also explain how to put the method into practice before asking students to do an initial investigation of a current sociopolitical reality.

- *Third movement:* I ask students to begin step one from the handout. I ask them to confront a specific reality or practice (Mountain Top Removal, Hydraulic Fracturing, Wall Street Business Practices, Immigration, Abortion, Addiction, HealthCare Reform) through the medium of documentary video. To encourage students to go more in-depth from what is learned from the documentary I ask them to use the Cardijn/Holland handout to gather additional empirical data related to the business practice, healthcare practice, environmental practice, or government policy under investigation. To facilitate this process, I provide students with web-links and texts to guide them toward economic, political, sociological, and ethnographic data relevant to the reality or practice under investigation.

- *Fourth movement:* I ask students to consider how Christian scripture presents an "eschatological imaginary" that can provide a way to critically reflect on the reality or practice under investigation. To facilitate their theological reflection, I unpack what Jesus' means when he invokes the phrase "Kingdom of God." To accomplish this, I present the scholarship of N.T. Wright, Joseph Ratzigner, Cardinal Donald Weurl, Ignacio

Ellacuria, Jon Sobrino, Vitor Westhelle, and Jean-Yves Lacoste. By presenting the work of these authors I not only teach students what Jesus means when he says the Kingdom of God is "at hand" (Mk 1:15) in his own cultural context, I also explain how his understanding of the Kingdom of God is alive and present in our twenty-first century global cultural context.

- *Fifth movement:* I invite students to travel to business such as a non-profit healthcare center, a non-profit hospitality house, a non-profit addiction and recovery center, a non-profit mission site in the Dominican Republic, and/or a non-profit environmental center, in order to learn how labor practices in a non-profit professional context carry the potential to historicize a Christian eschatological ethos.

- *Sixth movement:* students are asked to synthesize all the insights they have learned in previous movements in order to describe a future where their own professional practices and actions are understood as creatively realizing a Christian ethic.

One particular outcome of my pedagogical approach is that students are able to carve out an interdisciplinary agora where theology, philosophy, history, politics, economics, environmental studies, and ethnography enter into dialogue in such a way that critical thinking becomes the normative learning practice. To add depth to my explanation I provide a thicker description of my pedagogy below.

Movement One

In movement one, I introduce to students, via readings and lectures, to the epoch-defining Catholic turn to methods and methodologies of theological praxis, the interpretation of historical reality as a *locus theologicus,* the preferential option for the poor, and practical theology.

First, I discuss the contrast between Plato and Aristotle in regard to ethics and methodology. I then explain how Karl Marx revived classic discussions of Aristotelian praxis in modern philosophy. Next, I discuss Cardinal Joseph Cardijn and his See-Judge-Act method of praxis. I also explain that Pope John XXIII canonized Cardijn's See-Judge-Act method, and, how Cardijn's method was used in the production of *Gaudium et Spes*, the Pastoral Constitution of the Church in the Modern World, the sixteenth and final document produced at the Second Vatican Council.

I go on to explain how Pope Paul VI added canonical weight to Cardijn's See-Judge-Act method of theological praxis as he used it to turn the Church toward the historical reality of poverty as a *locus theologicus*. I further explain that the Latin American bishops (CELAM), including liberation theologians Gustavo Gutierrez, Clodovis Boff, Ignacio Ellacuria, and Jon Sobrino appropriated the turn to methods and methodologies of theological and philosophical praxis, which resulted in a prophetic call for the Catholic Church to convert its mission toward a preferential option for the poor.

I move toward the conclusion by telling students how this epoch-defining turn to methods of theological praxis, and the interpretation of historical reality, helped birth the paradigm of practical theology, which was first discussed in Catholic circles by Karl Rahner, followed by his student, Johann Baptist Metz. I then discuss how in the context of the United States the contributions of David Tracy, Joe Holland, Peter Henriot, and Thomas Groome, among many others, helped the field of practical theology flourish in various disciplines.

I conclude my lectures on the history of the Catholic Church's epoch-defining turn to methods of theological praxis by showing how Pope Francis, through his teachings in *Evangelii Gaudium* and *Laudato Si,* has added canonical weight to the turn toward a practical theology that interprets historical reality as a *locus theologicus* a la Cardijn's See-Judge-Act method. In sum, I assign readings and deliver lectures to students based on the content I chronicled in the first five chapters of this dissertation.

Movement Two

After explaining the history of the Catholic Church's epoch-defining turn to methods and methodologies of theological praxis, historical reality, a preferential option for the poor, and practical theology I provide a handout to students. The handout depicts an integrated model based on Cardinal Cardijn's See-Judge-Act method and Holland and Henriot's pastoral circle method.[8] I begin by asking students if they can tell me what appears to be the dominant theme of the handout. Typically, one student will correctly answer "questions."

The handout is designed to help students learn that a process of questioning is foundational to methods of practical theological praxis. Questions on the handout are categorized as: See (Empirical Data + Ethnographic Listening), Judge (Socio-Economic and Political Analysis), Theological Reflection (Biblical and Eschatological), and Act (*Poiesis*).

In the "See" section questions to provoke thought include: What is going on? What did you observe? Who are the people involved? What specific facts can you cite about this issue or experience? How did you feel about the issue? How does is touch you personally?

In the "Judge" section questions aim to provoke a more in-depth social analysis through a process of questioning related to four factors: (1) Economic factors: Who owns? Who controls? Who

---

8 Credit goes to Dee Laymen at St. Thomas Aquinas High School for developing the handout in dialogue with her students following a conversation about the See-Judge-Act method in a religious studies department meeting. See appendix.

pays? Who receives what? Why? (2) Political factors: Who decides? For whom do they decide? How do decisions get made? Who is left out of the process? Why? (3) Historical factors: What past events influence the situation today? What are the systemic and historical causes? (4) Cultural factors: What values are evident? What do people believe in? Who influences what people believe in? Who gains from this situation? Who loses? What is the situation doing to people? Why is it happening? Why does it continue?

In the theological reflection section questions include: What do you think ought to be happening? What Christian scriptures can be used to help us interpret reality? How can you correlate the data of social analysis with wisdom from the Christian eschatological tradition? How do biblical values help us to see reality in a different way? What does Catholic Social Teaching say about this issue? What key principles from Catholic Social Teachings apply to this issue?

In the "Act" section students must respond to questions such as: What can we do to bridge the gap between what is happening and what ought to be happening according to Christian scripture and Catholic Social Teaching? What action can be taken? Who can we involve? How can the structures involved be a place of transformation? How can you help those who are disadvantaged? After some class discussion I explain that everyone will put the method into practice in the next class meeting in order to confront a socio-political reality of ethical and moral import.

Movement Three

The students begin the third movement by confronting a reality or practice through the medium of documentary video. When students see the effects of particular business practices such as hydraulic fracturing,[9] mountain top removal,[10] or Wall Street practices,[11] or, see the affects governmental policies related to realities such as migration,[12] the health care industry,[13] especially addiction, [14] or death and dying,[15] their eyes become open to previously unknown political, economic, environmental, and sociocultural realities and practices in way that provokes the same comments semester after semester: "Why do they not show this on the news?" And, "how come I've never heard of this?"

The shock of watching real images and real people talk about realities and practices that crucify people and cause them to suffer, in some cases, to the point of death, helps me reinforce something students learn in movement two: Ignacio Ellacuria's analogy between the crucified Christ and the crucified people of our world today.

---

9 An excellent resource for this topic is the documentary *Gasland*, directed by Josh Fox (An International Wow Company Production, 2010).

10 An excellent resource for this topic is the documentary *The Last Mountain*, directed by Bill Haney (Uncommon Productions, 2011).

11 An excellent resource for this topic is the documentary *Inside Job*, directed by Charles Ferguson, (Sony Pictures Classic, 2011).

12 An excellent resource for this topic is the documentary *The Fence: La Barba*, directed by Rory Kennedy, (HBO Documentary Films, 2010). Another excellent resource for this topic is the documentary Which Way Home, directed by Rebecca Cammisa (HBO Documentary Films in association with Good and White Buffalo Entertainment).

13 An excellent resource for this topic is the documentary *Escape Fire: The Fight to Rescue American Healthcare*, directed by Matthew Heineman and Susan Froemke (Aisle C Productions & Our Time Projects, 2012). Another excellent resource for this topic is the documentary Sick Around the World: Other Rich Countries Have Universal Health Care. Why Don't We?, directed Jon Palfreman (Frontline with Palfreman Film Group, 2008).

14 An excellent resource for this topic is the documentary *The Big Lie: American Addict 2*, directed by Sasha Knezev, 2017).

15 An excellent resource for this topic is the documentary *#Play for 22: The Story of Lauren Hill*, (layup4lauren.org in conjunction with The Cure Starts Now, 2015).

After learning about a particular sociopolitical reality, and doing further social analysis, students are then guided through theological reflection. First, we review what Christian eschatology means. I explain that we will begin by looking at Jesus' own eschatopraxis but I first prime the students with a discussion of what it means to have an "eschatological imaginary" or "eschatological consciousness."

For example, I use Ratzinger's dissertation *The Theology of History in St. Bonaventure* to explain how Saint Francis of Assisi "was filled with that primitive eschatological mood" that "The Kingdom of God is at hand." (Mk. 1:15).[16] And, how "without this eschatological consciousness Francis and his message is no more understandable than is Christ and his message of the New Testament."[17] I use Ratzinger's discussion of an eschatological consciousness to lead into the next movement where the primary focus becomes Christian eschatology.

Movement Four

I describe movement four in more detail than the other movements because I believe it is what is novel about my practical theological approach to teaching ethics. To begin, I introduce students to the Christian eschatological tradition through readings, lectures, and class discussion. First, I present New Testament phrases and verses and explain what the Kingdom of God and eschatology means to Jesus in his own sociopolitical context and then I move on to contemporary descriptions of eschatology and the kingdom of God. To facilitate this process, I draw from the work of scholars such as N.T. Wright, Joseph Ratzinger, Cardinal Donald Wuerl,

---

16 Ratzinger, *Eschatology*, 39.

17 Ratzinger, *Eschatology*, 39-40.

Ignacio Ellacuria, Jon Sobrino, Vitor Westhelle, and Jean-Yves Lacoste. What follows is the crux of the first movement.

I begin the discussion of what of Jesus names the Kingdom of
God by drawing from the work of Joseph Ratzinger, Emeritus Pope
Benedict XVI. I tell students that according to Ratzinger: "The core
content of the Gospel,"[18] the "true *Leitmotiv* of Jesus' preaching" is
"the phrase 'Kingdom of God,' *basileia Tou Theou,* or 'Kingdom of
heaven,' *basileia tôn ouranōn.*"[19] I show students that Ratzinger supports his claim with an appeal to biblical data: "Looking at statistics
makes this plain. There are in all 122 occurrences of the word in the
New Testament, 99 being in the three Synoptic Gospels and 90 on
the lips of Jesus himself. This in itself makes it clear that the phrase
has a fundamental importance in the tradition stemming from Jesus."[20]

I also tell students that the phrase "Kingdom of God" is crucial
in the Christian religion beyond scripture. I explain to students that
"At Mass each week millions of Catholics profess belief in a kingdom that 'will have no end'" and "pray," as Jesus did, that "thy
Kingdom come."[21] Once I describe the centrality of Jesus' Kingdom
in scripture and liturgy I explain what Jesus meant when he invoked the phrase.

---

18 Pope Benedict XVI, *Jesus of Nazareth: From the Baptism in the Jordan to the
Transfiguration* (New York: Doubleday, 2007), 47.

19 Joseph Ratzinger, *Eschatology: Death and Eternal Life.* trans. Michael Waldstein
(Washington D.C.: The Catholic University of America Press, 1988), 24. Ratzinger
explains that the difference between the two phrases is that Matthew speaks of the
'Kingdom of heaven' because of the Jewish linguistic rule of not using the name of
God. 'Heaven' then is a periphrasis for "God."

20 Ratzinger, *Eschatology*, 24-25.

21 Cardinal Donald Wuerl, *Seek First the Kingdom: Challenging the Culture by Living
Our Catholic Faith,* (Huntington, IN: Our Sunday Visitor, Inc., 2012), 14-5.

To open the discussion of what Jesus means when he says the "Kingdom of God" I begin with a simple question. I ask: what is the kingdom? I tell the students that for Cardinal Weurl "the most basic definition is this: the kingdom of God is the presence of God."[22]

To add depth to Weurl's statement, I again draw from Ratzinger who uses Joachim Jeremias to explain "the affirmation that 'the Kingdom of God is at hand' can be paraphrased 'God is close.'"[23] I further explain that "what is at stake" when Jesus invokes the Kingdom of God is "not the beyond, but God, in his personal activity and living power."[24] And, "This observation gains in force if we add that in Jewish usage, the term *basileia*...does not signify a sphere of governance, but an active reality."[25] Following these insights, I tell students that there is a know-how that aids in the discernment of signs of the kingdom (presence of God) from signs of an anti-kingdom or the unkingdom.

To open the lecture of how to "see" a sign of the Kingdom, or the unkingdom, I introduce students to an exegesis of Luke 17:20-1, one by Joseph Ratzinger and the other by biblical scholar N.T. Wright. First, I tell students how Ratzinger explains that the gospel of Luke 17:20 "is so hard to translate that every translation must be an interpretation."[26] I then read the verse: "The kingdom of God is not coming with signs to be observed, *meta paratērēseōs*; nor will they say, 'Lo, here it is!' or 'There!' for behold, the kingdom of God is in the midst of you, *entos humōn estin*."[27]

---

22 Weurl, *Seek First the Kingdom*, 22.

23 Ratzinger, *Eschatology*, 26.

24 Ratzinger, *Eschatology*, 26.

25 Ratzinger, *Eschatology*, 26.

26 Ratzinger, *Eschatology*, 32.

27 Ratzinger, *Eschatology*, 33.

I then explain that in the "history of exegesis, three varieties of interpretation of Luke 17: 20 can be identified."[28] The first kind interprets *"entos humōn"* as "within you." The "meaning would then be: the Kingdom of God is not outside you, but inside. Its proper space is personal interiority."[29] A "second type" of interpretation of the text argues that "Jesus thought exclusively in terms of imminent eschatology, expecting the Kingdom in the form of a cataclysmic transformation of the very near future."[30] And, a "third interpretation" could be called "Christological" if it includes the "doctrine of the Holy Spirit."[31]

Ratzinger explains that this interpretation suggests "Jesus is speaking in the present tense; the Kingdom of God cannot be observed, yet, unobserved, it is among those to whom he is speaking. It stands among them – in his own person."[32] In the words of Origen, "Jesus is *hē autobasileia*, the kingdom in person."[33] Ratzinger sums up the third position by explaining "Jesus is the kingdom...through the Holy Spirit's radiant power flowing forth from him." And, "in his Spirit-filled activity...the Kingdom of God becomes reality."[34]

N.T. Wright similarly explains that the history of exegesis of Luke 17:20 reveals three different interpretations. Wright explains that the phrase *"within your grasp"* is a translation from the Greek *"Entos Hymon,"* which tends to be translated as 'within you' in the sense of 'in your heart, as opposed to in your political or material circumstances': that is, the kingdom is an inward, not an outward

28 Ratzinger, *Eschatology*, 33.

29 Ratzinger, *Eschatology*, 33.

30 Ratzinger, *Eschatology*, 33.

31 Ratzinger, *Eschatology*, 34.

32 Ratzinger, *Eschatology*, 34.

33 Ratzinger, *Eschatology*, 34n17.

34 Ratzinger, *Eschatology*, 34-35.

reality. However, Wright explains that *Entos Hymon* "has also been read as meaning 'in your midst': that is, the kingdom is already present, here among you. I explain that Wright concludes: "Of these two, the latter is closer to the meaning we would have guessed from the rest of Jesus' work." But, I also explain that Wright claims that "philologically the meaning is most likely to be a third option." Wright claims "Jesus seems to be saying" 'If you had eyes to see,' 'you could reach out and take hold of the new reality that is already at work.'"[35]

What is crucial to take away from the third type of interpretation is that, as Ratzinger explains, "the mystery of the Kingdom...calls out for another kind of seeing."[36] I explain to students that to develop this type of "vision" requires a *"metanoeite"*[37] a conversion where one's eyes are opened to seeing reality anew. I appeal to Ratzigner again to explain that a *metanoiete,* a conversion of one's way of seeing, carries an enormous value in regard to Christian ethics.

To support this argument I point to Ratzinger's claim that "Jesus' depiction of the Kingdom of God carries a categorical importance for ethics" because "the poor, the last and least," must be understood as "the bearers of the Kingdom and" are therefore "first and foremost among its citizens."[38] I explain that what this means is that Christian "Ethos, right behavior," requires a certain way of seeing Jesus, and his actions toward the poor, last, and least, as *hē autobasileia,* "the Kingdom in person."[39]

---

35 N.T. Wright, *Jesus and The Victory of God* (Minneapolis: Fortress Press, 1996), 469.

36 Ratzinger, *Eschatology*, 33.

37 Ratzinger, *Eschatology*, 29 n7.

38 Ratzinger, *Eschatology,*31.

39 Ratzinger, *Eschatology*, 34n17.

I then appeal to work of Leonardo Boff and Jon Sobrino[40] to support Ratzinger's claims. I tell students how these Latin American liberation theologians explain that the kingdom of God "demands...conversion" or "changing one's mode of thinking and acting."[41] But, the key question I pose is: conversion to what social imaginary? To the: "the *Acta* and *Facta* of Jesus (his praxis)" which "are to be seen as historifications of what the kingdom of God signifies concretely, i.e., a liberative change in the existing situation."[42] I explain that this shows Jesus' praxis with those who are poor and outcast demonstrate how to liberate those who suffer due to existing sociopolitical structures.[43] In short, students learn that Jesus' voluntary solidarity with the poor and outcast, his eschatopraxis, is the foundational *bonum morale* (ethical virtue) of Christian praxis.[44]

I then lecture about how to imitate and embody the praxis of Jesus, the *bonum morale* of Christianity. I explain that they must cultivate what protestant theologian Vitor Westhelle calls a "latitudinal eschatological perspective" that emphasizes a "topological awareness" ... that has "to do more with places than with eras, more with locations than with epochs, more with contexts than with ages."[45]

I explain to students how Westhelle's topological focus retrieves "the etymology of the word" *eschaton* in a way that "lifts up dimensions of what 'end' means that have been ignored."[46] For example, Westhelle draws from the Gospel to tease out a nuanced

---

40 Both Leonardo Boff and Jon Sobrino are censured by Ratzinger while he was head of the Congregation for the Doctrine of Faith.

41 Leonardo Boff *Jesus Christ Liberator*, 64.

42 Leonardo Boff, *Jesus Christ Liberator*, 282-3.

43 Sobrino, *Jesus in Latin America*, 144.

44 Sobrino, *Jesus in Latin America*, 145-7.

45 Westhelle, *Oxford*, 315.

46 Westhelle, *Oxford*, 320-1.

understanding of *eschaton*: "In the parable of the banquet in Luke 14:7-11, Jesus admonishes the disciples not to sit in the first places, but way back in the last place (*eschaton topon*) from where one will be invited to move up to a place of honor."[47] Here, the motif is the reversal that is often repeated elsewhere in the New Testament: the first (*protoi*) will be the last (*eschatoi*), and the last, first.[48] What Westhelle points out is that the "eschaton" is the marginal "location in which a reversal occurs."[49] In other words: "Margins…are the turning point to another world," a world that can be changed by those "who dare to stand at its threshold and remove the veil that hides the truth."[50]

I add that the key takeaway from Westhelle's work is how he links his theological focus on topology with Jesus' commitment to the Kingdom of God as a political reality, that the Kingdom is not a utopia…but *topia*, a place of happiness for all people.[51] And, that such an understanding of the eschatological Kingdom of God shifts the classic understanding from the "univocal transcendental or longitudinal" project to a multilayered topological perspective.[52]

In addition, I explain that the topological eschatological approach Westhelle describes carries a serious ethical urgency…because what is to be expected lies already here…the kingdom is lodged in the adjacency of a new reality and not solely in a future perennially postponed.[53] I also explain that if "The kingdom is topologically nearby," this shifts "eschatology" from a discourse about

---

47 Westhelle, *Oxford*, 321.

48 Westhelle, *Oxford*, 321.

49 Westhelle, *Oxford*, 321.

50 Westhelle, *Oxford*, 322.

51 Westhelle, *Oxford*, 318.

52 Westhelle, *Oxford*, 318.

53 Westhelle, *Oxford*, 318.

"'the last things' to 'those things in our midst.'"[54] In short, I introduce students to Westhelle because I side with his elevation of Pedro Casaldaliga's insight that a "reading of the signs of the times" needs to be balanced with a reading of the "signs of places."

To conclude the lecture on eschatology, I introduce students to Jean-Yves Lacoste, who, like Westhelle, thinks that "Eschatology thwarts all laws of topology."[55] I explain to students that if an "eschatological subversion of the topological entails a transgression, a redefinition of place"[56] then we cannot ignore the tension between the empirical I (what is), and the eschatological I (what ought to be), without losing all means of interpreting what is at stake in Christian Ethics and Moral Theology.[57] I add that, for Lacoste, the ability to distinguish between the "empirical I" and the "eschatological I" is what enables us to interpret and critique the present with the logic of another place.[58]

Movement Five

My experience teaching has shown me that immersion learning helps students realize that they can "change the world" through their praxis and *poiesis* in a professional context.[59] Thus, in the fifth

---

54 Westhelle, *Oxford*, 319n31.

55 Jean-Yves Lacoste, *Experience and the Absolute: Disputed Questions on the Humanity of Man*, trans. Mark Raftery-Skehan, (New York: Fordham University Press, 2004), 25

56 Lacoste, *Experience and the Absolute*, 25.

57 Lacoste, *Experience and the Absolute*, 66-67. Lacaoste adds that "Ethics itself has eschatological implications few would contest."

58 Lacoste, *Experience and the Absolute*, 58.

59 To understand how to "change the world" I like to look to Dorothy Day who, in 1946, in an article for the *Catholic Worker*, described what actions she thought could change the world. "What we would like to do is change the world--make it a little simpler for people to feed, clothe, and shelter themselves as God intended them to do. And, by fighting for better conditions, by crying out unceasingly for the rights of the workers, the poor...we can, to a certain extent, change the world. For more

movement, students travel to non-profit businesses and/or religious institutions that aim to change economic, sociocultural, and political signs of the unkingdom. For example, students travel to a non-profit Setonian healthcare center, a non-profit hospitality house, a Catholic mission site in the Dominican Republic, a non-profit environmental center, a non-profit foodbank, and/or a non-profit drug addiction and recovery center. The reason I choose to integrate a travel seminar and immersion activity in my pedagogical practices is best explained in my publication, "Liturgical Laboratories," in the *Journal of Religious Education*.[60]

By integrating a travel seminar component to the curriculum, I am able to move beyond status quo teaching practices that focus on disseminating ideas and propositions to "brains-on-a-stick."[61] Picture a traditional theology or religious studies classroom (or most classrooms for that matter). Is it a room filled with rows of chairs pointed at a podium, a chalkboard or projection screen where a professor stands and lectures or presents a PowerPoint slideshow?

James K. A. Smith points out that in western education circles, this type of instruction technique shows that reason has become reified and prized as the chief virtue of the American university. Smith adds that such pedagogical approaches tend to neglect the body and non-cognitive ways of being-in-the-world as nonessential in religious education. Paul Griffiths likewise notes that forms of religious learning today, when unchecked, can lead to a single-

---

articles by Day from the Catholic Worker see: http://www.catholicworker.org/doro-thyday/articles/425.html. Accessed July 10, 2015.

60 Robert Pennington, "Liturgical Laboratories: Consider a Case Study for an Extra Credit Component for Comparative Theology and World Religions Courses," *Journal of Religious Education*, (London: Springer Press, 2015).

61 James K.A. Smith, "Keeping Time in the Social Sciences: An Experiment with Fixed-Hour Prayer and the Liturgical Calendar," in *Teaching and Christian Practices: Reshaping Faith & Learning*, David I.Smith & James K.A. Smith, eds. (Grand Rapids: Eerdmans Publishing Company, 2011), 141.

minded idolatry of the intellect. Moreover, Griffith argues that universities have structurally and institutionally made the idolatry of the intellect evident. When idolatry of the intellect permeates the university context students cannot acquire an understanding of Christian or non-Christian religious practices and forms of knowledge that exist outside of traditional learning tools such as books, lectures, and PowerPoint presentations.

Obviously, there is much more to Christian education than the transfer of information through focused attention to books, lectures, and PowerPoint presentation. As Craig Dykstra points out, religious or theological education must integrate forms of participation in practices to engage students in forms of learning that introduce broad and complex non-rational ways of knowing.

The question that emerges for me from my reading of these theoretical reflections on the practice of teaching religion and theology is this: if such an intellectualist approach is the pedagogical habitus for religious education, then what must educators do to liberate learning practices from the privileged epistemic domain of intellectual knowledge? In my view, religious educators need to think more deeply about how the learning context affects the production of religious or theological knowledge.

Contemporary research provides bountiful evidence that shows how "travel seminars," a type of immersion learning where a group of students and one or more teachers leave the comfort of their institutional home to travel together to various contexts for the purpose of achieving specific educational aims. For several reasons, travel seminars tend to have profound influence on student learning because they involve the whole person and not simply the mind. Ultimately, travel seminars promote experience-based, context-situated, practice-centric forms of immersion learning, which help students transcend the boundary between the learning environment and "real life."

In sum, in the fifth movement, I use travel seminars to incorporate experiential and embodied forms of learning so that the essential *modus operandi* of the pedagogic action enables students' knowledge to emerge through a *poiesis-based* form of learning that overcomes the habit of seeking truth at the level of disembodied ideas and decontextualized sayings.

Movement Six

In this final movement students are asked to synthesize all the insights they have learned in previous movements in order to describe a future where their own professional practices and actions are understood as creatively realizing a Christian ethic. By reflecting on, and trying to integrate, everything they have been exposed to: the history of the Catholic turn to praxis, a practical theological method, actual historical realties and practices of moral importance, the idea of Jesus' "kingdom of God," and an immersion experience; students are able to envision a future where they creatively realize the kingdom through their professional praxis and *poiesis*. In this way, I think I honor, in my own classroom, the canonicity of Cardijn's See-Judge-Act method of theological praxis.

Conclusion

In this sixth chapter, I described how my work as a theologian, ethicist, and educator builds on the Catholic Church's epoch-defining turn to practical theological methods that are grounded in praxis and interpret historical reality as a *locus theologicus*. What I claim is novel about my approach is how I teach students about Jesus' eschatological social imaginary, the Kingdom of God, and how it can be used as a hermeneutic for the critical analysis of present day realities of ethical and moral import. In short, Chapter six introduces my pedagogy and method of eschatopraxis and how it helps students question realities of poverty and environmental damage through a focus on the Christian eschatological tradition that stems from what Jesus names the Kingdom of God.

CONCLUSION

I n this project, I argued that in the twentieth century the Catholic Church made an epoch-defining magisterial, philosophical, and practical theological turn from an "ahistorical" methodological "habitus" and toward a praxis-based methodology that interprets "historical reality," especially the reality of the poor, as a *locus theologicus*. In support of this claim I reviewed the contributions of a range of twentieth-century Catholic philosophers, theologians, and members of the Magisterium, all of whom who lived and worked in Western Europe, Latin America, and North America.[1] I presented the documentation in three parts.

In Part I, Chapter 1, I presented the work of three figures whose are foundational to the Catholic Church's initial turn toward the interpretation of historical reality as a *locus theologicus*. First, I discussed Pope Leo XIII (1810-1903), specifically his encyclical letter *Rerum Novarum*, and his focus on the plight of poor Western European workers affected by the Industrial Revolution. I then explained that Maurice Blondel (1861-1949) developed a philosophy of action to overcome the Catholic philosophical habitus rooted in

---

1 This study does not include additional and important contributions from philosophers, theologians, and magisterial voices in Africa and Asia, due to my limited knowledge of these regions of the world.

Neo-Scholastic Thomism. I concluded Chapter 1 with an explanation of how Rev. Joseph Cardijn (1882-1967) developed the See-Judge-Act method of theological praxis.

In Part I, Chapter 2, I showed that Pope John XXIII canonized Cardijn's method in his encyclical letter *Mater et Magistra*. I also explained how developments at the Second Ecumenical Council of the Vatican added further canonical weight to Cardijn's method since it was used to construct the Pastoral Constitution of the Church in the Contemporary World, better known by the first words of its Latin text, *Gaudium et Spes*. I concluded Chapter 2 with a discussion of how Pope Paul VI confirmed the canonization of Cardijn's method of theological praxis and made a strong turn to poverty as a locus theologicus.

In Part II, Chapter 3, I documented how the Latin American liberation theologians and the Latin American Episcopal Conference draw from Cardijn's method of praxis to interpret the historical reality of Latin America as a *locus theologicus*. In Chapter 3, I also showed that, as a result of the turn to praxis, the Latin American Church made an epoch-defining turn toward a preferential option for the poor.[2]

---

2 The origins of a Christian preference for the poor can be found in the words and actions of Jesus as described in the Bible. The origins of an option for the poor within contemporary papal teaching began with Pope Leo XIII. In his 1891 encyclical *Rerum Novarum* (On the Condition of Labor) Leo XIII claimed that the state "should safeguard the rights of all citizens, especially the weaker, particularly workers, women, and children." (no. 15) An option for the poor was elevated in papal teaching by Pope Paul VI, particulary in *Populorum Progressio*. The phrase "preferential option for the poor" gained theological traction with the Latin American Magisterium at post-conciliar meetings of the *Consejo Episcopal Latinoamericano* (CELAM) at Medellin, Colombia (1968), Puebla, Mexico (1979), Santo Domingo, Dominican Republic (1992), and Aparecida, Brazil (2014). Thus, the "preferential option for the poor" has since become a leitmotif in Catholic social thought on the level of the Magisterium, in social theology and ethics, and in much of the Church's pastoral discourse." For more see David Hollenbach, "Commentary

In chapter 4, I explained how Basque Jesuit theologian, and long-time resident in El Salvador, Ignacio Ellacuria (1930-1989) built on the work of his teachers Karl Rahner (1904-1984) and Xavier Zubiri (1898-1983), as well as the work of his friend Archbishop Oscar Romero (1917-1980), to argue for a preferential option for the "crucified people" of El Salvador.[3]

In Part III, Chapter 5, I argued that the turn to a praxis-based methodology that interprets historical reality, especially the reality of poverty, as a *locus theologicus,* actually makes it plausible to argue that the entire movement spurs the development of Catholic practical theology, a paradigm that emerged in Catholic discourse with the work of Karl Rahner, and, is presently embodied by Pope Francis, who has therefore added canonical weight to the Church's turn toward practical theology and a preferential option for the poor.

In Chapter 6 I described my ethics pedagogy. I ground my pedagogical approach upon three claims. First, that teaching ethics requires a discussion of "method—how theology should approach social questions."[4] Second, that "U.S. student culture," in the context of contemporary higher education, can be described as entrance into a "liminal communal space."[5] Third, that "Eschatology is a discourse on liminality, marginality, on that which is different

---

on *Gaudium et Spes,*" in *Modern Catholic Social Teaching: Commentaries and Interpretations,* Kenneth R. Himes, O.F.M, ed. (Georgetown University Press: Washington D.C., 2005), 287.

3 According to Ellacuria, the reality of the crucified people is the principal sign of the times that Christians must "become aware of," "grasp what is at stake," and "take charge of" in order to change what is counter to Jesus' notion of the Kingdom of God. For more see, Lassalle-Klein, *Blood and Ink,* 221n104, n105, n106.

4 Charles Curran, "Social Ethics: Agenda for the Future," in *Toward Vatican III: The Work that Needs to Be Done,* David Tracy with Hans Kung and Johann Baptist Metz, eds., (New York: The Seabury Press, 1978), 147.

5 Philip Bergman, *Catholic Social Learning: Educating the Faith that Does Justice.* (New York: Fordham University Press, 2011), 100n20.

in an ontological, ethical and also epistemological sense."[6] To move from these insights toward a fuller explanation of my pedagogy I explain how I teach ethics courses with a practical theological methodology that integrates a focus on praxis and eschatology in order to invite students to think about what it means to have a liminal experience, to cross a threshold, to have a *metanoia*, a conversion to seeing and judging reality with an "eschatological imaginary."

In the end, what I believe is most important about the Catholic turn toward a praxis-based theological methodology that interprets historical reality as a *locus theologicus* is how it can be used to facilitate the conversion (*metanoia*) of students moral and ethical standpoint toward a preferential option for the poor in a civic and political context. My belief stems from my experience teaching students how to master the craft of using a theological method I designed that draws mostly from Cardinal Joseph Cardijn's See-Judge-Act method and Joe Holland and Peter Henriot's Pastoral Circle Method.[7]

My method, what I named eschatopraxis,[8] is not unlike other practical theological methods. My method teaches students how to: gather empirical and ethnographic data about a present sociopolitical or economic reality with the goal of developing new cultural and historical knowledge in an interdisciplinary way; question and

---

6 Vitor Westhelle, *Eschatology and Space: The Lost Dimension in Theology Past and Present*, (New York: PalgraveMacMillan, 2012), 73.

7 My pedagogical project also builds on the teaching theories and practices of other scholars. The work of Thomas Groome is foundational to my project. Also, my focus on the crucified people is similar to the way Miguel de la Torre focuses on *Doing Christian Ethics from the Margins*, (Maryknoll: Orbis, 2014). And, like Christina Astorga, I argue for an ethical methodology that is rooted in Christian scripture and takes its point of departure in context-dependent sociocultural experience. For more see her *Catholic Moral Theology and Social Ethics: A New Method*. (Maryknoll: Orbis, 2014).

8 Carl E. Braaten, *Eschatology and Ethics: Essays on the Theology and Ethics of the Kingdom of God*, (Minneapolis: Augsburg Publishing, 1975), 121; 141.

judge historical realities with a critical eschatological hermeneutic, specifically through reflection on the Bible and Christian tradition; and, transform the critically integrated knowledge into ethical Christian action.

My ultimate insight is simple: by teaching students how to use an eschatopraxis-based practical theological methodology I am able to open students' eyes to historical realities they are unaware of; then juxtapose this reality to what Charles Taylor may say is Jesus' social imaginary: "the Kingdom of God." I believe that by focusing on the eschatological wisdom related to Jesus' phrase "Kingdom of God" students are able to learn how to question what actions ought to be embodied to show solidarity with the poor and outcast, actions that embody what Jon Sobrino calls the *bonum morale* (ethical virtue) of Christian morality.[9]

Thus, the "signature" of my pedagogy respects the turn toward historical reality and a preferential option for the poor that marks the epochal change in contemporary Catholic method and methodology toward practical theology.[10]

---

9 Jon Sobrino, *Jesus in Latin America*, (Maryknoll: Orbis, 1987), 140-145.

10 Giorgio Agamben, in *The Signature of All Things: On Method*, explicitly claims "the signature of all things: method." Quoted in Kristine Suna-Koro, In Counterpoint: Diaspora, Postcoloniality, and Sacramental Theology, (Eugene, OR: Pickwick, 2017), 278.

BIBLIOGRAPHY

Ahern, Kevin. *Structures of Grace: Catholic Organizations Service the Global Common Good*. Maryknoll: NY, Orbis Books, 2015

Alberigo, Giuseppe. *History of Vatican II: Vol. V*. Maryknoll: Orbis Press, 2006

_____. *A Brief History of Vatican II*. Orbis: Maryknoll, 2006.

Andreassi, Anthony D. "Pope Paul VI," In *The Modern Catholic Encyclopedia*. Edited by

Glazier, Michael and Monika K. Hellwig. Collegeville: Liturgical Press, 1994.

Ashley, J. Matthew. "Ignacio Ellacuria and the Spiritual Exercises of Ignatius of Loyola," *Theological Studies* 61/1 (March 2000).

Astorga, Christina. *Catholic Moral Theology and Social Ethics: A New Method*. Orbis: Maryknoll, 2014.

Beaudoin, Tom. The Theological Anthropology of Thomas Groome. *Religious Education* 100, No. 2, (Spring 2005): 127-137.

Bernstein, Richard. *Praxis & Action: Contemporary Philosophies of Human Activity*, Philadelphia: University of Pennsylvania Press, 1971

Bevans, Stephen. *Models of Contextual Theology: Revised and Expanded Edition*. Maryknoll, NY: Orbis Books, 2013.

de la Bedoyere, Michael. *The Cardijn Story: A Study of the Life of Mgr. Joseph Cardijn and the Young Christian Workers Movement Which He Founded*. The Bruce Publishing Company, 1959.

Bidegain, A.M. *From Catholic Action to Liberation Theology: The Historical Process of the Laity in Latin America in the 20th Century*, Working

Paper #48, Nov. 1985. The Helen Kellogg Institute for International Studies, Accessed from https://kellogg.nd.edu/sites/default/files/old_files/documents/048_0.pdf on January 5, 2014.

Blanchette, Oliva. "Introduction," in Maurice Blondel, *Action (1893): Essay on a Critique of Life and a Science of Practice*, 3-15. Notre Dame: University of Notre Dame Press, 1984.

Blondel, Maurice. *Action (1893): Essay on a Critique of Life and a Science of Practice.* Notre Dame: University of Notre Dame Press, 1984.

_____. *The Letter on Apologetics & History of Dogma.* Translated by Alexander Dru and Illtyd Trethowan. Grand Rapids: Eerdmans Publishing Company, 1964.

Boff, Clodovis. *Theology and Praxis: Epistemological Foundations.* Translated by Robert R. Barr. Eugene: Wipf & Stock, 1987.

_____. "Epistemology and Method of the Theology of Liberation." In *Mysterium*

Liberationis: Fundamental Concepts of Liberation Theology, 57-85. Maryknoll: Orbis Books, 1990.

Boff, Clodovis and Leonardo Boff. *Introducing Liberation Theology.* Translated by Paul Burns. Maryknoll: Orbis, 1987.

Boff, Clodovis and Leonardo Boff. *Salvation and Liberation: In Search of a Balance Between Faith and Politics.* Maryknoll: Orbis, 1979.

Boff, Leonardo. *Jesus Christ Liberator: A Critical Christology for Our Time.* Translated by Patrick Hughes. Maryknoll: Orbis, 1978.

Bokenkotter, Thomas. *A Concise History of the Catholic Church*, New York: Doubleday, 2005

Bourdieu, Pierre. *Outline of a Theory of Practice* Cambridge: Cambridge University Press, 1977.

Braaten, Carl E. *Eschatology and Ethics: Essays on the Theology and Ethics of the Kingdom of God.* Minneapolis: Augsburg, 1974.

Bracken, Joseph A. "Structures, Systems and Whiteheadian Societies: The Quest for Objectivity." *The Xavier Zubiri Review Review*, 12 (2010-2012): 19-32.

Brackely, Dean. "Theology and Solidarity: Learning From Sobrino's Method" in *Hope & Solidarity*. Edited by Stephen J. Pope. Maryknoll: Orbis, 2008.

Brigham, Erin M. *See, Judge, Act: Catholic Social Teaching and Service Learning*. Anselm Academic: Winona, 2013.

Burke, Kevin. *The Ground Beneath the Cross: The Theology of Ignacio Ellacuria*, Washington, D.C.: Georgetown University Press, 2000

Cahalan, Kathleen A. Locating Practical Theology in Catholic Theological Discourse and Practice. *International Journal of Practical Theology* 15, no. 1 (2011): 1-21.

_____. "Three Approaches to Practical Theology, Theological Education, and the Church's Ministry." *International Journal of Practical Theology* 9, no. 1 (2005): 63-94.

Cahalan, Kathleen A. and Gordon Mikowski. *Opening the Field of Practical Theology: An Introduction*. New York: Rowan & Littlefield, 2014.

Cardijn, Joseph. *Challenge to Action: Addresses of Monsignor Joseph Cardijn*. Fides: Chicago, 1995.

_____. *Laymen into Action*. Translated by Anne Heggie. London: Geoffrey Chapman LTD, 1964

Carr, Anne. "Karl Rahner," in *A Handbook of Christian Theologians*, edited by Martin E.   Marty and Dean G. Peerman, 519-542. Nashville: Abignon Press, 1965. 519-542.

Casaldaliga, Pedro. *Creio na Justiça e na Esperança*. Rio de Janiero: Civilização Brasileira, 1978.

Chenu, M.D. "Les signes du temps." *Nouvelle revue theologique* 90 (1965): 29-39.

_____. "Vatican II and the Church of the Poor." *Concilium* 104 (1977): 56-61.

Christiansen, Drew. "Commentary on *Pacem in terries*." In *Modern Catholic Social Teaching: Commentaries and Interpretations*, edited by

Kenneth R. Himes, O.f.M, 217-243. Georgetown University Press: Washington D.C., 2005.

Comblin. Jose. *People of God*. Maryknoll. Orbis, 2004. Conde-Frazier, Elizabeth. "Participatory Action Research," in *The Wiley-Blackwell Companino to Practical Theology*, edited by Bonnie J. Miller-McLemore, 234-243. Wiley-Blackwell: Oxford, 2012.

Congar, Yves. *The Meaning of Tradition*. Translated by A.N. Woodrow. San Francisco: Ignatius Press, 1964.

de la Torre, Miguel. *Doing Christian Ethics from the Margins*. Maryknoll: Orbis, 2014.

Dennis, Marie, Renny Golden, Scott Wright. *Oscar Romero: Reflections on His Life and   Writings*. Maryknoll: Orbis, 2000.

Dru, Alexander. "Introduction: Historical and Biographical." In Maurice Blondel, *The Letter on Apologetics & History of Dogma*, translated by Alexander Dru and Illtyd Trethowan, 13-116. Grand Rapids: Eerdmans Publishing Company, 1964.

Dubois, Francis and Josef Klee, ed., *Pacem in Terris: Its Continuing Relevance for the Twenty-First Century*. Washington D.C.: Pacem in terris Press, 2013.

Dussel, Enrique D. *A History of the Church in Latin America: Colonialism to Liberation* (1492-1979). Translated by Alan Nely. Grand Rapids, MI: Eerdmans, 1981.

Eagleson, John and Philip Scharper, eds. *Puebla and Beyond: Documentation and Commentary*. Maryknoll: Orbis, 1979.

Ellacuria, Ignacio. *Freedom Made Flesh: The Mission of Christ and His Church*. Maryknoll: Orbis, 1976.

_____. "Christian Spirituality (1983)," in *Ignacio Ellacuría: Essays on*

History, Liberation, and Salvation, edited Michael E. Lee, 275-284. Orbis: Maryknoll,   2013.

_____. "Laying the Philosophical Foundations of Latin American Theological Method (1975)." In *Ignacio Ellacuría: Essays on*

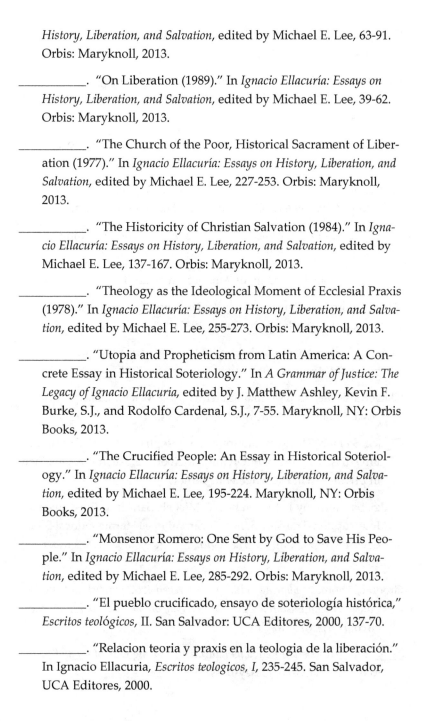

History, Liberation, and Salvation, edited by Michael E. Lee, 63-91. Orbis: Maryknoll, 2013.

_____. "On Liberation (1989)." In *Ignacio Ellacuría: Essays on History, Liberation, and Salvation*, edited by Michael E. Lee, 39-62. Orbis: Maryknoll, 2013.

_____. "The Church of the Poor, Historical Sacrament of Liberation (1977)." In *Ignacio Ellacuría: Essays on History, Liberation, and Salvation*, edited by Michael E. Lee, 227-253. Orbis: Maryknoll, 2013.

_____. "The Historicity of Christian Salvation (1984)." In *Ignacio Ellacuría: Essays on History, Liberation, and Salvation*, edited by Michael E. Lee, 137-167. Orbis: Maryknoll, 2013.

_____. "Theology as the Ideological Moment of Ecclesial Praxis (1978)." In *Ignacio Ellacuría: Essays on History, Liberation, and Salvation*, edited by Michael E. Lee, 255-273. Orbis: Maryknoll, 2013.

_____. "Utopia and Propheticism from Latin America: A Concrete Essay in Historical Soteriology." In *A Grammar of Justice: The Legacy of Ignacio Ellacuria*, edited by J. Matthew Ashley, Kevin F. Burke, S.J., and Rodolfo Cardenal, S.J., 7-55. Maryknoll, NY: Orbis Books, 2013.

_____. "The Crucified People: An Essay in Historical Soteriology." In *Ignacio Ellacuría: Essays on History, Liberation, and Salvation*, edited by Michael E. Lee, 195-224. Maryknoll, NY: Orbis Books, 2013.

_____. "Monsenor Romero: One Sent by God to Save His People." In *Ignacio Ellacuría: Essays on History, Liberation, and Salvation*, edited by Michael E. Lee, 285-292. Orbis: Maryknoll, 2013.

_____. "El pueblo crucificado, ensayo de soteriología histórica," *Escritos teológicos*, II. San Salvador: UCA Editores, 2000, 137-70.

_____. "Relacion teoria y praxis en la teologia de la liberación." In Ignacio Ellacuria, *Escritos teologicos, I*, 235-245. San Salvador, UCA Editores, 2000.

Endean, Philip. *Karl Rahner: Spiritual Writings*. Maryknoll: Orbis, 2004.

Figueroa Deck, Allan. "Commentary on *Populorum Progressio*." In *Modern Catholic Social Teaching: Commentaries and Interpretations*, edited by

Kenneth R. Himes, O.f.M, 292-314. Washington DC: Georgetown University Press: 2005.

Foote, Peter. *Laymen: Vatican II's Decree on the Apostolate of the Laity: Text and commentary*. Catholic Action Federations, Chicago, 1966.

Fritz, Peter Joseph. *Karl Rahner's Theological Aesthetics*. Washington, D.C.:

The Catholic University of America Press, 2014.

Ganss, George, ed. *Ignatius of Loyola: The Spiritual Exercises and Selected Works*, New York: Paulist Press, 1991

General Conference of the Bishops of Latin America and the Caribbean. *The Aparecida Document: V.* Lexington, 2014.

Glazier, Michael and Monika K. Hellwig. *The Modern Catholic Encyclopedia*. Collegeville: Liturgical Press, 1994.

Gigacz, Stefan. "The Role and Impact of Joseph Cardijn at Vatican II." PhD diss., University of Divinity, Melbourne, Australia. Obtained in private email exchange with author.

Godzieba, Anthony J., Lieven Boeve, Michele Saracino. "Resurrection-Interruption-Transformation: Incarnation as Hermeneutical Strategy: A Symposium," in *Theological Studies* 67, no. 4 (December 2006).

Groome, Thomas. *Sharing Faith: A Comprehensive Approach to Religious Education and Pastoral Ministry: The Way of Shared Praxis*. San Francisco: HarperCollins, 1991.

_____. *Christian Religious Education: Sharing Our Story and Vision*. San Francisco: Jossey-Bass, 1980.

_____. "Theology on Our Feet: A Revisionist Pedagogy for Healing the Gap between Academia and Ecclesia." In *Formation and Reflection: The Promise of*

Practical Theology, edited by Lewis S. Mudge and James N. Poling, 55-78. Fortress Press: Philadelphia, 1987.

_____. "Practices of Teaching: A Pedagogy for Practical Theology." In *Invitation to Practical Theology: Catholic Voices and Visions*, edited by Claire E. Wolfteich, 277-300. New York: Paulist Press, 2014.

Gudorf, Christine. "Commentary on *Octogesima adveniens*." In *Modern Catholic Social Teaching: Commentaries and Interpretations*, edited by Kenneth R. Himes,

O.f.M, 315-332. Georgetown University Press: Washington D.C., 2005.

Gutierrez, Gustavo. *A Theology of Liberation: History, Politics, and Salvation*. Maryknoll: Orbis, 1988.

_____. *The God of Life*. Maryknoll: Oribs, 1991.

_____. *The Power of the Poor in History*. Maryknoll: Orbis, 2010.

_____. *We Drink from Our Own Wells*. Maryknoll: Orbis Books, 2009.

Heidegger, Martin. *Being and Time*. Translated by John Macquarrie and Edward Robinson. New York: Harper and Row, 1962.

Hobsbawm, Eric. *The Age of Revolution 1789-1848*. New York: New American Library, 1962.

Holland, Joe. *Modern Catholic Social Teaching: The Popes Confront the Industrial Age*, New York: Paulist Press, 2003

Holland, Joe and Peter Henriot, S.J. *Social Analysis: Linking Faith and Justice*. Washington D.C.: Dove Communications and Orbis Books, 1988.

Holland, Joe. "Introduction," in *The Pastoral Circle Revisited: A Critical Quest for Truth and Transformation*, edited by Frans Wijsen, Peter Henriot, and Rodrigo Mejia, 1-12. Maryknoll: Orbis, 2005.

_____. *Pacem in Terris: Summary & Commentary for the 50ᵗʰ Anniversary of the Famous Encyclical Letter of Pope John XIII on World Peace*, Washington DC: Pacem in Terris Press, 2012.

_____. *Social Analysis II - End of the Modern World: The Need for a Postmodern Global Ecological Civilization and a Call for a Postmodern Ecological Renaissance* (unpublished manuscript), 2014.

Hollenbach, David. "Commentary on *Gaudium et spes*," in *Modern Catholic Social Teaching: Commentaries and Interpretations*, edited by Kenneth R. Himes, O.F.M, 266-291. Georgetown University Press: Washington D.C., 2005.

Hughson S.J., Thomas. "Interpreting Vatican II: 'A New Pentecost,'" *Theological Studies* 69, no. 1 (March 2008): 3-37.

Husserl, Edmund. *Ideas: General Introduction to Pure Phenomenology*. New York: Routledge Classics, 2012.

Johnson, Elizabeth A. *Quest for the Living God: Mapping Frontiers in the Theology of God*. New York: Continuum, 2007.

Justaert, Kristien "Cartographies of Experience: Rethinking the Method of Liberation Theology." *Horizons* 42, no. 2 (December 2015): 237-261.

Karecki, Madge. "Teaching Missiology in Context: Adaptations of the Pastoral Circle." In *The Pastoral Circle Revisited: A Critical Quest for Truth and Transformation*, edited by Frans Wijsen, Peter Henriot, and Rodrigo Mejia, 137-150. Maryknoll: Orbis, 2005.

Kelly, Thomas M. *When the Gospel Grows Feet: Rutilio Grande, SJ, and the Church in El Salvador, An Ecclesiology in Context*. Collegeville, MN: Liturgical Press, 2013.

Kelly, Thomas M. *Rutilio Grande, SJ: Homilies and Writings*. Collegeville, MN: Liturgical Press, 2015.

Langdale, Eugene. "Introduction," in *Challenge to Action: Addresses of Monsignor Joseph Cardijn*, 7-12. Chicago: Fides, 1955.

Lassalle-Klein, Robert and Burke, Kevin, eds. *Love That Produces Hope: the Thought of Ignacio Ellacuria*. Collegeville: Michael Glazier/Liturgical Press, 2006.

Lassalle-Klein, Robert. *Blood and Ink: Ignacio Ellacuria, Jon Sobrino, and the Jesuit Martyrs of the University of Central America*. Maryknoll: Orbis, 2014.

_____, ed. *Jesus of Galilee: Contextual Christology for the 21st Century*. Orbis: Maryknoll, 2011.

_____. "The Jesuit Martyrs of the University of Central America: An American Christian University and the Historical Reality of the Reign of God." PhD diss., Graduate Theological Union, July 26, 1995.

_____. "The Christian University for a Globalized World: Ignacio Ellacuria's Vatican II Advance on Cardinal Newman's Classic Statement," in *A Grammar of Justice: The Legacy of Ignacio Ellacuria*, edited by J. Matthew Ashley, Kevin F. Burke, S.J., and Rodolfo Cardenal, S.J., 173-188. Maryknoll: Orbis Books, 2014.

_____. "Rethinking Rahner on Grace and Symbol: New Proposals for the Americas," in *Rahner Beyond Rahner*, edited by Paul G. Crowley, 87-99. Lanham: Sheed and Ward, 2005.

_____. "Introduction," in *Love That Produces Hope: The Thought of Ignacio Ellacuria*. Edited by Kevin Burke, xii-xxxv. Collegeville: Michael Glazier/Liturgical Press, 2006.

_____. Personal correspondence, June 3, 2017.

Lonergan, Bernard. *Method in Theology*, Toronto: University of Toronto Press, 1990.

Luciani, Rafael. "Hermeneutics and Theology in Sobrino's Christology." In *Hope & Solidarity*, edited by Stephen J. Pope, 105-118. Maryknoll: Orbis, 2008.

MacReamoinn, Sean. "John XXIII, Pope." In *The Modern Catholic Encyclopedia*, edited by Michael Glazier and Monika K. Hellwig, Collegeville: Liturgical Press, 1994.

Mejia, Rodrigo. "The Impact of the Pastoral Circle in Teaching Pastoral Theology." In *The Pastoral Circle Revisited: A Critical Quest for*

Truth and Transformation, edited by Frans Wijsen, Peter Henriot, and Rodrigo Mejia, 127-136. Maryknoll: Orbis Books, 2005.

Metz, Johannes Baptist. *Faith in History and Society: Toward a Practical Fundamental Theology.* New York: Crossroad, 1980.

Mich, Marvin L. "Commentary on *Mater et magistra,*" in *Modern Catholic Social Teaching: Commentaries and Interpretations,* edited by Kenneth R. Himes,   O.F.M. Georgetown University Press: Washington D.C., 2005.

Miller-McLemore, Bonnie, ed. *The Wiley-Blackwell Companion to Practical Theology.* Malden: Wiley-Blackwell, 2012.

Montgomery, Tommie Sue. *Revolution in El Salvador: From Civil Strife to Civil Peace.* Boulder, CO: Westview Press, 1995

Moschella, Mary Clark. "Ethnography," in *The Wiley-Blackwell Companino to Practical Theology,* edited by Bonnie J. Miller-McLemore, 224-233. Wiley-Blackwell: Oxford, 2012.

Mosely, LaReine-Marie. "Negative Contrast Experience: An Ignatian Appraisal," *Horizons* 41, no. 1 (June 2014): 74-95.

Nieman, James R. "Congregational Studies," in *The Wiley-Blackwell Companino to Practical Theology,* edited by Bonnie J. Miller-McLemore, 133-142. Wiley-Blackwell: Oxford, 2012.

O'Connor, Edward. *Pope Paul and the Spirit: Charisms and Church Renewal in the Teaching of Paul VI.* Notre Dame: Ave Maria Press, 1978

O'Donovan, Leo J. "Orthopraxis and Theological Method in Karl Rahner," in *Proceedings of the Thirty-Fifth Annual Convention: The Catholic Theological Society of America* 35 (1980): 47.

O'Meara, Thomas F. and Paul Philibert. *Scanning the Signs of the Times: French Dominicans in the Twentieth Century.* Adelaide: ATF Press, 2013.

Phan, Peter. *Eternity in Time: A Study of Karl Rahner's Eschatology.* Selinsgrove: Susquehanna University Press, 1988

Pope Leo XIII. *Rerum Novarum.* Accessed July 15, 2015. Vatican.va.

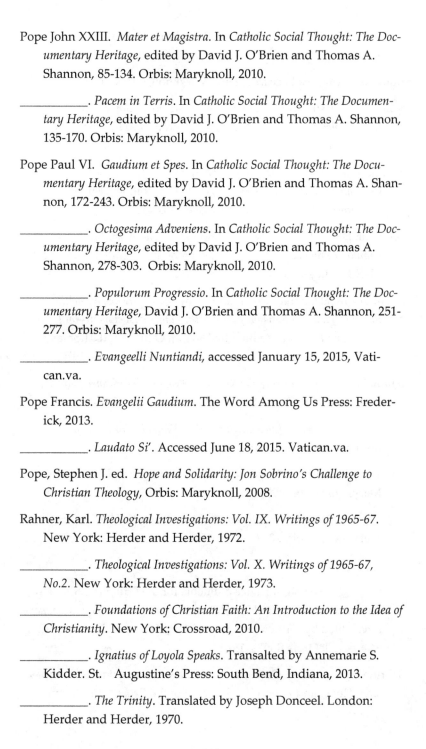
Pope John XXIII. *Mater et Magistra.* In *Catholic Social Thought: The Documentary Heritage,* edited by David J. O'Brien and Thomas A. Shannon, 85-134. Orbis: Maryknoll, 2010.

_____. *Pacem in Terris.* In *Catholic Social Thought: The Documentary Heritage,* edited by David J. O'Brien and Thomas A. Shannon, 135-170. Orbis: Maryknoll, 2010.

Pope Paul VI. *Gaudium et Spes.* In *Catholic Social Thought: The Documentary Heritage,* edited by David J. O'Brien and Thomas A. Shannon, 172-243. Orbis: Maryknoll, 2010.

_____. *Octogesima Adveniens.* In *Catholic Social Thought: The Documentary Heritage,* edited by David J. O'Brien and Thomas A. Shannon, 278-303. Orbis: Maryknoll, 2010.

_____. *Populorum Progressio.* In *Catholic Social Thought: The Documentary Heritage,* David J. O'Brien and Thomas A. Shannon, 251-277. Orbis: Maryknoll, 2010.

_____. *Evangeelli Nuntiandi,* accessed January 15, 2015, Vatican.va.

Pope Francis. *Evangelii Gaudium.* The Word Among Us Press: Frederick, 2013.

_____. *Laudato Si'.* Accessed June 18, 2015. Vatican.va.

Pope, Stephen J. ed. *Hope and Solidarity: Jon Sobrino's Challenge to Christian Theology,* Orbis: Maryknoll, 2008.

Rahner, Karl. *Theological Investigations: Vol. IX. Writings of 1965-67.* New York: Herder and Herder, 1972.

_____. *Theological Investigations: Vol. X. Writings of 1965-67, No.2.* New York: Herder and Herder, 1973.

_____. *Foundations of Christian Faith: An Introduction to the Idea of Christianity.* New York: Crossroad, 2010.

_____. *Ignatius of Loyola Speaks.* Transalted by Annemarie S. Kidder. St. Augustine's Press: South Bend, Indiana, 2013.

_____. *The Trinity.* Translated by Joseph Donceel. London: Herder and Herder, 1970.

_____. *The Spiritual Exercises*. New York: Herder and Herder, 1965.

Romero, Oscar. *The Violence of Love*. Maryknoll: Orbis, 2004.

Schaaren, Christian and Aana Marie Vigen, eds. *Ethnography as Christian Theology and Ethics*. New York: Continuum International Publishing Group, 2011.

Schilderman, Hans. "Quantitative Method," in *The Wiley-Blackwell Companino to Practical Theology*, edited by Bonnie J. Miller-McLemore, 123-132. Wiley-Blackwell: Oxford, 2012.

Schipani, Daniel S. "Case Study Method," in *The Wiley-Blackwell Companino to Practical Theology*, edited by Bonnie J. Miller-McLemore, 91-101. Wiley-Blackwell: Oxford, 2012.

Second General Conference of Latin American Bishops, *Medellin, Justice Document*. In *Renewing the Earth: Catholic Documents on Peace, Justice and Liberation*, edited by David J. O'Brien and Thomas A. Shannon, 549-560. Garden City: NY, Image   Books, 1977.

Smith, James K.A. *Desiring the Kingdom: Worship, Worldview, and Cultural Formation*. Grand Rapids: Baker Academic, 2009.

_____. *Imagining the Kingdom: How Worship Works* Grand Rapids: Baker Academic, 2013.

Sobrino, Jon. *Spirituality of Liberation: Toward a Political Holiness*. Maryknoll: Orbis,1988.

_____. *No Salvation Outside the Poor: Prophetic-Utopian Essays*. Maryknoll: Orbis, 2008.

_____. *Jesus in Latin America*. Maryknoll: Orbis, 1987.

_____. "The Significance of Puebla for the Catholic Church in Latin America." In *Puebla and Beyond: Documentation and Commentary*, edited by John Eagleson and Philip Scharper, 289-309. Maryknoll: Orbis Books, 1979.

Sobrino, Jon. "Jesus of Galilee from the Salvadoran Context: Compassion, Hope, and Following the Light of the Cross." *Theological*

Studies 70, no. 2 (2009): 449, special issue; edited by Robert Lassalle-Klein.

Suna-Koro, Kristine. In Counterpoint: Diaspora, Postcoloniality, and Sacramental Theology. Eugene: Pickwick, 2017.

Taylor, Charles. *A Secular Age*. Cambridge, MA: Belknap Press of Harvard University Press, 2007.

Tetlow, Joseph A. "The Most Postmodern Prayer: American Jesuit Identity and the Examen of Conscience, 1920-1990," *Studies in the Spirituality of Jesuits* 26/1 (1994): 1-67.

Third General Conference of the Bishops of the Latin American Episcopate. "Final Document: Puebla de Los Angeles, Mexico." In *Puebla and Beyond: Documentation and Commentary*, edited by John Eagleson and Philip Scharper, 122-285. Maryknoll: Orbis, 1979

Tracy, David. "The Foundations of Practical Theology," in *Practical Theology*, edited by Don Browning, 61-82. New York: Harper and Row, 1983.

_____. *The Analogical Imagination: Christian Theology and the Culture of Pluralism*. New York: Crossroad, 1986.

_____. "A Correlational Model of Practical Theology Revisited," in *Invitation to Practical Theology: Catholic Voices and Visions*, edited by Claire E. Wolfteich. New York: Paulist Press, 2014.

_____. *Plurality and Ambiguity: Hermeneutics, Religion, and Hope*. Harper & Row: San Francisco, 1987.

Valiente, O. Ernesto. "The Reception of Vatican II in Latin America." *Theological Studies*, 73 (2012): 795-823.

van der Ven, Johannes. *Practical Theology: An Empirical Approach*. Leuven, Belgium: Peeters Publishers, 1998.

Vidaurrazaga, Jaime. "Appropriating the Bible as 'Memory of the Poor.'" In *The Bible and Catholic Theological Ethics*, edited by Yiu Sing Lúcás Chan,

James F. Keenan, and Ronaldo Zacharias, 183-192. Maryknoll: NY, Orbis Books, 2017.

Wiarda, Howard J. and Harvey F. Kline. *An Introduction to Latin American Politics and Development*, Boulder: Westview Press, 2001.

Wijsen, Frans, Peter Henriot, and Rodrigo Mejia, eds. *The Pastoral Circle Revisited: A Critical Quest for Truth and Transformation*. Maryknoll: Orbis Books, 2005.

Woeftlich, Claire, ed. *Invitation to Practical Theology: Catholic Voices and Visions*, New York: Paulist Press, 2014.

Zotti, Mary Irene. *A Time of Awakening: The Young Christian Worker Story in the United*

States, 1938 to 1970. Chicago: Loyola University Press, 1991.

Zubiri, Xavier. *Dynamic Structure of Reality*. Urbana: University of Illinois Press, 2003

Zynda, Damian. *Archbishop Oscar Romero: A Disciple Who Revealed the Glory of God*. Scranton, PA: Scranton University Press, 2010.

OTHER BOOKS
FROM PACEM IN TERRIS PRESS

PADRE MIGUEL
A Memoir of My Catholic Missionary Experience in Bolivia
amidst Postcolonial Transformation of Church and State
Michael J. Gillgannon, 2018

POSTMODERN ECOLOGICAL SPIRITUALITY
Catholic-Christian Hope for the Dawn of a Postmodern Ecological Civilization Rising from within the Spiritual Dark Night of Modern Industrial Civilization
Joe Holland, 2017

JOURNEYS TO RENEWED CONSECRATION
Religious Life after Fifty Years of Vatican II
Emeka Obiezu, OSA & John Szura, OSA, Editors, 2017

THE CRUEL ELEVENTH-CENTURY IMPOSITION OF
WESTERN CLERICAL CELIBACY
A Monastic-Inspired Attack on Catholic Episcopal & Clerical Families
Joe Holland, 2017

LIGHT, TRUTH, & NATURE
*Practical Reflections on Vedic Wisdom & Heart-Centered Meditation
In Seeking a Spiritual Basis for Nature, Science, Evolution, & Ourselves*
Thomas Pliske, 2017

THOMAS BERRY IN ITALY
Reflections on Spirituality & Sustainability
Elisabeth M. Ferrero, Editor, 2016

PETER MAURIN'S
ECOLOGICAL LAY NEW MONASTICISM
*A Catholic Green Revolution Developing
Rural Ecovillages, Urban Houses of Hospitality,
& Eco-Universities for a New Civilization*
Joe Holland, 2015

PROTECTION OF RELIGIOUS MINORITIES
A Symposium Organized by Pax Romana at the United Nations
and the United Nations Alliance of Civilizations
Dean Elizabeth F. Defeis & Peter F. O'Connor, Editors, 2015

BOTTOM ELEPHANTS
Catholic Sexual Ethics & Pastoral Practice in Africa:
The Challenge of Women Living within Patriarchy
& Threatened by HIV-Positive Husbands
Daniel Ude Asue, 2014

CATHOLIC LABOR PRIESTS
Five Giants in the United States Catholic Bishops Social Action Department
Volume I of US Labor Priests During the 20th Century
Patrick Sullivan, 2014

CATHOLIC SOCIAL TEACHING & UNIONS
IN CATHOLIC PRIMARY & SECONDARY SCHOOLS
The Clash between Theory & Practice within the United States
Walter "Bob" Baker, 2014

SPIRITUAL PATHS TO
A GLOBAL & ECOLOGICAL CIVILIZATION
Reading the Signs of the Times with Buddhists, Christians, & Muslims
John Raymaker & Gerald Grudzen, with Joe Holland, 2013

PACEM IN TERRIS
Its Continuing Relevance for the Twenty-First Century
(Papers from the 50th Anniversary Conference at the United Nations)
Josef Klee & Francis Dubois, Editors, 2013

PACEM IN TERRIS
Summary & Commentary for the Famous Encyclical Letter
of Pope John XXIII on World Peace
Joe Holland, 2012

100 YEARS OF CATHOLIC SOCIAL TEACHING
DEFENDING WORKERS & THEIR UNIONS
Summaries & Commentaries for Five Landmark Papal Encyclicals
Joe Holland, 2012

HUMANITY'S AFRICAN ROOTS
Remembering the Ancestors' Wisdom
Joe Holland, 2012

THE "POISONED SPRING" OF ECONOMIC LIBERTARIANISM
Menger, Mises, Hayek, Rothbard: A Critique from
Catholic Social Teaching of the Austrian School of Economics
Pax Romana / Cmica-usa
Angus Sibley, 2011

BEYOND THE DEATH PENALTY
The Development in Catholic Social Teaching
Florida Council of Catholic Scholarship
D. Michael McCarron & Joe Holland, Editors, 2007

THE NEW DIALOGUE OF CIVILIZATIONS
A Contribution from Pax Romana
International Catholic Movement for Intellectual & Cultural Affairs
Pax Romana / Cmica-usa
Roza Pati & Joe Holland, Editors, 2002

This book and other books from Pacem in Terris Press,
are available at:

www.amazon.com/books

219

CPSIA information can be obtained
at www.ICGtesting.com
Printed in the USA
LVHW011640111221
705947LV00017B/1407

9 780999 608845